The Seafood Cookbook

The *Seafood* Cookbook

Choosing, Preparing and Savoring the Bounty of the Sea

Jean-Paul Grappe

A FIREFLY BOOK

A FIREFLY BOOK

Published by Firefly Books Ltd. 1999

First Printing

LIBRARY OF CONGRESS CATALOGUING IN PUBLICATION DATA

Grappe, Jean-Paul.
   The seafood cookbook : choosing, preparing and savoring the bounty of the sea / Jean-Paul Grappe; Brenda Guild Gillespie.–1st U.S. ed.
[384] p. : col. Ill.; cm.
Originally published : Quebec : Les Editions de l'Homme, 1997.
Includes index and glossary.
ISBN 1-55209-401-4
1. Cookery (Fish). 2. Cookery (Seafood). I. Gillespie, Brenda Guild. II. Title.
641.6/92 —dc21   1999   CIP

Published in the United States in 1999 by
Firefly Books (U.S.) Inc.
P.O. Box 1338, Ellicott Station
Buffalo, New York, USA
14205

Published in Canada in 1999 by Key Porter Books Limited.

Electronic formatting: Jean Peters
Computer graphics: Johanne Lemay
Translation: Linda Hilpold

Printed and bound in Canada

Credits

Illustrations: © Brenda Guild Gillespie
Illustrations on pages 120, 128, 132, 216, 220, 222, 224, 228, 232, 236, 238, 240, 246: reproduced with the permission of Recreational Fishing, Fisheries and Oceans Canada.
Photographs of recipes, utensils and techniques: Pierre Beauchemin, ITHQ.
Photographs: Sylvain Majeau, pages 2, 50, 96, 146, 214, 334, 364, 384; MAPAQ, Marc Lajoie, pages 34, 124, 170, 252, 352; MAPAQ, pages 74, 266, 278, 282, 286, 356

We would like to thank Dr. William Scott of Huntsman Marine Science Centre, for allowing us to reproduce in this work, extracts from the book Fishes of the Atlantic Coast of Canada, A.H. Leim and W.B. Scott, Fisheries Research Board, 1972.

We would like to thank the MAPAQ for allowing us to reproduce in this work, extracts from the Guide des produits de la pêche, La Direction générale des publications gouvernementales, 1985.

To the

culinary

profession

and to all those

who make

eating seafood

possible.

Contents

Introduction

People have always been interested in what lies just below the water's surface. With its mythical beings and monsters that symbolize adventure and challenge, the sea has been the source of many stories pitting the power of man against the mysteries of this unfathomable vastness. Even though the sea still holds many mysteries, we (or most of us) no longer believe in these quasi-magical creatures that instilled fear in the hearts of sailors past. However, given the growing number of human beings that need to be fed, we are trying to keep the sea as our ally in the great battle to sustain the human race. The sea, lakes and rivers have always provided us with food. Water, grain and fish have allowed whole nations to maintain a certain dietary independence. But, in this race against time, we seem to have forgotten to show consideration: we must ensure that our underwater pantry remains in good condition by not polluting, not overharvesting and not wasting a resource that is not as inexhaustible as we want to believe it is.

For example, faced with the dramatic decline in cod stocks, we must, of course, react, not by eliminating fish from our diet, but by substituting fish that is more abundant, at least until nature has replenished its stock of cod. It is true that changing our habits requires a certain amount of effort, and the risk of disappointment often prevents us from venturing beyond the familiar.

This book, we hope, will lead to the discovery and enjoyment of the numerous species of fish, mollusks and crustaceans that are available commercially in North America. Some of these species do not exist locally, but are nonetheless consumed in numerous households and are routinely used in professional kitchens. Others are part of our culinary heritage and our gastronomical history.

Far from wanting to produce the authoritative word in the classification of fish, mollusks and crustaceans, and to add a scientific work to the literature, we have opted to offer an approach that appreciates the gastronomical value and the gustatory quality of each species discussed in this book.

The dishes contained in this work are new and inventive, simultaneously simple, daring and easy for all to prepare. The descriptions are clear and the techniques can easily be performed at home. The illustrations are based on detailed research to ensure that each species discussed is readily recognizable at the moment of purchase, and that the description is true to life.

Lastly, we wanted this recipe book to be fun to use and to serve as a reference for all practitioners of the culinary arts and for professional fishers, to be a learning tool for students in gastronomy and a stimulant for food lovers. We also wanted it to be a guide for the hobby fisher who wants to secure for his or her catch an honorable fate and to make his or her fishing stories both enjoyable and true.

Fish Consumption

In the past, fish as a main course was a religious and family obligation, often difficult to accept. Every Friday, a day of fasting for the Catholic community, this "duty" required that the family sit down in front of a meal then considered to be "second-rate."

Today, we are rediscovering the value of seafood, even though some concerns exist regarding fish in general, and some types of marine products in particular. However, fish should be considered to be as "noble" as lobster, crab or shrimp. Moreover, fine cuisine has always reserved a special place for fish in its menus. All cookbooks, both old and new, devote as much space to describing the careful preparation of seafood as they do of meat. A few great chefs have even devoted themselves to preparing only dishes based on fish and crustaceans.

There are regions rich in seafood, and countless species of freshwater and sea fish. Markets teem with fish imported from other areas such as the southern oceans. On the other hand, sadly, there is a general lack of knowledge among most people regarding products from the sea. Generally, we know the names of some fish but cannot describe their shape or their color. We hesitate to cook them, for various reasons, but primarily because we do not know how to prepare them.

Over the last decade, often the only fish available commercially was frozen. A few years ago, a handful of pioneers—fishmongers and a small number of innovative restaurateurs—decided to promote fish and to once again inspire consumers to try them. Moreover, these restaurateurs, much to their credit, are increasingly choosing fresh fish. Modern transportation ensures that fresh products are available all year long. Fish is delivered to its final destination within 24 to 36 hours of its arrival at the dock. Of course, the distance of some major centers from port can make the prompt delivery of fresh fish difficult. In this case, vigilance is called for when selecting and checking potential purchases to determine whether they have been fast-frozen, for example. Care is needed to ensure that the fish being bought is fresh and not previously frozen.

Since nutrition has become a prime concern among people who watch their health and since dieticians and nutritionists have been spreading their knowledge, fish has regained its rightful dietary place. Like meat and poultry, fish contains many proteins. It can, therefore, easily replace beef, pork or chicken and serve as the basic ingredient of several meals throughout the week.

Some people are under the impression that fish is less nutritious than meat. This illusion stems from the fact that fish is more easily digested than meat. The flesh of a fish contains only 5% connective tissue, compared with 14% in meat. In addition, fish does not contain indigestible fibers. Laboratory tests have proven, moreover, that 90% of fish proteins are digested.

For those who watch their weight, fish offers the advantage of supplying far fewer calories than meat. Obviously, this depends on the fish being prepared in a simple way and cooked in a *court-bouillon*, on the grill or steamed. Of course, frying is not a technique recommended for those who follow a low-calorie diet. In addition, it can be advantageous for those who are watching their calorie intake to be selective when choosing the type of fish they eat as fish are divided into two categories: lean and fatty.

Guide to Purchasing Fresh Fish
In order to determine the quality of fresh fish, certain characteristics need to be observed, which indicate the level of freshness.

Body: The body of a fresh fish must be rigid, firm and glossy.
Eye: The eye of a fresh fish is clear, bright, glossy and convex in shape, and occupies the entire eye socket.
Flesh: When pressed, the flesh of a fresh fish must be firm and elastic. It may be white, pink or red, as is the case with some species of tuna. When cut, the flesh of larger sea fish appears satiny.
Gills: Fresh fish gills must be shiny, moist, and blood-red or pink in color. Nevertheless, some sea fish,

such as sole, have gills that are less brightly colored, tending to a blackish-brown.

Odor: Most fresh sea fish give off a light seawater smell, except skate, which sometimes has a slight ammonia smell. Freshwater fish give off a scent of seaweed.

Scales: When fresh, fish are covered in shiny scales that lie very close to the skin.

Skin: The skin of a fresh fish is taut and adheres well to the bones.

Guide to Purchasing Frozen Fish

Care is needed when buying frozen or deep-frozen fish. Usually, it is preferable to purchase vacuum-packed fish clearly marked "deep-frozen product." Ideally, the date of freezing should appear on the label as that will enable you to determine the shelf life of the fish (see table, page 16). Some fish may have been poorly frozen, and others may have been refrozen. Therefore, carefully check the appearance of frozen fish: it should never appear brownish or bear any burn marks from contact with ice on the thinner parts of the fish.

Method for Storing Fresh Fish

After carefully checking the freshness of the fish when buying it, it is important that you store it properly.

Of course, fish cannot be kept "fresh" for more than 4 or 5 days, even if it was wrapped carefully and transported under the best conditions, at a constant temperature of between 32°F (0°C) and 39.2°F (4°C). Since few of us have a refrigerator equipped with a drawer designed specifically to store fish (a fish compartment), the fish must be wrapped and packed in ice. Cover a rack with a cloth and lay it in a plastic (or other) container, then place the fresh fish on top. Drape another cloth over the fish, and bury under crushed ice or ice cubes. Take care that the fish does not come in direct contact with the ice as it might "burn" the flesh. In addition, the fish must not lie in the water produced by the melting ice. Therefore, the water should be drained regularly, new ice added as needed, and everything chilled.

Storing Frozen Fish

All fish bought frozen must be kept at a temperature of 4°F (-18°C) in order to stop any microbial activity. However, frozen fish should not be kept too long as the flesh hardens and spoils. It is beneficial to glaze the fish by dipping it into water once thawed to stop dehydration and oxidation.

Storage Times for Fresh and Frozen Fish

	FRESH FISH			FROZEN FISH			
	Above 50°F (10°C)	50°F (10°C) (fresh)	32° to 39.2°F (0° to 4°C) (refrigerated)	14° to 0°F (-10° to -18°C) (frozen)	0°F (-18°C) (deep-frozen)	-13°F (-25°C) (deep-frozen)	-22°F (-30°C) (deep-frozen)
Shelf Life: Fatty fish	short	5–30 days	5–30 days	2 months	4 months	8 months	12 months
Shelf Life: Lean fish	short	5–30 days	5–30 days	1 1/2 months	8 months	18 months	24 months
Shelf Life: Flatfish	short	5–30 days	5–30 days	4 months	10 months	24 months	23 months
Development of pathogenic microbes[1]	rapid	slow	stopped	stopped	stopped	stopped	stopped
Development of spoilage microbes[2]	rapid	fairly rapid	fairly rapid	very slow	stopped	stopped	stopped
Chemical Reactions: Browning and rancidification[3]	rapid	fairly rapid	fairly rapid	slow	very slow	very slow	very slow

1. Pathogenic microbes: These microbes produce toxins that can result in food poisoning.
2. Spoilage microbes: These microbes produce waste that is responsible for a bad taste, smell or appearance; results in food spoilage and a decrease in shelf life.
3. Chemical reactions such as browning and rancidification: In the case of poor deep-freezing, freezing or packaging, the fish can show traces of brown on the thinner parts due to "freezer burn."

Freezing and Deep-Freezing

The principal goal of freezing and deep-freezing is to transform the maximum amount of water into ice and noticeably improve the shelf life of food. Freezing and deep-freezing can be carried out just as easily on raw material to be processed later on as on products ready for consumption. These two techniques require sufficient application of freezing and deep-freezing procedures as well as proper storage and reheating.

While freezing is a gentle and slow method, deep-freezing is quicker. Deep-freezing offers certain advantages over freezing. Deep-freezing involves "freezing" a product in a chiller at very low temperatures, i.e., -40°F (-40°C), in order to quickly exceed the zone from 30.2°F (-1°C) to 5°F (-15°C), called "the crystallization zone." This zone is the most important one when freezing and deep-freezing, as it is at that moment that the water contained in fish (80–90%) is transformed into ice crystals.

When freezing is done slowly, the crystals are large; when freezing is rapid, the crystals are smaller. The large crystals tend to spoil a food product more than do small crystals. Large crystals also lead to a greater quantity of liquid being formed, resulting in drier meat or fish. A fish that has been properly deep-frozen will keep its freshness better than a poorly preserved or frozen fish. It should be noted that fish should be deep-frozen shortly after leaving the water and not after a long waiting period.

Ideally, deep-freezing fish is preferable if the goal is to keep it for a long time. But, even lacking the proper chilling equipment, it is possible to adequately freeze fish.

These two techniques require that certain precautions be taken to ensure a good quality product.

It is important, therefore, that the following conditions be respected:

- Always wash, drain and scale the fish.
- Choose good packaging before freezing or deep-freezing fish.
- Ideally, opt for the vacuum-packaging method.
- If vacuum-packaging is not possible, use plastic wrap instead of aluminum foil or another wrap to ensure a minimum of air space around the fish.
- Remember to affix a sticker indicating the date of freezing.
- Never refreeze a thawed fish.

Cooking Methods and Times

There are basic rules and precise methods for cooking fish. In general, the cooking methods for meat can be applied to fish. However, fish should never be cooked too long as over-cooking can dry and harden the flesh and leave it tasteless. Fish can be prepared in different ways and used in the preparation of different dishes such as soups, pâtés, breads or mousses.

Various Cooking Methods

Anglaise (à l'): This method involves flouring, dipping in an egg-wash and milk preparation, and breading the fish, then cooking it in butter in a skillet.

Bake: Some large pieces of fish can be baked in the oven with butter and a vegetable garnish. It is important to baste often with the cooking juices.

Bake *en papillote*: Fish cooked *en papillote* is wrapped in aluminum foil along with a *brunoise* of vegetables as well as a little white wine or fish fumet. The *papillote* is placed in the oven and the fish is "braised."

Double boiler (*bain-marie*): This method is used to prepare mousse and fish loaf. The container holding the preparation to be cooked is put in a *bain-marie* and placed in the oven or on the stove.

Fry: Before frying fish or a piece of fish, it must first be dipped in batter or simply dredged in flour. It is then submerged in a bath of hot cooking oil.

Grill: The method is for thinner fish. They should be dried off to remove as much moisture as possible, then dipped in oil before being cooked on a grill.

Meunière (à la): This method, which is used primarily with smaller fish, involves flouring the fish, then cooking in butter in a skillet.

Poach (braise): This method applies primarily to large pieces of fish and involves cooking the fish in a little bit of liquid (white wine or fish fumet) with a vegetable garnish. This method works best with a covered pot, in the oven.

Poach with a *court-bouillon*: The fish is cooked in a liquid called a *court-bouillon* made with white wine, fish fumet or water, carrots, onion, a *bouquet garni*, lemon juice, salt and pepper.

Steam: The fish is steamed in a *court-bouillon*, white wine or fish fumet, using a basket steamer or a rack placed in a container with a cover. A pressure cooker may also be used.

Regarding Herbs

In the recipes, we always suggest using fresh herbs, which in most cities can be found all year round. The quantities indicated are for fresh herbs. It is, of course, possible to use dried herbs; however, in that case, a smaller quantity should be used.

Cooking Time

During cooking, the protein substance (albumin) tends to coagulate. The fish is cooked when this substance (a white liquid) slightly escapes from the fish. Cooking time can vary from 9 to 11 minutes for fresh fish 1 inch (2.5 cm) thick and from 12 to 22 minutes for frozen fish. Cooking times also vary depending on the type and the quality of the fish. Therefore, a lean fish can cook faster than a fatty fish. NOTE: The cooking times indicated in the recipes always depend on the thickness, the quality, the freshness and the type of fish used.

Morphology of a non-cartilaginous fish

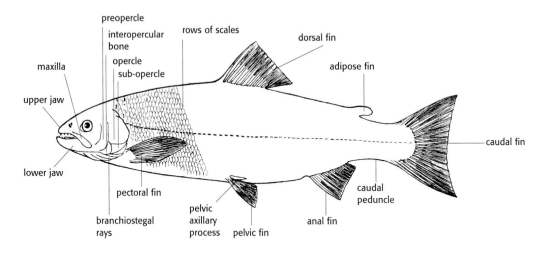

Side view and body parts of a non-cartilaginous fish with soft rays

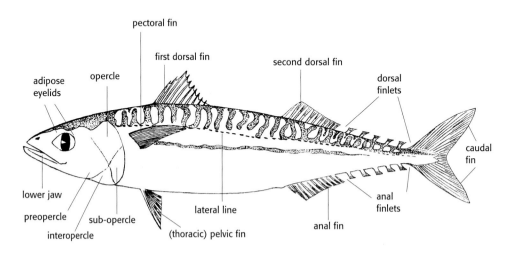

Side view and body parts of a non-cartilaginous fish with spiny rays

Basic Ingredients for Some Recipes

Fish Fumet

1 1/2 Tbsp (25 mL)	Butter
1 3/4 lbs (800 g)	Bones and trimmings (preferably from flatfish)
2 1/2 oz (75 g)	Onion, sliced thin
4 oz (125 g)	Leek, sliced thin
4 oz (125 g)	Celery, sliced thin
6 Tbsp (30 g)	Shallots
5 oz (150 g)	Mushrooms, sliced thin
3 1/2 oz (100 mL)	Dry white wine
4 tsp (20 mL)	Lemon juice
4 cups (1 L)	Cold water
1 pinch	Thyme
1/2	Bay leaf
10	Peppercorns

• Heat the butter in a saucepan, add the fish bones and trimmings and all the vegetables. Let the entire mixture sweat for 4 to 5 minutes. Moisten with the wine, the lemon juice and the cold water. Add the thyme, bay leaf and pepper. Bring to a boil and let simmer for 25 minutes. Strain through cheesecloth, let cool and set aside for later use.

NOTE: This fish fumet will keep in the refrigerator for up to 2 or 3 months. Avoid using carrots in the preparation since they generally give it a sweeter taste. Never add salt as the fish fumet is sometimes reduced to produce a fish "concentrate."

Court-bouillon

The court-bouillon is seldom used. However, it is a high-quality, aromatic ingredient for preparing fish (small or large pieces).

10 cups (2.5 L)	Water
3 1/2 oz (100 mL)	Dry white wine
3 1/2 oz (100 mL)	Good-quality white vinegar
1 3/4 Tbsp (30 g)	Coarse salt
2 cups (300 g)	White onion, sliced into thin rounds
2 2/3 cups (300 g)	Carrot, sliced into thin rounds
1	*Bouquet garni*
10	Black peppercorns

• Combine all the ingredients and cook until the carrots and the onions are tender. If the *court-bouillon* is to be used immediately, reserve the vegetables to use as a garnish for the fish, mollusks or crustaceans. If it is not for immediate use, strain the *court-bouillon* through cheesecloth or a fine mesh strainer and reserve.

Vegetable Essences

Vegetable essences are flavor concentrates that can be made from one ingredient such as celery, or from several different vegetables. Simply cook the ingredient(s) in water, then, when they are cooked, reduce the liquid.

Fish Velouté

2 cups (500 mL)	Fish fumet (see recipe above)
As needed	White roux (see recipe below)
1/4 cup (60 g)	Butter
approx. 2/3 cup (150 mL)	Cream (35%)
To taste	Salt & pepper

- Heat the fish fumet. Gradually add the cold white roux and cook 10 minutes until the desired consistency is reached. Add the butter, the cream, salt and pepper.
- Strain through cheesecloth or a fine mesh strainer.

White Roux

3 cups (500 g)	Butter
3 1/2 cups (500 g)	Flour

- Melt the butter in the microwave oven, add the flour and mix well. Cook in 20-second intervals, stirring well after each one. The roux is cooked once it begins to bubble.

NOTE: A roux is a basic ingredient in both the family and the professional kitchen. The microwave oven is ideal for preparing a roux.
- A roux can be kept in the refrigerator for at least one month and can be used as needed.
- A roux is preferable to *beurre manié* (see glossary entry) since the flour is cooked.

Beurre blanc

1	Lemon (juice)
3 Tbsp (40 mL)	White wine
To taste	Salt & white pepper
7 oz (200 g)	Melted butter

- In a metal mixing bowl placed in a *bain-marie*, heat the lemon juice and the white wine, then add the salt and pepper. Whisk vigorously. Add the warm melted butter.

NOTE: The salt and pepper should always be added before the butter, as the acid present in the wine and the lemon dissolves them before the butter is added. The *beurre blanc*, which is easy to prepare, should be served immediately. Unlike *beurre nantais* (see below), it does not have the binding properties that cream has.

Beurre nantais

2	Shallots, minced
3 1/2 oz (100 mL)	White wine vinegar
3 1/2 oz (100 mL)	White wine
To taste	Salt and ground pepper
7 oz (200 mL)	Cream (35%)
approx. 1 cup (200 g)	Cold sweet butter

- Combine the minced shallots, vinegar, white wine, salt and pepper in a saucepan. Reduce by 3/4 at high heat. Add the cream and reduce this mixture by half. Add the butter in stages, whipping constantly with a whisk. Remove the saucepan from the heat once the butter is completely incorporated. Store in a cool place.

Hollandaise Sauce (Quick Method)

There are two ways to prepare hollandaise sauce: the quick method and the classic method. The classic method produces better results.

1 cup (175 g)	Sweet butter
4	Egg yolks
3 Tbsp (40 mL)	White wine
To taste	Salt & pepper
1/2	Lemon (juice) (Optional)

- Melt the butter. Whisk together the egg yolks, white wine, salt and pepper in a round mixing bowl that can be placed on a heat source.
- In a warmed *bain-marie*, emulsify the mixture until it sticks to the spoon (like whipped cream). This step is very important as it is the egg yolk combined with the acid from the white wine that ensures the success of this sauce.
- Once the mixture has emulsified, slowly incorporate the melted butter. The mixture should be creamy. Add lemon juice as needed.

NOTE: Sweet butter should always be used as it is higher in fat content.

Hollandaise Sauce (Classic Method)

3 1/2 oz (100 mL)	White wine
5 Tbsp (35 g)	Shallots, chopped
2 tsp (10 mL)	White vinegar
4	Egg yolks
To taste	Salt & pepper
1 cup (175 g)	Lemon (juice) (Optional)

- Combine the white wine, the chopped shallots and the white vinegar and reduce by 9/10. Let the liquid cool, then add the egg yolks. Strain the sauce through cheesecloth or a fine mesh strainer.
- Melt the butter. Using a whisk, combine the egg yolks, the white wine, the salt and the pepper in a round mixing bowl that can be placed on a heat source.
- In a warmed *bain-marie*, emulsify the mixture until it sticks to the spoon (like whipped cream). This step is very important as it is the egg yolk combined with the acid from the white wine that ensures the success of this sauce.
- Once the mixture has emulsified, slowly incorporate the melted butter. The mixture should be creamy. Add lemon juice as needed.

NOTE: Sweet butter should always be used as it is higher in fat content.

Variations of Hollandaise Sauce for Fish, Mollusks and Crustaceans

Maltese sauce: Hollandaise + orange juice + zest
Mikado sauce: Hollandaise + juice and blanched julienne of tangerine peel
Mousseline sauce: Hollandaise + whipped cream
Mustard sauce: Hollandaise + white mustard seed or old-style (Meaux) mustard
Sabayon sauce: Hollandaise + crustacean, tomato, pepper or fennel coulis

Béarnaise Sauce

3 Tbsp (40 mL)	Wine vinegar
3 1/2 oz (100 mL)	White wine
2 tsp (5 g)	Peppercorns, crushed
1 Tbsp (15 g)	Fresh tarragon, chopped
4 Tbsp (30 g)	Dried shallots, chopped
1 1/4 cups (300 g)	Melted butter
3	Egg yolks
To taste	Salt & pepper
1 Tbsp (15 g)	Tarragon, chopped
1 Tbsp (5 g)	Parsley, chopped
2 Tbsp (5 g)	Chives, cut with scissors

- Pour the vinegar and the wine into a saucepan; add the pepper, tarragon and the shallots. Reduce the liquid by half and let cool. Decant the melted butter, leaving the white sediment in the bottom of the saucepan. Set the clarified butter aside, keeping it warm. Add the vinegar and wine mixture to the egg yolks, then whisk yolks in a *bain-marie* until thick and creamy. Check that the butter is not too hot, then add it gently to this mixture.
- Strain the sauce through a fine sieve and adjust the seasoning. If the sauce is too thick, add a little warm water to dilute it. Garnish with the tarragon, parsley and chives. Serve.

Béarnaise Sauce (Alternative Method)

This béarnaise sauce is a hollandaise sauce prepared according to the classic method and to which chopped chives and tarragon must be added. The sauce is not strained.

Variations of Béarnaise Sauce

Choron sauce: Béarnaise + reduced tomato fondue, chopped or blended tomatoes (no tarragon or chervil)

Coral sauce: Béarnaise, with coral (the eggs from lobsters, scallops or sea urchins) substituted for the egg yolks. Coral has the same binding properties as egg yolks.

Paloise sauce: Béarnaise + chopped mint leaves instead of tarragon

Valois sauce: Béarnaise + meat glaze

Fines Herbes Sauce with Crayfish Garnish

16	Crayfish
3 Tbsp (45 mL)	Oil
approx. 3/4 lb (325 g)	Onions, chopped
2 Tbsp (15 g)	Fresh shallots, chopped
3 Tbsp (30 g)	Carrots, chopped
1 pinch	Thyme
1	Bay leaf
3 1/2 oz (100 mL)	Cognac
14 oz (400 mL)	Fish fumet
7 oz (200 mL)	White wine
To taste	Salt & pepper
1 hint	Cayenne pepper
1/4 cup (60 g)	Butter
3/4 cup (100 g)	Flour
1/2 cup (125 mL)	Cream (35%)
FINES HERBES	
1 tsp (5 mL)	Chives
1 tsp (5 mL)	Parsley, chopped
1/2 tsp (2 mL)	Tarragon

- Eviscerate the crayfish. (In fact, remove the digestive system. The tip of the crayfish tail is made up of three fan-like segments. Hold the middle one between two fingers and give it a quarter turn while gently pulling; the long black filament should come out in one piece.)
- Heat the oil at high heat in a high-sided frying pan, then brown the vegetables and the crayfish with the thyme and the bay leaf. Once the crayfish turn red, flambé with the cognac, then moisten with the hot fish bouillon and the white wine. Season and cook for approximately 10 minutes. Remove the crayfish from the sauté pan. Shell the crayfish and keep the tails to decorate the dish.
- Crush the crayfish shells and the claws in the remaining cooking liquid and strain through cheesecloth or a fine mesh strainer. Keep the resulting liquid warm.
- Prepare a roux with the butter and the flour. Moisten with the liquid and thicken, stirring with a wooden spoon. Simmer for 8 minutes, keeping a watchful eye. Add the cream to the liquid. Cook until the sauce is very creamy. Add the *fines herbes* and adjust the seasoning.

It is possible to purchase good-quality lobster bisque commercially if lobster coulis is unavailable. Crab, shrimp and crayfish bisques are also available. It is also possible to find fish veloutés, demi-glace, hollandaise and béarnaise sauces, as well as veal stocks. Obviously, the quality of these products cannot compare with the quality of fresh products.

Lobster or Crab Fumet

approx. 1 lb (500 g)	Lobster or crab
1/4 cup (60 mL)	Oil
1/4 cup (60 mL)	Carrots, diced
3 Tbsp (45 mL)	Onions, diced
3 Tbsp (45 mL)	Celery, diced
1/4 cup (60 mL)	Leek (white part only), diced
1/2 cup (125 mL)	Fresh tomato, diced
4 cups (1 L)	Fish fumet (see recipe at beginning of this chapter)
4 tsp (20 mL)	Cognac
4 tsp (20 mL)	Tomato paste
2	Garlic cloves
1 pinch	Thyme, chopped
1	Bay leaf
To taste	Salt & pepper

- Roughly cut the lobster and its shell into large pieces (see "How to" photographs); remove the intestines and the stomach. Brown the lobster pieces in the oil. Add the vegetables and cook for 4 to 5 minutes.
- Pour off the oil remaining in the saucepan, then flambé the lobster pieces and vegetables with cognac. Moisten with the fish fumet. Add the tomato paste, then the other ingredients. Let simmer for 30 minutes.
- Crush or chop the lobster and the vegetables, then strain through cheesecloth or a fine mesh strainer. Let simmer for 1 to 2 minutes, then adjust the seasoning.

NOTE: This fumet can be frozen. It can also be prepared using crab.

Lobster Coulis

2 lbs (900 g)	Lobster
1/4 cup (60 mL)	Olive oil
4 Tbsp (45 g)	Sweet butter
4 Tbsp (30 g)	Shallots, chopped
1/2	Garlic clove, chopped
7 oz (200 mL)	White wine
1/2 cup (125 mL)	Cognac
2/3 cup (150 mL)	Fish fumet (see recipe above)
2 Tbsp (30 g)	Tomato paste
1 Tbsp (5 g)	Parsley, roughly chopped
3 oz (90 mL)	*Demi-glace* (see glossary)
To taste	Cayenne pepper and salt

- Cut the lobster into sections and crack the claws. Split the lobster in two lengthwise. Remove the stomach sac, located near the head. Set aside the creamy parts (see "How to" photographs).
- Heat the oil and the butter in an ovenproof pan; sear the lobster pieces until they turn red. Remove the excess fat. Add all the other ingredients. Cover the saucepan and let cook in a hot oven for approximately 20 minutes. Drain the lobster pieces, remove the flesh and set aside for another use. Crush the shells and return them to the sauce along with the creamy parts of the lobster. Cook at high heat and reduce the liquid, constantly whipping with a whisk. Strain through cheesecloth or a fine mesh strainer.

NOTE: This recipe may also be prepared using crab, large shrimp or crayfish instead of lobster.

Lobster Bisque

1/4 cup (30 g)	Carrots, diced
1/4 cup (30 g)	Onions, diced
1/4 cup (30 g)	Celery, diced
1/2 cup (45 g)	Leek, diced
approx. 1/3 cup (90 g)	Butter
4 tsp (20 mL)	Cognac
1/4 cup (55 mL)	White wine
2 Tbsp (40 g)	Tomato paste
1/3 cup (200 g)	Fresh tomatoes, diced
1 3/4 lbs (800 g)	Lobster carcass
3 cups (750 mL)	Fish fumet (see recipe above)
3 cups (750 mL)	White chicken stock (see recipe in this chapter)
To taste	Salt & pepper
To taste	Cayenne pepper
approx. 3 oz (100 g)	Lobster meat
As needed	Rice flour
1/3 cup (75 mL)	Cream (35%)

- Cook the *mirepoix* (diced vegetables) in the butter until tender. Deglaze with the cognac and the white wine. Add the tomato paste and the fresh tomato. Add the lobster carcass. Moisten with the fish fumet and the white chicken stock. Season. Let simmer for 1 hour.
- Strain through cheesecloth or a fine mesh strainer. While cooking the lobster meat at low heat, combine the rice flour and the cream, and bind as desired. Strain once again through cheesecloth. Dice the lobster meat and add to the cream mixture.

NOTE: When should the word "bisque" be used? Only in the case of bases made from crustaceans (crayfish, crab, scampi, shrimps, etc.). To bind, use only rice flour since it is odorless and preserves the delicate flavor of crustaceans.

Lobster Sauce

2 lbs (900 g)	Lobster or lobster carcass
1/4 cup (60 mL)	Olive oil
3 Tbsp (45 mL)	Sweet butter
2 Tbsp (30 mL)	Shallots, chopped
1/4 tsp (1 mL)	Garlic, chopped
1/2 cup (125 mL)	Cognac
3 1/2 oz (100 mL)	White wine
3 1/2 cups (850 mL)	Fish fumet (see recipe above)
2 Tbsp (30 g)	Tomato paste
1 Tbsp (5 g)	Parsley, roughly chopped
1/2 tsp (1 g)	Cayenne pepper
1/2 tsp (5 g)	Salt

- Cut the lobster tail into sections and crack the claws. Split the body in two lengthwise. Remove the stomach sac, located near the head, and set aside the creamy parts and the meat.
- In a sauté pan, heat the oil and the butter, then sear the pieces of shell until they turn red. Remove the excess fat and add all the other ingredients.
- Cover and cook at 400° to 450°F (200° to 230°C) for approximately 30 minutes. Drain the pieces of shell, crush, and return them to the sauce with the creamy parts and the meat. Cook at high heat and reduce while whisking. Strain through cheesecloth or a fine mesh strainer, then set aside in the refrigerator until ready to use.

Lobster Butter

approx. 1 lb (500 g)	Lobster scraps (chest with coral and creamy parts, small legs and shell, excluding the large claws)
3 cups (500 g)	Sweet butter
As needed	Ice water

- Grind the lobster scraps using a pestle and mortar. Add the butter and mix until creamy. Place the mortar in the double-boiler insert and heat at low heat for 30 minutes. Pour approximately 1 inch (2.5 cm) of ice water into the bottom of a tall, straight-sided container.
- Strain the melted butter through cheesecloth or a fine mesh strainer, then through a cloth placed over the container holding the water. Press the lobster scraps through the cheesecloth or the strainer in order to collect the maximum amount of melted butter. Let sit until the butter has floated to the surface of the water. Place the container and contents in the refrigerator to allow the butter to congeal.
- Separate the hardened butter from the water, dry off and melt again. Strain and decant into a container that can be tightly sealed. Set aside in the refrigerator until ready to use.

NOTE: Store the butter in the refrigerator, where it can be kept for several weeks; use on canapés, to decorate cold dishes and to thicken fish or crustacean sauces. Another crustacean (crab, scampi or crayfish) can be substituted for the lobster, if you prefer.

– This butter can be frozen.

White Chicken Stock

4 1/2 lbs (2 kg)	Chicken bones (or bones of other poultry)
2 cups (300 g)	Carrots, in small dice
1 1/3 cups (200 g)	Onions, in small dice
1 cup (100 g)	Leek (white part only), in small dice
approx. 3 oz (100 g)	Celery, in small dice
3	Garlic cloves, chopped
1	Clove
To taste	Black pepper

BOUQUET GARNI

1 sprig	Thyme
1/2	Bay leaf
20 stems	Parsley

- Soak the chicken bones to remove impurities.
- Place the *mirepoix* (finely diced vegetables), the garlic and the seasonings in a stockpot along with the soaked bones. Cover with water and bring to a boil. Skim if necessary. Cook for 45 minutes if using chicken bones. Strain through cheesecloth or a fine mesh strainer, and reduce if the flavor is not strong enough.

NOTE: This recipe can be prepared using other poultry. The principle is always the same. If using a hen or a rooster, boil the entire bird. The longer the cooking time, the more flavor can be drawn out. If using chicken bones, soak them in order to remove any impurities (blood).

Brown Chicken Stock

- To prepare brown chicken stock, the same ingredients for the white chicken stock are used; however, the method is slightly different.
- Using a cleaver, crush the bones and brown them on a lightly oiled baking sheet in the oven until golden. At the same time, sweat the vegetables in oil. Combine the two and season. Cover with water and cook for 45 to 60 minutes. If the stock is not brown enough, add a little tomato paste, then strain through cheesecloth or a fine mesh strainer.

Brown Veal Stock

This brown veal stock was used extensively in the 16th, 17th and 18th centuries with fish, mollusks and crustaceans. Often, the marriage of the two ingredients was a happy one. Stocks can be prepared in winter and frozen for use later on. As they cook, they give off a pleasant aroma and add humidity to the air.

As needed	Vegetable fat to cover bottom of roasting pan
22 lbs (10 kg)	Veal bones (preferably the knuckle), diced by a butcher
As needed	Vegetable oil
2 1/4 lbs (1 kg)	Onions, diced (large cubes)
2 1/4 lbs (1 kg)	Carrots, diced (large cubes)
approx. 1 lb (500 g)	Celery stalks, cut into 2-inch (5-cm) pieces

10 oz (300 g)	Leeks (green part only), cut into pieces
4	Garlic bulbs, skin on
2	Bay leaves
2 pinches	Thyme sprigs
25	Black peppercorns
3/4 cup (200 g)	Tomato paste

- In a roasting pan, heat the vegetable fat in the oven at 400°F (200°C). Once the fat is sufficiently hot, add the veal bones and roast until completely golden. This step is very important, as the juice will give the stock its beautiful color.
- At the same time, in a sufficiently large saucepan, let the vegetables sweat in vegetable oil. Add the garlic, the seasoning and the tomato paste, and cook.
- Once these two steps have been completed, combine the two preparations in a large stockpot and completely cover with water, as the stock needs to simmer for at least 6 hours.

NOTE: Never add salt to a stock that is to be reduced as it will then be too salty. During cooking, skim regularly and, if too much liquid has evaporated, add more water. When cooked, strain through cheesecloth or a fine mesh strainer, chill in a cool place, then transfer to smaller containers if it is to be frozen.

- Reducing the stock produces a *demi-glace*; reducing it further will produce a glaze, in other words, a concentrated juice.
- This is not a thick veal stock. Using a white roux produces a brown veal stock.

Glazes

Glazes are concentrations of flavor that are used to improve a sauce. A glaze is produced when a stock, whether from chicken, veal or fish, is reduced by 95%. For example, 20 cups (5 liters) of chicken stock cooked for 40 to 60 minutes, strained through cheesecloth or a fine mesh strainer, and reduced by 95% will leave 1 to 2 cups (250 to 500 mL) of liquid. This is a highly concentrated glaze. If the stock is reduced less, leaving, for example, 4 cups (1 liter) of liquid, the glaze will have less flavor. When the stock has been reduced, store in ice-cube trays and freeze. Once frozen into cubes, store in small bags. If a sauce needs extra flavoring, add one small cube of glaze.

Garlic Cream

Although garlic should be used as little as possible with fish, mollusks and crustaceans, some can tolerate this marriage. Garlic cream is simply a thickener made from 35% cream whipped to produce garlic butter.

Garlic Butter

approx. 1 lb (500 g)	Unsalted butter (sweet butter), whipped
1 oz (30 g)	Garlic
approx. 1/4 cup (30 g)	Shallots or onions
approx. 1 cup (70 g)	Parsley
approx. 1 Tbsp (20 g)	Dijon mustard
approx. 2 Tbsp (20 g)	Roasted almonds
2 tsp (10 mL)	Pernod or Ricard
To taste	Salt & pepper

- In a food processor, blend all the ingredients, salt and pepper to taste.

Basic Fish Mousse

2 ¼ lbs (1 kg)	Pike, sole or pollock (Boston bluefish), filleted
4 or 5	Egg whites
To taste	Salt & freshly ground pepper
To taste	Nutmeg
4 cups (1 L)	Cream (35%)
2 cups (375 g)	Sweet butter

- Pound the fish flesh in a mortar. During this procedure, blend in the egg whites and the seasoning. Strain through a fine sieve and wrap (see "Method for Storing Fresh Fish," page 15) in a high-sided frying pan placed on ice. Let sit for approximately 2 hours.
- With the pan still on ice, gradually dilute the forcemeat by adding in the cream and the butter, gently stirring with a wooden spoon. Chill overnight in a cool place before serving.

Panada for Fish

1 cup (125 g)	Flour
4	Egg yolks
½ cup (90 g)	Melted butter
To taste	Salt, pepper and nutmeg
1 cup (250 mL)	Milk, at boiling point

- In a saucepan, work the flour and the egg yolks together, then add the melted butter, salt, pepper and nutmeg. Dilute gradually by adding the boiling milk. Beat with a whisk to thicken while cooking for 6 to 8 minutes. Once the preparation is thick enough, remove and let cool.

Pike Forcemeat Quenelles (Garnish)

2 ¼ lbs (1 kg)	Pike meat, filleted
5	Egg whites
To taste	Salt & ground pepper
½ tsp (2 mL)	Grated nutmeg
14 oz (400 g)	Choux pastry
4 cups (1 L)	Cream (35%)
½ lb (225 g)	Sweet butter, whipped
8 cups (2 L)	Fish fumet (see recipe at beginning of this chapter)

- When buying the fish, request meat that has been perfectly filleted and skinned. Cut into small pieces and purée with the egg whites and the seasoning in a food processor.
- In a bowl, combine the mixture of pike meat and egg whites with the choux pastry and blend well. Strain through a fine sieve. Transfer the forcemeat to a mixer and work with the flat spatula at low speed. Gradually incorporate the cream and the whipped butter. Increase the speed and beat for approximately 1 minute in order to obtain a smooth, creamy forcemeat. Chill overnight in the refrigerator. Using 2 moistened spoons, shape into dumplings the size of a large egg (approximately 3 oz or 90 g) and place in a buttered dish.
- Lightly cover with fish fumet and bake for approximately 10 minutes at low heat (approximately 300°F or 150°C), adding fumet as needed. Drain the dumplings and repeat until all the forcemeat has been used up.

Mayonnaise

4	Egg yolks
1 Tbsp (15 mL)	Dijon mustard
To taste	Salt & pepper
As needed	Good-quality white vinegar
4 cups (1 L)	Oil (olive, peanut, canola, corn, sunflower, walnut, hazelnut, pistachio, etc.)

- In a blender or with a whisk, combine the egg yolks and the mustard, salt, pepper and a few drops of the vinegar. The salt must be added at this stage to allow it to dissolve. Gradually incorporate the oil. If the mixture is too firm, add a few more drops of vinegar or water to dilute before adding more oil.

Varieties of Mayonnaise

Aïoli (quick): Mayonnaise + crushed garlic + lemon juice + olive oil (mandatory)

Almonds & Ginger: Sour cream + mayonnaise + chopped roasted almonds + finely chopped ginger

Andalouse: Mayonnaise + cooked tomato paste + finely diced peppers + seasoning

Mousseline: Mayonnaise + whipped cream + seasoning

Mustard: Mayonnaise + Dijon or Meaux mustard (there are now Beaujolais, violet, Champagne and other mustards that go well with some fish, mollusks and crustaceans)

Rouille (quick): Mayonnaise + chopped garlic + saffron powder + lemon juice

NOTE: For *aïoli* and *rouille* mayonnaises, mashed potatoes or stale bread may be added.

Cold Yogurt or Sour Cream Sauces

Curry Sauce: Mayonnaise + curry + sour cream + salt & pepper

Japanese Pickled Ginger Sauce: Sour cream + sake + chopped pickled ginger + chopped parsley + salt & pepper

Laniel Sauce: Sour cream + yogurt + whitefish eggs + lemon juice + salt & pepper

Muscovite Sauce: Sour cream + vodka + sturgeon caviar + salt & pepper

Piquante Sauce: Mayonnaise + sour cream + tomato paste + chili paste + chopped coriander

Poseidon Sauce: Sour cream + sea urchin roe + finely chopped nettle + salt & pepper

Saffron and Orange Blossom Sauce: Sour cream + saffron threads + orange blossom water + salt & pepper

Seaweed Sauce: Rehydrated seaweed (kelp, rockweed, fucus) + sour cream + lime juice + salt & pepper

Watercress Sauce: Mayonnaise + sour cream + puréed watercress + lemon juice + salt & pepper

NOTE: These sauces are generally served with cold dishes. It is important that they do not mask the flavor of the fish, mollusks or crustaceans.

– Yogurt can be substituted for the sour cream.

Lemon Herb Butter

approx. 2/3 cup (150 g)	Butter
2 Tbsp (30 mL)	Lemon juice
1/3 cup (20 g)	Parsley, chopped
1/2 cup (20 g)	Chives, chopped
1/3 cup (10 g)	Tarragon, chopped
To taste	Salt & pepper

• Soften the butter, then mix with all the other ingredients. Store the butter at room temperature until ready to use. Can be frozen.

NOTE: This recipe may be prepared using the juice of other citrus fruits, such as oranges and grapefruit.

Varieties of Flavored Butter for Fish, Mollusks and Crustaceans

Anchovy: Butter + chopped anchovies + pepper

Coconut: Butter + condensed coconut milk + lime juice

Crustacean: Butter + cooked and chopped shellfish meat (lobster, shrimp, scampi or crayfish) + salt & pepper

Fennel: Butter + chopped fresh fennel + Ricard or Pernod + salt & pepper

Garden Herb: Butter + lemon juice + tarragon + chives + parsley + sorrel + salt & pepper

Glasswort: Butter + chopped glasswort + lemon + pepper

Lemongrass: Butter + chopped lemongrass + chopped parsley

Maître d'hôtel: Butter + lemon juice + chopped parsley + salt & pepper

Marchand de vin: Butter + reduced red wine with chopped shallots + salt & pepper

Mustard: Butter + white wine + mustard + salt & pepper

Orange-Lime: Butter + orange and lime juice + salt & pepper

Papaya: Butter + concentrated papaya juice + lime juice + salt & pepper

Purslane: Butter + chopped purslane + lemon juice

Saffron: Butter + lime juice + minced saffron + salt & pepper

Saltwater Cordgrass: Butter + saltwater cordgrass + pepper

Sweet Basil: Butter + lime juice + chopped fresh basil + salt & pepper

Tarragon: Butter + finely chopped tarragon + lemon juice + salt & pepper

Flavored butters are generally served with grilled fish, mollusks and crustaceans.

NOTE: Always use unsalted butter.

Standard Equipment

KITCHEN EQUIPMENT

Every day, new equipment, large and small, appears on the market. However, to prepare the recipes in this book, you can easily use the equipment you already own.

Whenever parchment paper is specified in a recipe, aluminum foil can be used instead.

Fish kettle

Trout kettle

Round stewpot and stockpot

Saucepans

Sauté pan (for sautéed fish)

High-sided frying pan (for sauces)

Oval fish pan

Round frying pan

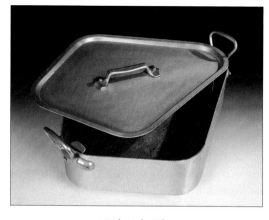

Turbot kettle

Braising pan

To steam: Basket steamer, steamer, Chinese wood steamer

To grill: Grill (for gas, wood or coal flame), grill pan, fish grilling basket for braising

To cook quickly and at high heat: Wok, sheets for broiling or grilling

To drain or sift: Colander, sifter, strainer, cheesecloth

To drain: Perforated spoons, skimmers, wire skimmer

To mix: Round metal mixing bowls, whisks

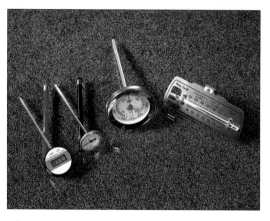

Thermometers
From left to right: electronic thermometer, thermometer for small pieces, thermometer for large pieces, refrigerator thermometer

Cooking utensils
From left to right: salmon cutter, filleting knife, chef's knife, fish knife, small knife

Cooking utensils
Left: cleaver, fork, steel
Right, from top: perforated spatula for fish, spatula, oyster knife, peeler, knife for turning vegetables, paring knife

Cooking utensils
From left to right: oyster knife, peeler, zester, grapefruit knife, scissors, garlic press, shrimp deveiner
Top: fish scaler

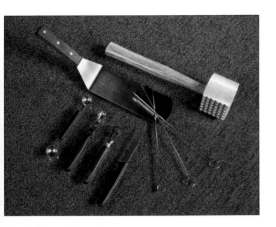

Cooking utensils
Top: tenderizing hammer, fish spatula, skewers
Bottom, from left to right: *noisette* and *parisienne* knife, queen scallop knife, zester, paring knife

Small baking and aspics molds
First row at right, from top to bottom: *dariole* mold, *savarin* mold, ramekin
Second row: ramekins of different sizes
Third row, from top to bottom: brioche mold, *barquette* mold

Cooking utensils
From left to right: brush, pastry bag and nozzles, wooden spoons, plastic spatula, plastic scraper

How to Prepare Fish and Seafood

How to fillet a sole

Beard.

Scale the white skin.

Make an incision in the black skin at tip of the tail.

Lift the black skin to remove.

Pull back the black skin.

Pull the skin away completely.

Cut into the center of the sole.

Lift the fillets.

Remove the fillets.

The fillets.

How to flatten a flounder or sole fillet

Place the fillets between two sheets of aluminum foil.

Tap gently.

Flattened fillet.

How to prepare sole or flounder fillet *goujonnettes*

Stretch out the fillet.

Fold the fillet in the middle.

Roll to form a tongue.

Loop the tongue around and tuck inside.

The goujonnette.

How to prepare a sole or flounder fillet roulade

Stretch out the fillet and lay the asparagus tips on top.

Roll carefully.

The roulade, ready to cook.

How to prepare sole or flounder fillet *en portefeuille*

Place the garnish on the flattened fillet.

Fold in thirds.

The sole or flounder fillet pocket.

How to prepare sole or flounder soufflé

Fillet the fish.

Cut the bones using scissors.

Slide a knife under the bones to remove.

Remove the bones.

Sole or flounder without the bones.

Stuff the sole or the flounder.

43

How to fillet a flounder

Fillet the fish.

Remove the black skin.

NOTE: The black skin cannot be pulled off by hand, as it can with sole. Using a knife, separate the black skin from the fillet. All other procedures regarding sole can be adapted to flounder, yellowtail flounder and fourspot flounder.

How to prepare halibut

Individual section.

Section for several guests (right).

Fillet the fish.

How to cut salmon steaks

Cut off the head.

Cut a steak.

The steak.

How to fillet a salmon

Cut the length of the backbone.

Fillet the fish.

Remove the skin.

Cut the fillets into portions.

How to remove the bones from a spindle-shaped fish through the stomach to stuff it (here, we are using a trout)

Run a knife under the bones on one side, then the other.

Remove the backbone.

A trout without the bones.

Stuff using a pastry bag.

NOTE: All spindle-shaped fish can be boned through the stomach.

How to skin a dogfish

Remove the skin by hanging on to the head and pulling on the skin.

NOTE: Can also be applied to conger, American and moray eels.

How to prepare a lobster for grilling or for the oven

Put the lobster to sleep (a lobster can also be put to sleep before boiling).

Insert the tip of the knife and push down quickly and firmly.

Holding the tail, cut half the body in two.

Insert the knife just above the tail and cut.

The lobster cut in half.

The lobster with the coral (left) and the stomach sac (right).

Crack the claws with the blunt edge of the knife.

Cut the end of the claw.

How to cut up a cooked lobster

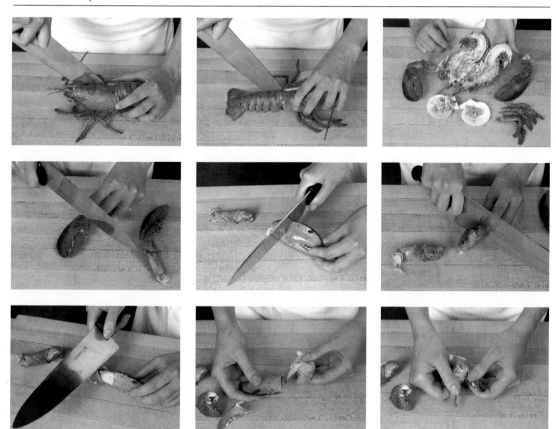

Same method as for live lobster.

How to cut up a cooked crab

Divide the crab by separating the legs from the body.

Cut the legs.

Remove the flesh.

How to remove the flesh from a whelk

Remove the whelk from the shell using a sharp instrument.
NOTE: Can also be applied to periwinkles.

How to remove the flesh from a razor clam

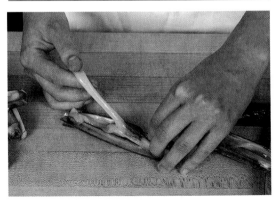

Open the clam and gently remove the flesh.

How to open an oyster

Plunge the knife into the back of the shell.

Pry apart the two halves of the shell.

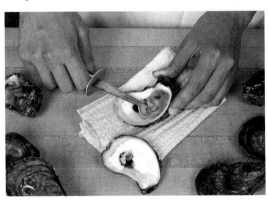

Remove the oyster from the shell.

How to open a scallop shell

Open by running the oyster knife between the two halves of the shell.

How to open a sea urchin and remove the roe

Make an incision using scissors.

Open the sea urchin with the scissors.

Remove the "cover."

The roe.

TURBOT, FLOUNDER, HALIBUT AND OTHERS

Flatfish

Very compressed, flatfish have both eyes on the same side of their head. Their long dorsal and anal fins are well developed.

At the beginning of their life, these fish swim normally. Very early on, however, they change and, rather than swimming in a vertical position, they swim on their side. The eye located on the lower side moves to the upper. This change leads to a modification of the head's structure and of the muscular and the nervous tissues. The eyes may bulge slightly and move independently, thereby increasing the field of vision of these fish.

Flatfish are carnivores that feed on several animal substances. A ground species of continental coastal waters, flatfish can be found in abundance in tropical and temperate seas. Some species can also be found in Arctic waters.

The order includes approximately 500 species classified under 6 families. More than 60 species belonging to 2 families (*Bothidae* and *Pleuronectidae*) can be found in North America. Several of these species play an important role in commercial fishing.

In this chapter, we discuss those fish that can be found commercially in some areas of North America as well as those we would like to see more of.

Windowpane
Brill
Sole
Witch flounder
American plaice
Yellowtail flounder
Fourspot flounder
Halibut
Greenland halibut
Thorny skate

WINDOWPANE

Scophthalmus aquosus (Mitchill) 1815
Incorrect names: turbot, sole, flounder

Flesh: Very thin, tasty and firm

Habitat: North Atlantic coast

Where & When to Find It: Regularly available where imported fish is sold

Processed & Sold: Whole, as fillets and in sections

Cooking Method: *Meunière*, poached, steamed, grilled, braised or in sauces

Value: One of the best sea fishes, but 60% is unsuitable for consumption.

Comments: Not to be confused with turbot. The fish we call turbot is, in fact, Greenland halibut, which is of lesser quality than the windowpane.

$$$$$

Characteristics: Coloring varies from reddish to brownish-gray on one side and white on the other. Average size is approximately 22 inches (56 cm) and weight ranges from 1 1/4 to 2 1/4 lbs (600 g to 1 kg) for young windowpane, and to 22 lbs (10 kg) for the adult.

Soufflé of Young Windowpane in Champagne Sauce *

2 1/4 lbs (1 kg)	Cultured mussels
3 1/2 oz (100 mL)	White wine
2	Shallots, dried and chopped
3 1/2 oz (100 mL)	Fish fumet (see "Basic Ingredients for Some Recipes")
approx. 3 oz (100 g)	Pike fillet
To taste	Salt & pepper
1	Egg white
6 oz (170 mL)	Cream (35%)
To taste	Nutmeg
2 3/4 lbs (1.2 kg)	Fresh young windowpane
As needed	Butter

As needed	Champagne
4 oz (120 g)	Pink shrimp
1/2	Lemon (juice) (Optional)

- Cook the mussels with the white wine, one shallot and the fish fumet. Remove the cooked mussels from the saucepan, shell and set aside. Reduce the cooking liquid almost completely; set aside.
- To prepare the forcemeat, chop the pike fillet in a food processor. Season with salt and pepper and add the egg white while kneading in the processor. Gradually add approx. 1/3 cup (70 mL) of cream and a little ground nutmeg.
- Strain the forcemeat through a sieve and set

aside. Open the young windowpane from the black side and remove the backbone. Season the fish with salt and pepper, then stuff, using a pastry bag. Seal the windowpane and place on a buttered baking sheet.

- Pour the champagne and the fish fumet onto the baking sheet. Add the other shallot, salt and pepper, and bake covered at 350°F (180°C) for 12 to 20 minutes, until small white droplets appear on the fish. Remove the black skin and the small bones immediately; set the windowpane aside on a serving dish and keep warm. Cover with a damp cloth to prevent the fish from drying out.
- Reduce both the remaining cream and the

cooking liquid from the windowpane by ¾. Add the cooking juice from the mussels to the cooking liquid from the windowpane, then incorporate the reduced cream. Strain this sauce through cheesecloth or a fine mesh strainer.

- Add the mussels and the drained pink shrimp, which have been dried off, to the sauce. Reheat at low heat. Add a little lemon juice to the sauce, if so desired. Cover the young windowpane with hot sauce.

Accompaniment: Steamed potatoes
* In memory of chef André Bardet.

Preparation time: 1 hour 20 minutes	
Cooking time: 12 to 20 minutes	
Servings: 4	**Cost:** $$$$$

Windowpane Fillets with Steamed Seaweed and Lemon Butter

approx. 1 cup (160 g)	**Butter**
1	**Lemon**
To taste	**Salt & pepper**
2 cups (500 mL)	*Court-bouillon* (see "Basic Ingredients for Some Recipes")
7 oz (200 g)	**Fresh kelp or rock-weed (seaweed)**
4 × 6 oz (180 g)	**Windowpane fillets**

- **Lemon butter:** Combine the butter with the lemon juice, salt and pepper and store at room temperature.
- **Cooking:** Using a three-part steamer (with lid), put the *court-bouillon* in the bottom; the seaweed in the middle; and the windowpane fillets in the top. The steam will take on the aroma of the seaweed before cooking the fillets. When small droplets of white liquid escape from the fish, the fillets are cooked. Serve very hot with the lemon butter.

Accompaniment: Wild rice cooked in the water used to steam the seaweed

Preparation time: 15 minutes	**Cooking time:** 8 to 15 minutes
Servings: 4	**Cost:** $$$$$

Photo on next page →

BRILL

Scophthalmus rhombus (Linnaeus) 1758
Incorrect names: sole and turbot

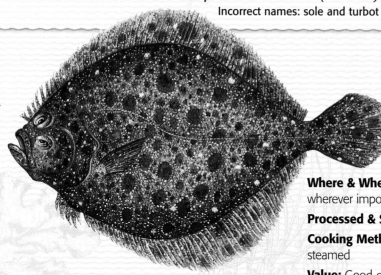

Where & When to Find It: Available all year round wherever imported fish is sold

Processed & Sold: Whole and as fillets, frozen

Cooking Method: *Meunière*, grilled, poached or steamed

Value: Good quality, but not as good as window-pane

Comments: Rarely used in some regions

$$$

Characteristics: Oval-shaped flatfish 50 cm (20 inches) in length. Lives near sand-and-gravel beds. Yellowish-gray or brownish in color

Flesh: Thin, tasty, lean and somewhat soft

Habitat: English Channel and the North Sea

Brill Fillets in Port

³/₄ cup (120 g)	Butter
2	Shallots, chopped
1 ¹/₂ cups (120 g)	Mushrooms, finely sliced
4 × 4 oz (120 g)	Brill fillets
To taste	Salt & pepper
1 cup (240 mL)	Port
¹/₂ cup (120 mL)	Fish fumet (see "Basic Ingredients …")
¹/₂ cup (120 mL)	Brown chicken stock (see "Basic Ingredients …")

1	Lemon (juice)

- Using half the butter, grease the sides and bottom of the ovenproof dish. Sprinkle chopped shallots and finely sliced mushrooms in the dish. Lay the brill fillets in the dish, season and pour in the port and the fish fumet. Cover with aluminum foil.

- Bake at 375°F (190°C) until white droplets escape from the fish. Remove the fillets and keep warm. Reduce the cooking liquid by ⁹/₁₀. Add the brown chicken stock. Reduce, add the remaining butter and the lemon juice and season to taste.

- Pour the very hot sauce over the fish fillets.

Accompaniment: Carrots and rice

Preparation time: 20 minutes	**Cooking time:** 20 minutes
Servings: 4	**Cost:** $$$

Braised Brill with Fiddleheads

approx. 1 cup (160 g)	Butter
6 Tbsp (40 g)	Shallots, chopped
approx. 1 cup (120 g)	Raw mushrooms, chopped
4 × 6 oz (170 g)	Brill sections
To taste	Salt & pepper
1/2 cup (120 mL)	Dry white wine
3 1/2 oz (100 mL)	Fish fumet (see "Basic Ingredients for Some Recipes")
approx. 1 cup (200 g)	Cooked fiddleheads
1/3 cup (60 g)	Tomatoes, diced

Preparation time: 15 minutes   **Cooking time:** 15 minutes
Servings: 4   **Cost:** $$$

- Grease an ovenproof dish, using half the butter. Lay the shallots, the chopped mushrooms and the brill sections in the dish and season.
- Pour in the white wine and the fish fumet, cover with aluminum foil and bake at 350°F (180°C). The brill is ready when small white droplets escape from the fish. Reduce the cooking liquid by 9/10. Gently braise the fiddleheads in the reduction and add the remaining butter in little knobs.
- On a plate, arrange the brill sections and pour the braised fiddlehead preparation over the fish. Sprinkle with the diced tomato.

Accompaniment: Steamed rice or potatoes

COMMON SOLE

Solea solea and solea lascaris risso
Incorrect names: winter flounder, Dover sole

Habitat: Europe

Where & When to Find It: Available all year round, deep-frozen and sometimes fresh, wherever imported fish is sold

Processed & Sold: Whole

Cooking Method: *Meunière*, grilled, poached or steamed

Characteristics: This fish, which rarely measures more than 18 inches (45 cm) and rarely weighs more than 2 lbs (1 kg), lives near sand and clay beds. The head is small and rounded. Its color is light brown.

Flesh: Lean and firm

Value: Very good culinary quality because of its delicate white flesh

Comments: Not found off the Atlantic coast of North America. The sole is imported from the English Channel and the North Sea. Often incorrectly referred to as "Dover Sole."

$$$$$

Fillets of Sole with Almond Milk

12 × 1 ¹/₂ oz (approx. 40 g)	Sole fillets
To taste	Salt & pepper
¹/₃ cup (40 g)	Chopped toasted almonds
²/₃ cup (100 g)	Butter
3 ¹/₂ oz (100 mL)	Almond milk
¹/₃ cup (80 mL)	Brown veal stock (see "Basic Ingredients for Some Recipes")
To taste	Lemon juice
4 oz (120 g)	Cooked lentils

- In order to break the fillet fibers to prevent shrinking, take a sheet of aluminum foil and, one by one, wrap the sole fillets, then tap gently, using the flat of the knife blade. The fillet will flatten without being crushed (see "How to" photos).

- Lay the fillets out on a table; salt, pepper and sprinkle with the chopped almonds. Roll up the fillets. Grease an ovenproof dish with butter. In the dish, place the fillets so that they touch, to prevent them from rolling over.
- Pour in the almond milk. Cover with a sheet of buttered aluminum foil and bake at 350°F (180°C). When they are cooked, remove the fillets and keep warm. Incorporate the brown veal stock in the cooking liquid and emulsify with the remaining butter. Add the lemon juice and season to taste.
- Heat the lentils and spoon onto each plate. In the middle, arrange three sole fillets and cover with sauce.

Accompaniment: *Cocotte* potatoes cooked in almond milk

Preparation time: 20 minutes	**Cooking time:** 8 to 12 minutes
Servings: 4	**Cost:** $$$$$

Sole à la meunière

4 × 1/2 lb	Sole fillets
(approx. 220 g)	
To taste	Salt & pepper
1 3/4 cups (300 g)	Butter
3 1/2 oz (100 mL)	Peanut oil
As needed	Flour
2	Lemons

- Dry off the sole. Salt and pepper.
- Heat 2/3 cups (100 g) of the butter and oil in a heavy-bottomed skillet. Flour the fillets and lay in the hot fat, skin side first. Once golden, turn and brown other side. Generally, sautéing 4 to 5 minutes per side is adequate.

- Once the sole is cooked, remove the cooking fat and sprinkle the remaining butter over the sole. Heat and serve, or transfer the fillets to a smaller plate. Serve with lemon wedges on the side.

Accompaniment: *Cocotte* potatoes prepared in butter

NOTE: To ensure success:
– Dry off the sole to remove as much moisture as possible.
– Why use half butter, half oil for cooking? Butter combined with oil takes longer to burn than butter alone. This mixture is ideal for cooking "à la meunière."
– The white skin of sole is always retained, but it must be scaled.

Preparation time: 10 minutes	**Cooking time**: 15 minutes
Servings: 4	**Cost**: $$$$

WITCH FLOUNDER

Glyptocephalus cynoglossus (Linnaeus) 1758
Incorrect names: sole and gray sole

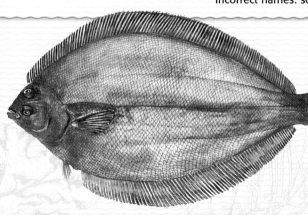

Characteristics: Grayish-brown on one side and grayish-white with dark spots on the other, this fish reaches a maximum length of 25 inches (64 cm) and weight of approximately 1 1/2 lbs (700 g). A small mouth and eyes on the right side of the head distinguish the witch flounder from other flatfish, except the smooth flounder and the winter flounder.

Flesh: Lean and fairly firm

Habitat: Both sides of the Atlantic Ocean

Where & When to Find It: Available wherever fish is sold. Available deep-frozen all year round

Processed & Sold: Whole and as fillets

Cooking Method: *Meunière*, poached, steamed or grilled

Value: From a culinary standpoint, of all fish, witch flounder most resembles sole.

Comments: In Europe, referred to as sole (*Miecrostomus kit*).

$$$

Witch Flounder Fillets en Portefeuille *with Scallop Coral Cream*

12 × 2 oz (60 g)	Flounder fillets
2/3 cup (100 g)	Butter
To taste	Salt & pepper
1/3 cup (40 g)	Shallots, chopped
1/2 cup (120 mL)	White wine
4 oz (120 g)	Scallop coral
2/3 cup (160 mL)	Cream (35%)
1	Lemon
4 sprigs	Dill

• Flatten the fillets (see "Fillets of Sole with Almond Milk," page 58). Fold to form a *portefeuille* (see "How to" photographs). Place the fillets in a buttered dish, salt and pepper. Sprinkle with the chopped shallots, pour in the wine and cover with aluminum foil. Bake at 375°F (190°C).

• At the same time, mix the scallop coral, the cream and the lemon juice. Remove the cooking liquid from the cooked fillets and keep the fillets warm. Pour the cooking liquid into the coral-cream preparation and heat gently. Season to taste and pour over the fillets. Garnish with the dill.

Accompaniment: Baby pasta shells

NOTE: Scallop coral is a liaison or binder like butter or cream. As the coral degrades at 160°F (70°C), care is required when heating the sauce.

Preparation time: 25 minutes		**Cooking time:** 12 minutes	
Servings: 4		**Cost:** $$$	

Witch Flounder Fillets with Lobster Mousseline *and Seaweed Sauce*

7 oz (200 g)	Cooked lobster meat
1	Egg white
14 oz (400 mL)	Cream (35%)
1 ¾ lbs (800 g)	Witch flounder fillets
To taste	Salt & pepper
14 oz (400 mL)	White wine
3	Dried shallots, chopped
2 cups (500 mL)	Fish fumet (see "Basic Ingredients for Some Recipes")
2 tsp (30 g)	Dried seaweed
1	Lemon (juice)

- In a food processor, purée the lobster meat. Incorporate the egg white and half the cream. Strain through a sieve and set aside.
- Make an incision into the center of each fillet, lift the edge and season with salt and pepper. Spoon the forcemeat into a pastry bag and stuff the fillets, using a fluted pastry nozzle.
- Place the fillets in an ovenproof dish. Add the wine and the shallots. Cover with aluminum foil and bake at 350°F (180°C) for 7 to 10 minutes. Remove the fillets from the dish and keep warm.
- Reduce the cooking liquid from the fillets with the fish fumet. Strain through cheesecloth or a fine mesh strainer. Heat the remaining cream in a saucepan and reduce by half. Combine the cream and liquid reductions.
- Soak the seaweed in water for 2 hours; drain and add to the sauce with the lemon juice.

Presentation: Arrange 3 fillets on each plate and cover with very hot sauce.

Preparation time: 1 hour	**Cooking time**: 7 to 10 minutes
Servings: 4	**Cost**: $$$

AMERICAN PLAICE

Hyppoglossoides platessoides (Fabricus) 1780
Incorrect names: sole, sand dab, hen fish

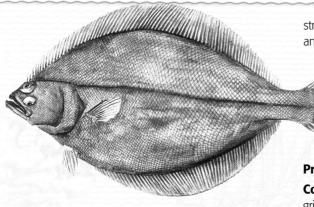

straight lateral line, a rounded tail, a large mouth, and eyes located on the right side of the head.

Flesh: Lean

Habitat: Both sides of the North Atlantic

Where & When to Find It: From April to October, in abundance. Available deep-frozen all year round

Processed & Sold: Whole and as fillets

Cooking Method: *Meunière*, poached, steamed or grilled

Characteristics: Grayish-brown on one side and white or bluish-white on the other. Maximum length is 27 inches (70 cm) and average weight is 2 to 3 lbs (900 g to 1.4 kg). This flatfish has an almost

Value: The culinary quality is somewhat less than that of witch flounder.

Comments: In Europe, referred to as dab (*Limanda limanda*).

$$

American Plaice Roulades with Yogurt Sauce and Chives

12 × 2 oz (60 g)	American plaice fillets
To taste	Salt & pepper
1/2 cup (120 mL)	White wine
1/2 cup (50 g)	Shallots, chopped
5 oz (140 mL)	Lobster juice
As needed	White roux (see "Basic Ingredients for Some Recipes")
6 oz (160 mL)	Plain yogurt
2/3 cup (100 g)	Butter
1/2 bunch	Chives, cut with scissors

- Salt and pepper the plaice fillets. Roll them up to form roulades. Pour the white wine and the chopped shallots into a saucepan. Place a basket steamer in the pan and position the roulades in the steamer.
- Cover and steam for 3 to 4 minutes. Remove the roulades and keep warm. Reduce the cooking liquid by 9/10. Add the lobster juice and lightly bind with the roux.
- Add the yogurt sauce. Strain through cheesecloth or a fine mesh strainer. Incorporate the butter and the cut chives. Pour over the plaice roulades.

Accompaniment: Potatoes cooked in the lobster juice

Preparation time: 20 minutes **Cooking time:** 7 minutes
Servings: 4 **Cost:** $$

American Plaice Goujonnettes *with* Tomato and Onion Compote

TOMATO AND ONION COMPOTE

3 cups (450 g)	Red onions, finely sliced
approx. 1/2 cup (80 g)	Butter
1/2 sprig	Thyme
1	Garlic clove, chopped
5 cups (900 g)	Diced tomatoes, blanched, peeled and seeded
approx. 2 oz (50 mL)	White wine
1	Lemon

GOUJONNETTES

1 3/4 lbs (800 g)	American plaice fillets
As needed	Flour
As needed	Cooking oil
4 servings	Tomato and onion compote
As needed	Parsley

- **Compote**: Cook the onions, thyme and garlic in butter at low heat. Add the tomatoes, wine and lemon juice to 3/4 of the preparation. Set this mixture aside and keep warm.
- *Goujonnettes*: Slice the fillets into long strips 1/2 inch (1 cm) wide. Dry off and dredge in the flour. Fry the strips in oil at 400°F (200°C). Arrange the tomato and onion compote in a circle on each plate. Place the plaice *goujonnettes* in the center to form a pyramid.
- Fry the parsley and sprinkle over the *goujonnettes*. Serve immediately.

Preparation time: 25 minutes	**Cooking time:** 2 to 3 minutes
Servings: 4	**Cost:** $$

YELLOWTAIL FLOUNDER

Limanda ferruginea (Storer) 1839
Incorrect names: greater amberjack and sole

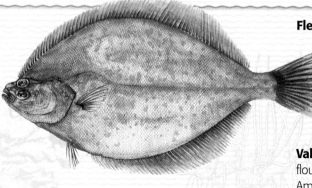

Flesh: Lean and soft

Where & When to Find It: From April to October, in abundance. Available as deep-frozen fillets all year round

Processed & Sold: Whole and as fillets

Cooking Method: *Meunière*, poached, steamed or grilled

Value: Given its somewhat soft flesh, the yellowtail flounder is not as good as the witch flounder or the American plaice, but better than the summer flounder.

$

Characteristics: A brownish-olive green with orange spots on 1 side and white on the other, this fish can measure up to 28 inches (72 cm) in length (16 inches or 40 cm on average) and can weigh on average 1 1/4 lbs (600 g).

Fried Yellowtail Flounder Goujonnettes *with Irish Moss Sauce*

approx. 1 1/4 lbs (600 g)	Yellowtail flounder fillets
1 1/4 tsp (20 g)	Dried Irish moss seaweed (carrageen)

BATTER

4	Eggs
3 1/2 cups (500 g)	Flour
1 bottle (12 oz or 330 mL)	Beer
To taste	Salt & pepper

Preparation time: 10 minutes **Cooking time:** 5 to 8 minutes
Servings: 4   **Cost:** $$$

SAUCE

1 1/4 cups (300 mL)	Fish *velouté* (see "Basic Ingredients ...")

- Cut the yellowtail flounder fillets into strips and form *goujonnettes*. Set aside. Rehydrate the Irish moss with a little bit of water.
- **Batter:** Separate the whites from the yolks. Create a basin in the flour and gently incorporate the yolks and the beer. Season with salt and pepper and strain through cheesecloth or a fine mesh strainer. Stiffen the whites and, just before cooking the *goujonnettes*, incorporate them into the preparation.
- **Sauce:** Chop the seaweed and add to the fish *velouté*.
- Dip the *goujonnettes* in the batter and deep fry. Serve with the sauce on the side.

Accompaniment: Sautéed potatoes

Yellowtail Flounder Paupiettes *with Blue Mussels*

1 ³/₄ lbs (800 g)	Blue mussels
1 cup (100 g)	Shallots, chopped
7 oz (200 mL)	White wine
4 × 4 oz (120 g)	Yellowtail flounder fillets
6 cups (600 g)	Crushed tomatoes, peeled and drained
5 ¹/₄ cups (600 g)	Potatoes, diced
²/₃ cup (160 mL)	Cream (35%)
1 cup (60 g)	Fresh parsley, chopped

- Carefully wash the mussels and place in a saucepan with the chopped shallots and the white wine. Cover and cook until the mussels open. Remove them from the cooking liquid and set aside.
- Roll the yellowtail flounder fillets and cook in the mussel liquid. Remove and set aside.
- Shell the mussels and keep warm. Add the crushed tomatoes and the diced potatoes to the cooking liquid and simmer until the potatoes are cooked, then incorporate the cream. Pour this mixture over the yellowtail flounder *paupiettes* and the reheated mussels. Sprinkle with the chopped parsley.

Preparation time: 25 minutes **Cooking time:** 25 minutes
Servings: 4 **Cost:** $$

FOURSPOT FLOUNDER

Paralichthys oblongus (Mitchill) 1815

Incorrect name: plaice

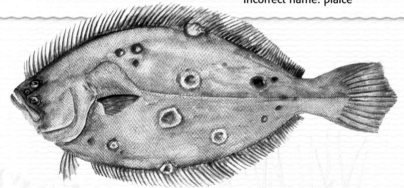

Characteristics: The body is gray in color. This fish can measure up to 43 inches (110 cm) in length and weigh up to 25 lbs (11.5 kg). It eats small fish, squid, crab, shrimp and clams.

Flesh: Lean and soft

Habitat: North Atlantic (from Georges Bank to the South Carolina coast)

Where & When to Find It: From April to October, in abundance. Available deep-frozen all year round.

Processed & Sold: Whole and as fillets

Cooking Method: *Meunière*, steamed, poached or grilled

Value: Its soft flesh makes it an ordinary fish.

$ (It is the least expensive fish of the flatfish family.)

Fourspot Flounder with Green Peas

1	White onion
approx. ²/₃ cup (140 g)	Butter
14 oz (400 g)	Unshelled wild or cultured green peas
¹/₂	Garlic clove
To taste	Salt & pepper
4 × 4–5 oz (120–150 g)	Fourspot flounder fillets

Preparation time: 15 minutes **Cooking time:** 10 minutes
Servings: 4 **Cost:** $

- Mince the onion. Heat ¹/₃ cup (60 g) of butter and gently braise the onion, then cook the peas with their pods in this preparation. Mince the garlic and add to the preparation once it is cooked. Season with salt and pepper and set aside.
- Fold the fourspot flounder fillets into *portefeuille* (see "How to" photographs). Season with salt and pepper.
- Pour half the peas into a saucepan or onto a baking sheet. Arrange the fourspot flounder fillets and cover with the remaining peas. Sprinkle with knobs of butter. Cover and cook gently. Serve very hot.

Fourspot Flounder Fillets with Glasswort

4	Potatoes
10 oz (300 g)	Glasswort
1/3 cup (80 mL)	Sunflower oil
To taste	Salt & pepper
3 1/2 oz (100 mL)	Brown veal stock (see "Basic Ingredients for Some Recipes")
3 1/2 oz (100 mL)	Lobster juice
1 1/4 lbs (600 g)	Fourspot flounder fillets

- Boil the potatoes in their skins in salted water and set aside.
- Quickly sauté the glasswort at high heat in the sunflower oil and season with salt and pepper.
- Heat the veal stock and lobster juice together.
- Slice the potatoes into rounds into an oven-proof dish, then add the fillets as roulades. Cover with the glasswort. Pour the brown veal stock and lobster juice over the roulades. Cover with aluminum foil and bake gently at 300°F (150°C). Serve directly in the ovenproof dish.

NOTE: Glasswort, sometimes called "saltwort," must be used sparingly as it is often very salty.

Preparation time: 25 minutes	**Cooking time:** 12 minutes
Servings: 4	**Cost:** $$$

GREENLAND HALIBUT

Reinhardtius hippoglossoides (Walbaum) 1792

Incorrect names: turbot and Greenland turbot

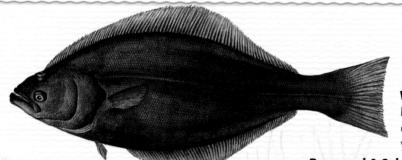

Where & When to Find It: From March to September, in abundance. Available deep-frozen all year round.

Processed & Sold: Whole and as fillets

Cooking Method: *Meunière*, steamed, poached or grilled

Value: Depending on where the fish is caught, the flesh is often tender after cooking. Identical in quality to the summer flounder.

Characteristics: This fish likes to live in deep water in the coldest coastal regions. Its body color ranges from yellowish to grayish-brown on one side and pale gray on the other. Capable of reaching 45 inches (115 cm) in length, the Greenland halibut can weigh as much as 25 lbs (11.3 kg), usually averaging between 10 and 25 lbs (4.5 to 11.5 kg).

Flesh: Lean and soft

Habitat: Deep water in the Arctic regions and North Atlantic

Comments: Incorrectly identified as the Greenland "turbot." There is no comparison in terms of quality between the turbot, which is one of the best of the sea fish, and the Greenland halibut, which is an ordinary fish.

Baked Greenland Halibut

As needed	Butter
2 1/4 lbs (1 kg)	Greenland halibut
2 cups (500 mL)	Plain yogurt, lightly whipped
2 Tbsp (30 mL)	Lemon juice
1/4 cup (60 mL)	White wine
1/4 tsp (1 mL)	Mace, ground
2	Egg yolks, lightly beaten
To taste	Salt & pepper
1 cup (250 mL)	Fresh bread crumbs
As needed	Butter
1 cup (60 g)	Parsley, finely chopped

- Butter an ovenproof dish and lay the fish in the dish. The black skin of the halibut should have been removed (see "How to" photographs) and the fish bearded. Combine the yogurt, lemon juice, wine, mace and the egg yolks. Pour over the fish.
- Season. Cover with a mixture of butter and bread crumbs and bake in an oven preheated to 350°F (180°C) for approximately 15 minutes. Garnish with the parsley and serve hot.

Preparation time: 20 minutes	**Cooking time:** 15 minutes		
Servings: 6		**Cost:** $	

Greenland Halibut with Chanterelle Mushrooms

2 oz (160 g)	Chanterelles
As needed	Vinegar
approx. 4 oz (110 mL)	Olive oil
To taste	Salt & pepper
8 × 2 oz (60 g)	Greenland halibut fillets
As needed	Flour
³/4 cup (120 g)	Butter
3 Tbsp (40 mL)	White wine
1	Lemon (juice)
¹/2	Garlic clove
3 Tbsp (12 g)	Fresh parsley, chopped

- Wash the chanterelle mushrooms with water and a little vinegar. Drain well. Quickly sauté them in ¹/4 cup (60 mL) of olive oil, and season with salt and pepper. Set aside. Dry off the Greenland halibut fillets, flour and cook *à la meunière* with 4 ¹/2 Tbsp (50 g) of butter and 3 Tbsp (50 mL) of olive oil until golden. Season with salt and pepper.
- Once they are cooked, remove the fillets and keep warm. Remove fat from the pan and deglaze with the white wine and lemon juice. Reduce the liquid by half. Add the remaining butter, mushrooms, chopped garlic and chopped parsley.
- On each hot plate, arrange a bed of chanterelles with the fillets on top. Serve hot.

Accompaniment: *Noisette* potatoes sautéed in butter

NOTE: Care should be taken when cooking this fish, as the flesh is often very soft.

Preparation time: 25 minutes	**Cooking time:** 5 to 8 minutes
Servings: 4	**Cost:** $$$

HALIBUT (ATLANTIC HALIBUT)

Hippoglossus hippoglossus (Linnaeus) 1758

Incorrect names: topknot and flounder

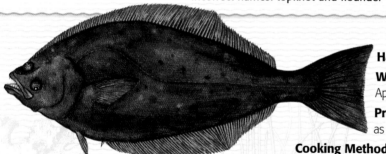

Characteristics: Halibut lives in the frigid waters stretching from the North Atlantic almost to the Arctic. Brown on one side, and usually white on the other, halibut can reach lengths of 8 ft (240 cm) and weigh up to 400 lbs (181.5 kg). Its average weight ranges from 5 to 44 lbs (2.3 to 20 kg).

Flesh: Lean and firm

Habitat: Both sides of the Atlantic

Where & When to Find It: From April to October (in abundance)

Processed & Sold: In sections and as fillets

Cooking Method: Poached, steamed, grilled or *meunière*

Value: High culinary quality, especially when fresh

Comments: More popular in North America than in Europe, this fish can easily replace the windowpane. It is vastly superior when fresh.

$$** (in season) **$$$ (out of season)

Halibut with Quiaude

1 ¹/₂ cups (200 g)	Chopped onions
3 Tbsp (50 mL)	Oil
¹/₃ cup (50 g)	Flour
4 cups (800 g)	Potatoes, finely chopped
To taste	Salt & pepper
1 ¹/₂ lbs (700 g)	Diced halibut

PASTRY

1 cup (125 g)	Flour
1 ¹/₄ tsp (7 g)	Baking powder
As needed	Salt
¹/₄ tsp (1 g)	Baking soda
¹/₃ cup (80 mL)	Water

- Cook the onions in oil, covered and at low heat. Sprinkle with flour and brown.
- Add the potatoes, then cover with water. Bring to a boil. Season with salt and pepper. Cook for 10 minutes.
- Add the halibut and drop in the pastry prepared in advance, 1 tsp (5 mL) at a time. Cook covered for 10 to 15 minutes. Serve hot.
- Pastry: Combine the flour, baking powder, salt and baking soda. Incorporate the water. Drop into the preparation, as indicated.

NOTE: This recipe can also be prepared using cod.

Preparation time: 20 minutes **Cooking time:** 25 to 30 minutes
Servings: 6 **Cost:** $$

Grilled Halibut Steaks with Early Vegetables and Laniel Sauce

3 oz (90 mL)	Oil
To taste	Salt & pepper
6 × 6 oz (180 g)	Halibut steaks
18	Parsnips, trimmed in the shape of olives
18	Carrots, trimmed in the shape of olives
approx. 1 cup (120 g)	Green beans
1/3 cup (60 g)	Butter

PRESENTATION

3	Lemons
6 stems	Parsley

Preparation time: 45 minutes   **Cooking time:** 15 minutes
Servings: 6   **Cost:** $$

6 servings	Laniel sauce (see "Basic Ingredients …")

- Combine the oil, salt and pepper and marinate both sides of the steaks for several minutes. Heat the grill until very hot. Place the previously drained steaks on the grill (in order to get a nice crisscross pattern, rotate the steaks clockwise). The fish is done when the backbone can be removed easily with the tip of a paring knife.
- Boil or steam the vegetables separately. Set aside. Sauté in butter just before serving.
- **Presentation**: Arrange the steaks on the plates and decorate with the spring vegetables, lemon and parsley. Serve with Laniel sauce.

THORNY SKATE

Raja radiata (Donovan) 1807

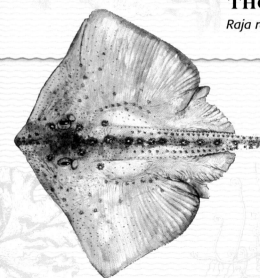

Flesh: Thin, lean and somewhat firm

Habitat: Both sides of the Atlantic. There are 325 species.

Where & When to Find It: Available occasionally, where fish is sold.

Processed & Sold: As wings

Cooking Method: *Meunière*, steamed or poached

Value: Because of its texture, skate is a surprising fish. Either you like it or you don't.

Comments: A fish that should be better known. Only the "wings" are used for cooking. Peeled, the flesh of the wings does not tolerate contact with either water or ice.

$$

Characteristics: A cartilaginous fish, its skin light brown to gray in color on the one side and white with spots on the other, the thorny skate lives in deep water. It can reach 2 ft (62 cm) in length.

Skate Wings with Capers and Mushrooms

2 1/2 cups (325 g)	Raw mushrooms
To taste	Salt & pepper
7 oz (200 mL)	Fish fumet (See "Basic Ingredients for Some Recipes")
approx. 1/2 cup (75 g)	Chopped capers
1 3/4 cup (800 g)	Skate wings
approx. 3/4 cup (150 g)	Butter
1	Lemon (juice)
As needed	Chopped parsley

- Chop the mushrooms in a food processor; sauté until almost all of their moisture has evaporated. Season with salt and pepper, then add 4 tsp (20 mL) of fish fumet and 1/3 of the capers. Set aside and keep warm.

- Poach the skate wings in the remaining fish fumet for 10 to 15 minutes, depending on their thickness. When cooked, dry the wings to remove as much liquid as possible. Heat the butter until light brown.

- Add the remaining capers and the lemon juice to the butter. Arrange the chopped mushrooms on hot plates. Lay the skate wings on top of the mushrooms, cover with the buttered capers, then add the parsley.

Accompaniment: Small, boiled *cocotte* potatoes

Preparation time: 30 minutes	**Cooking time:** 15 minutes
Servings: 4	**Cost:** $$

Skate Wings with Pink Cider

1 cup (240 mL)	**Pink cider**
To taste	**Salt & pepper**
7 oz (4 x 200 g)	**Skate wings cut in sections**
1/3 cup (80 mL)	**Veal glaze (see "Basic Ingredients for Some Recipes")**
1/2 cup (80 g)	**Saltwater cordgrass**
1/3 cup (60 g)	**Butter**

• Pour the cider and 1/2 cup (120 mL) of water into a fairly large but not too deep saucepan, as the skate sections take up a lot of room. Place a basket steamer in the saucepan. Season each skate section with salt and pepper, then arrange in the steamer. Cook covered for approximately 8 to 10 minutes, depending on the thickness of the sections. If the black skin has not been removed, do so while the sections are hot as this fish is very gelatinous and the skin will stick. Keep warm.

• Reduce the cooking liquid by 9/10, then add the veal glaze and the saltwater cordgrass. Season to taste and add the butter. Arrange the skate sections on hot serving plates and pour the sauce over the fish.

NOTE: It is preferable to leave the backbone in the skate during cooking to prevent the flesh from shrinking too much. The bones can be easily removed after cooking.

– Beware of the salt content of the saltwater cordgrass. If it is too salty, rinse in water first.

– The fishmonger should also be able to remove the black skin.

Preparation time: 15 minutes **Cooking time:** 8 to 10 minutes
Servings: 4   **Cost:** $$$

Gadidae (Cod Type)

Gadidae are a cold-water sea fish. They can be found in northern seas, although some species also live in the southern hemisphere. More numerous in shallow water, these fish can also be found in deep water. These are soft ray fish with small scales and large mouths; certain fins may be threadlike.

Atlantic cod consume many other fish and invertebrates. This family of fish has long been a staple of the North Atlantic fisheries. Several of its 59 species are of enormous commercial value.

From a culinary standpoint, all these fish share one thing in common: upon cooking, the flesh becomes flaky, which enables any sauce or butter to slide between the "flakes."

Some of these fish, in particular, cod, are famous around the world. Others are less well known. It is important that, as well hoping for the cod stock to return, we use other members of this family more often, especially since they are also very tasty.

Other fish that make up the *Gadidae* family can be prepared by adapting each of the recipes contained in this chapter, including Arctic cod, blue antimora, ogac, silver rockling, threebeard rockling and blue whiting.

Atlantic cod
Haddock
Pollock
Cusk
Squirrel hake
Silver hake
Whiting
Atlantic tomcod

ATLANTIC COD

Gadus morhua (Linnaeus) *1758*

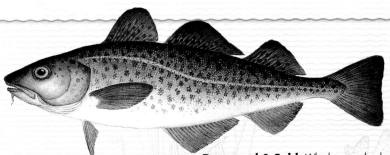

Characteristics: The color of this fish can vary from gray to green or brown to red. Average weight is approximately 5 lbs (2.3 kg).

Flesh: Dense and nutritious, flakes in large V-shaped sections

Habitat: Both sides of the Atlantic

Where & When to Find It: From January to March, May to July, and in September (in abundance)

Processed & Sold: Whole, smoked, as steaks and fillets

Cooking Method: *Meunière*, roasted, poached or steamed

Value: Long considered an ordinary fish, Atlantic cod is once again gaining in popularity.

Comments: When fresh, Atlantic cod is referred to as "codfish." "Cod" normally refers to the salted product.

$$

Atlantic Cod Fillets with Red Peppers and Capers

approx. 1 lb (500 g) or 8	Small endives
1 ¼ cup (300 mL)	Fish fumet (see "Basic Ingredients for Some Recipes")
1 ¼ lbs (600 g)	Potatoes, peeled and shaped
approx. ½ cup (115 g)	Butter
approx. 1 cup (125 g)	Red peppers, diced
approx. 1 cup (125 g)	Onion in a fine *brunoise*
¼ cup (40 g)	Capers
1	Lemon (juice)
4 stems	Parsley, chopped
To taste	Salt & pepper
8 × 3 oz (90 g)	Fresh Atlantic cod fillets
As needed	Butter and oil

- Remove the stem end of the endives to make them less bitter. Cook them or steam them in a basket steamer with a little of the fish fumet. Keep warm (endives should always be well cooked).
- Steam the potatoes. Set aside and keep warm.
- Sweat the peppers, onions and capers in butter. Add the lemon juice and parsley once the vegetables are cooked.
- Season the cod fillets, and cook in butter and oil until golden. Remove from the heat when white droplets escape from the fish. Arrange the pieces of fish on hot plates. Place the endives and potatoes on the plates.

- Add butter to the pepper and caper mixture, and pour onto the fish. Serve immediately.

Preparation time: 30 minutes **Cooking time:** 30 minutes
Servings: 4 **Cost:** $$$

Photo on next page →

Atlantic Cod Crumble with Vegetables and Tomato Sauce

approx. 3 lbs (1.4 kg)	Fresh tomatoes
3 Tbsp (50 mL)	Vegetable oil
3/4 cup (100 g)	Celery *brunoise*
1 1/2 cups (200 g)	Onions *brunoise*
2 cups (200 g)	Leeks *brunoise*
1 3/4 cups (250 g)	Carrots *brunoise*
To taste	Salt & pepper
2 Tbsp (30 g)	Tomato paste
1	Lemon (juice)
3	Anchovy fillets, minced
1/3 cup (20 g)	Chervil sprigs
1 1/4 lbs (600 g)	Fresh Atlantic cod fillets
3 1/2 oz (100 mL)	Fish fumet (see "Basic Ingredients for Some Recipes")
3 1/2 oz (100 mL)	White wine

Preparation time: 30 minutes **Cooking time:** 2 to 5 minutes
Servings: 4 **Cost:** $$$

- Peel and seed the tomatoes, then dice. Sweat the diced tomatoes and *brunoise* vegetables in oil. Season with salt and pepper, then continue to cook at low heat for 10 minutes. Add the tomato paste, lemon juice and the anchovies. Remove from the heat and let cool. Add the chervil to the cooled mixture and set aside.
- Salt and pepper the fresh Atlantic cod fillets. Heat the fish fumet and the white wine in a saucepan. Place a basket steamer in the pan and steam the fillets for 2 to 5 minutes. Let the cooked fish cool, then crumble. Reduce almost all of the fumet and the wine, then let cool.

Presentation: Arrange the tomato sauce and the vegetables in a ring on the plate. Place the crumbled cod in the center, and pour the fumet and wine reduction on top.

NOTE: This recipe, which is served cold here, may also be served hot.

HADDOCK

Melanogrammus aeglefinus (Linnaeus) *1758*
Incorrect names: cod

Characteristics: The head and back of this fish are violet-gray in color to the black lateral line, eventually becoming silvery-gray with pinkish highlights on the abdomen.

Flesh: Thin and light-tasting

Habitat: Both sides of the Atlantic

Where & When to Find It: Irregular availability where fish is sold. November and December, in abundance

Processed & Sold: As steaks, fillets and whole

Cooking Method: *Meunière*, steamed, poached or baked whole

Value: To be cooked gently as the flesh is not very solid

Comments: Haddock is used in the preparation of "fish and chips."

$$

Haddock Steaks with Endives and Saltwater Cordgrass

7 oz (200 mL)	Fish fumet (see "Basic Ingredients for Some Recipes")
1	Dried, chopped shallot
1 lb (450 g)	Endives, sliced thin
1/3 cup (80 g)	Butter
3 Tbsp (35 g)	Saltwater cordgrass
2 cups (500 mL)	Cream (35%)
1	Lemon (juice)

4 × 6 oz (180 g)	Fresh haddock steaks

- Pour the fish fumet into a deep saucepan. Add the shallot and cook for 5 minutes. Sweat the endives in butter along with the saltwater cordgrass.
- Add the cream and reduce until the desired consistency is achieved. Add the lemon juice. Place a basket steamer in the saucepan containing the fumet.
- Place the haddock slices in the steamer. Cover and steam for 5 to 6 minutes. Heat the plates. Arrange a haddock steak on each plate. Pour the endive sauce over the fish.

Preparation time: 20 minutes **Cooking time:** 8 to 10 minutes
Servings: 4 **Cost:** $$

Haddock Steaks with Cucumber

³/4 cup (150 g)	Butter
approx. ¹/2 lb (250 g)	*Parisienne* cucumbers (in small balls)
1 cup (250 mL)	Cream (35%)
6 × 6 oz (180 g)	Haddock steaks
As needed	Flour
2	Eggs, beaten
To taste	Salt & pepper
2	Lemons
¹/4 cup (15 g)	Parsley, chopped fresh
6	Anchovies
12	Black olives

- Braise the *parisienne* cucumbers in half the butter. Add the cream. Dredge the steaks in the flour, then in the seasoned, beaten eggs. Cook them *à la meunière* in the remaining butter, arrange them on a serving dish and surround with the cucumbers.
- Sprinkle with the lemon juice, then the butter used in the cooking. Sprinkle with the chopped parsley. Garnish with the anchovies wrapped around the black olives.

Preparation time: 30 minutes	**Cooking time:** 8 to 12 minutes
Servings: 6	**Cost:** $$

POLLOCK (BOSTON BLUEFISH, SAITHE [GB])

Pollachius virens (Linnaeus) *1758*
Incorrect names: hake, whiting

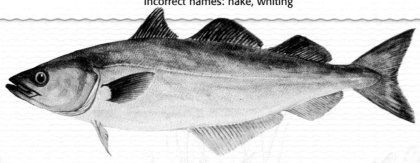

Characteristics: The back is a brownish-green that gradually becomes yellowish; has a silvery-gray abdomen; measures 20 to 35 inches (50 to 90 cm) and weighs from 2 1/4 to 15 1/2 lbs (1 to 7 kg).

Flesh: Thin, light and delicate

Habitat: Both sides of the Atlantic

Where & When to Find It: July, August and September, in abundance

Processed & Sold: Smoked, whole, as steaks or fillets

Cooking Method: *Meunière*, poached, steamed or roasted whole

Value: A good fish for lunch; tends to fall apart when cooked

Comments: This fish is referred to as coalfish and hake in Europe. It is primarily used to produce surimi, which are imitation crabmeat, shrimp and scallops. Commonly found in supermarkets.

$$

Pollock Brandade

1 3/4 lbs (800 g)	Salted pollock
3/4 lb (350 g)	Potatoes
To taste	Salt
1 cup (250 mL)	Olive oil
2 1/2 Tbsp (30 g)	Garlic, chopped
1 1/2 cups (350 mL)	Cream (35%)
To taste	Ground pepper and grated nutmeg
1/2 cup (60 g)	Fresh bread crumbs
6 slices	Sandwich bread
1/3 cup (60 g)	Butter

- Desalt the pollock under cold running water the night before. The next day, cut into pieces and poach in boiling water for approximately 6 minutes from the moment the water has reached boiling point. Drain the pollock, then remove the skin and bones.

- Cook the potatoes, unpeeled, in boiling, salted water. Peel, and grind with a vegetable mill.

- In a sauté pan, heat the oil and add the garlic, pollock and the potatoes. Mix well with a wooden spoon, stirring until a paste is obtained with the consistency of mashed potatoes. Purée in a blender and return to the sauté pan.

- Add the cream, pepper and nutmeg to this mixture, then work with the spoon. Pour 1 cup (250 mL) of this preparation into individual oval *au gratin* dishes. Dust with fresh bread crumbs and bake in the oven.

Presentation: Serve with triangles of sandwich bread fried in butter and a buttered green vegetable, such as spinach or green beans. May be served with lemon herb butter (see "Basic Ingredients for Some Recipes") as an accompaniment.

Preparation time: 40 minutes **Cooking time:** 20 to 35 minutes
Servings: 6   **Cost:** $$

Pollock Fillets with Steamed Seaweed and Lemon Butter

As needed	Water and salt
approx. 2 cups (150 g)	Fresh seaweed (kelp or rockweed)
or	
1/3 cup (30 g)	Dried seaweed
1 1/4 lbs (600 g)	Green cabbage, sliced thin
6 oz (180 g)	Carrot, sliced thin
6 oz (180 g)	Leek, sliced thin
6 × 50 oz (150 g)	Pollock fillets

3 Tbsp (40 mL)	Lemon juice
1 cup (180 g)	Diced butter

- In a stockpot, combine the water, salt and seaweed. Bring to a boil. Place a basket steamer in the stockpot. Lay the vegetables in the basket and half cook, covered. Place the pollock fillets in the basket and cook for 6 minutes.
- During this time, reduce the lemon juice by 1/3. Set a skillet on low heat and gradually add the diced butter, whisking constantly. Serve the lemon butter with the fish, vegetables and the seaweed.

Preparation time: 10 minutes **Cooking time:** 6 to 10 minutes
Servings: 6   **Cost:** $$

CUSK

Brosme brosme (Müller) *1776*

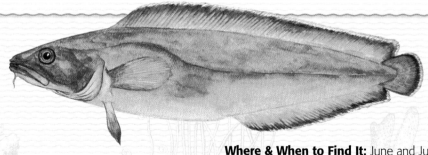

Characteristics: The color of the body can vary according to the environment, ranging from dark red to brownish-green or pale yellow. This fish can reach 3 1/4 ft. (1 m) in length and weigh 27 lbs (12.2 kg).

Flesh: Lean and firm

Habitat: North Atlantic

Where & When to Find It: June and July, in abundance; rarely available where fish is sold

Processed & Sold: Whole or as fillets

Cooking Method: *Meunière*, poached or steamed

Value: Because it is new on the market, there is a certain culinary interest. Its flesh resembles that of cod.

$$

Cusk, Redfish and Smelt in Beurre blanc

5 1/2 lbs (2.5 kg)	Cusk
1 1/2 lbs (750 g)	Redfish
8 × 2 oz (60 g)	Smelt
To taste	Salt & pepper
approx. 1/2 cup (60 g)	Carrot (medium-sized), julienned (in thin strips)
1/2 cup (60 g)	Celery, julienned
2/3 cup (60 g)	Leek (white part only), julienned
4 cups (1 L)	Water
4	Whole mushrooms
As needed	Lemon juice
1 cup (160 g)	*Beurre blanc* (see "Basic Ingredients for Some Recipes")

• Fillet the cusk and the redfish. Cut off the heads of the smelts, drain them from the stomach, then remove the bones by pulling toward the tail while sliding the knife blade under the bones. Keep the tail intact. Season and roll up the smelts.

• Cook the vegetables, excluding the mushrooms, in boiling salted water; set aside and keep warm. Save the water used for cooking. Steam the fish fillets in a basket steamer using the water in which the vegetables were cooked. Steam until the fish are done (3 minutes for the redfish and the cod, 1 minute for the smelts).

• Garnish the plate with the vegetables, and esthetically arrange the fish and the previously blanched mushrooms (i.e., cooked for several minutes in boiling salted water with lemon).

• Pour the *beurre blanc* into the middle of the plate and serve immediately.

Preparation time: 30 minutes	**Cooking time:** 5 minutes
Servings: 4	**Cost:** $$$

Cusk Fillets Creole

1/3 cup (80 mL)	Peanut oil
1 1/4 cup (175 g)	Onion, chopped
2 1/3 cups (250 g)	Celery, chopped
1 cup (175 g)	Green chili, chopped
1	Garlic clove, chopped
1 1/3 cup (240 g)	Fresh tomatoes, blanched, peeled, seeded and diced
To taste	Salt & pepper
6 × 5 oz (150 g)	Cusk fillets

- Cook the celery, onion, chili and garlic in 1/4 cup (60 mL) of oil at low heat. Add the tomatoes and let cook for 10 minutes. Remove from the heat. Season to taste, set aside and keep warm.
- Clean the cusk fillets, then place them in an oiled ovenproof dish. Cover with the cooked vegetables. Bake at 400°F (200°C) for 10 minutes.

Accompaniment: Sautéed *parisienne* chayote

Preparation time: 15 minutes **Cooking time:** 25 minutes
Servings: 6 **Cost:** $$$

SQUIRREL HAKE

Urophycis chuss (Walbaum) *1792*
Incorrect names: whiting, pollock, European hake

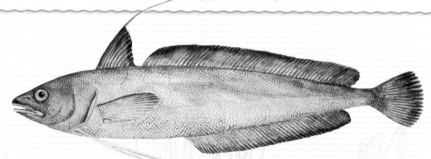

Characteristics: The color of the body varies: from a reddish- to a brownish-black with faint metallic highlights on the jowls; a pale gray abdomen. This fish may reach 4 1/2 ft (1.4 m) in length and weigh up to 44 lbs (20 kg).

Flesh: Lean and firm

Habitat: North Atlantic

Where & When to Find It: June to November, in abundance

Processed & Sold: Whole or as fillets. Rarely found on the market

Cooking Method: *Meunière*, steamed, poached or roasted whole

Value: Some culinary interest, particularly as a fish to be served for lunch

$$

Squirrel Hake Raclette

4 × 8–10 oz (250–300 g)	Squirrel hake
To taste	Salt & pepper
2	Lemons (juice)
4	Very ripe tomatoes
3 Tbsp (50 mL)	Olive oil
To taste	Whole nutmeg
9 oz (250 g)	Raclette cheese, cut into very fine slices
approx. 2/3 cup (140 mL)	Cream (35%)

- Clean the squirrel hake (beard, remove the head and the fine black film located inside the stomach). Remove the bones through the stomach.

- Season with salt and pepper, then place in a dish. Sprinkle with the lemon juice and marinate for at least 30 minutes, turning the fish often.
- During this time, blanch, peel, seed and crush the tomatoes.
- Grease an ovenproof dish with the olive oil. Lay the fish in the dish, season with salt and pepper and sprinkle with a little nutmeg. Arrange the tomatoes uniformly on top of the fish. Cover with the cheese slices, then pour in the cream. Bake at 400°F (200°C) for 25 to 35 minutes. Serve immediately in the ovenproof dish.

Accompaniment: Tagliatelle prepared *al dente*

Preparation time: 20 minutes **Cooking time:** 25 to 35 minutes
Servings: 4   **Cost:** $$$

Braised Squirrel Hake with Onions and Potatoes

2 × 1 lb (approx.500 g)	Squirrel hake
1 1/2 cups (200 g)	Spanish or red onions
3 1/2 oz (100 mL)	Olive oil
1/3 cup (60 g)	Butter
2/3 cup (160 mL)	White wine
1 1/4 cup (300 mL)	Fish fumet (see "Basic Ingredients for Some Recipes")
approx. 2 cups (240 g)	Potatoes, diced small

Preparation time: 30 minutes   **Cooking time:** 25 minutes
Servings: 4   **Cost:** $$

To taste	Salt, pepper and whole nutmeg

- Clean the squirrel hake and set aside.
- Thinly slice the onions. Heat the oil and the butter, then gently braise the onions for approximately 10 minutes. Add the white wine, fish fumet and the diced potatoes. Let simmer for 5 minutes. Salt, pepper and add some grated nutmeg.
- Place the squirrel hake in an ovenproof dish and pour the preceding mixture over the fish.
- Cover with aluminum foil and bake at 400°F (200°C) for 10 minutes. Serve as is on a plate.

SILVER HAKE

Merluccius bilinearis (Mitchill) *1814*
Incorrect names: pollock, whiting, European hake, hake

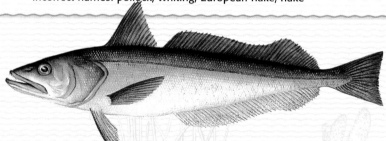

Characteristics: Silver-colored when out of water, this fish can measure 35 inches (90 cm) in length and weigh 5 lbs (2.3 kg). On average, its length ranges from 9 to 14 inches (24 to 35 cm) and its weight is 1 1/2 lbs (700 g).

Flesh: Thin, light and very tasty

Habitat: Continental shelf off the eastern coast of North America

Where & When to Find It: June to November, in abundance

Processed & Sold: Whole or as fillets

Cooking Method: *Meunière*, steamed or poached

Value: Delicate flesh, ideal for serving at lunch

Comments: Should not come in contact with ice

$$

Silver Hake à l'armoricaine *or* à l'américaine

4 × 8–10 oz (240–280 g)	Silver hake slices
To taste	Salt & pepper
As needed	Flour
1/4 cup (60 mL)	Virgin olive oil
1/3 cup (60 g)	Butter
1/2 cup (130 mL)	Cognac
approx. 1/2 cup (60 g)	Shallots, chopped
3/4 cup (100 g)	Carrot *brunoise*
3/4 cup (100 g)	Celery *brunoise*
4	Tomatoes, blanched, peeled, seeded and diced
1/4 tsp (1 g)	Saffron
1 Pinch	Cayenne pepper
1/2 cup (30 g)	Flat-leafed parsley, minced
1/2	Garlic clove, chopped
1 cup (250 mL)	Dry white wine
1 tsp (2 g)	Thyme sprigs
1/2	Bay leaf
2/3 cup (160 mL)	Lobster sauce (see "Basic Ingredients for Some Recipes")

- Drain and dry the silver hake slices. Season with salt and pepper, then flour. Heat the olive oil and the butter in a sauté pan. Sauté until the fish slices are golden. Set aside. Drain the excess fat and flambé with cognac. Cover and set aside.
- In a saucepan, cook the chopped shallots, carrot and celery *brunoise* in the excess fat until tender, then add the diced tomatoes, saffron, cayenne pepper, parsley and garlic.

Cook for 3 to 4 minutes. Add the white wine, thyme and the bay leaf. Adjust the seasoning.

- Pour this preparation over the fish slices and bake for 12 to 15 minutes at 400°F (200°C).

- Heat the lobster sauce.
- Remove the fish preparation from the oven, and place a fish slice and garnish on each plate. Cover with the hot lobster sauce. Serve with boiled potatoes.

Preparation time: 50 minutes **Cooking time:** 12 to 20 minutes
Servings: 4   **Cost:** $$$

Silver Hake Butterfly Fillets with Vegetable Garnish

2/3 cup (160 mL)	White wine
3	Dried shallots, minced
4 1/2 Tbsp (75 g)	Tomato paste
1 cup (250 mL)	Fish fumet (see "Basic Ingredients for Some Recipes")
As needed	White roux (see "Basic Ingredients …") and butter
1 3/4 cup (200 g)	Carrots
approx. 1 cup (200 g)	Red beets
1 1/2 cups (250 g)	Potatoes
As needed	Water
To taste	Salt & pepper
4 × 12 oz (350 g)	Whole silver hakes
As needed	Flour and oil

- Heat the wine and the shallots. Reduce completely. Incorporate the tomato paste and cook in order to reduce the level of acidity. Add the fumet and cook for 10 minutes.

- Bind the sauce with the white roux, then thicken with butter. Set the sauce aside and keep warm.
- Carve the carrots, beets and potatoes into the shape of an olive. Cook the vegetables separately in boiling, salted water. Set aside.
- Split the silver hakes open, starting at the stomach and stopping 1 inch (3 cm) from the tail. Remove the backbone and dry off the fish as well as possible. Season with salt and pepper. Dredge the hakes in flour and cook in butter and oil in a skillet until golden, approximately 5 to 7 minutes, to prevent overcooking.
- Reheat the vegetables in the butter. Heat the tomato-fish sauce, then pour onto hot plates. Lay a fish on each plate and arrange the vegetables in the middle of each fish. Serve immediately.

Preparation time: 45 minutes **Cooking time:** 12 to 15 minutes
Servings: 4   **Cost:** $$$

Photo on next page →

WHITING

Merlangius merlangus (Linnaeus) *1758*
Incorrect names: European hake, hake

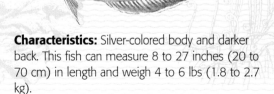

Characteristics: Silver-colored body and darker back. This fish can measure 8 to 27 inches (20 to 70 cm) in length and weigh 4 to 6 lbs (1.8 to 2.7 kg).

Flesh: Lean and soft

Habitat: South Atlantic

Where & When to Find It: Imported year round

Processed & Sold: Whole

Cooking Method: *Meunière* or poached

Value: Lean and easily digested. An excellent fish

Comments: Whiting is called "hake" in the Mediterranean region, which is the origin of the confusion surrounding the true hake.

$$

Whiting Fillets à la dijonnaise

1 ¹/₂ cups (250 g)	Sweet butter
4 × 5–6 oz (160–180 g)	Whiting fillets
As needed	Dijon mustard
4	Tomato rounds, peeled and seeded
1 ¹/₃ cups (160 g)	Bread crumbs
4	Shallots, chopped
1 ¹/₄ cups (300 mL)	White wine
1 ¹/₄ cups (300 mL)	White wine vinegar
To taste	Salt & pepper
¹/₂ cup (30 g)	Parsley, chopped
³/₄ cup (20 g)	Tarragon leaves, chopped
¹/₂ cup (25 g)	Chives, chopped

- In a skillet, sear the whiting fillets in 4 ¹/₂ Tbsp (50 g) of butter until golden. Brush an ovenproof dish with 4 ¹/₂ Tbsp (50 g) of whipped butter. Lay the whiting fillets in the dish and coat with the Dijon mustard. Cover each fillet with tomato rounds and sprinkle with bread crumbs. Set aside.
- In a saucepan, reduce the shallots with the white wine and the white wine vinegar. Pepper and reduce until a syrupy consistency is obtained. Set aside.
- Bake the whiting fillets at 400°F (200°C) for 8 to 12 minutes, depending on the thickness of the fillets.
- Incorporate the remaining butter and cooking juice from the fish into the reduction, whisking vigorously. Adjust the seasoning and incorporate the parsley, tarragon and chives.

Presentation: Place a whiting fillet in the middle of each plate. Pour the sauce around it and serve with hot, boiled white rice.

Preparation time: 30 minutes	**Cooking time:** 12 to 18 minutes
Servings: 4	**Cost:** $$

Stuffed Whiting Baked in the Oven

approx. 3 lbs (1.3 kg)	Whiting
To taste	Salt & pepper
2/3 cups (150 g)	Butter
2	Egg whites
approx. 5 oz (140 g)	Basic fish mousse (see "Basic Ingredients for Some Recipes")
1 1/3 cups (150 g)	Carrot sticks, cooked
1 cup (100 g)	Green beans, cooked
1 cup (240 mL)	*Fines herbes* sauce garnished with shrimp (see "Basic Ingredients …")

Preparation time: 20 to 30 minutes
Cooking time: 30 to 35 minutes
Servings: 6   **Cost:** $$$$

- Scale the fish. Remove the bones through the stomach. Season the inside and the outside of the fish. Place the fish on a sheet of buttered aluminum foil and brush with the egg whites. Lay the sheet on a rack.
- Using a spatula, cover the fish with half of the fish mousse.
- On this same aluminum sheet, place the previously cooked carrot sticks and green beans. Cover the remaining area with the rest of the mousse, using a pastry bag and a fluted pastry nozzle. Seal the edges of the aluminum foil around the fish. Place everything on a baking sheet and bake at 350°F (180°C) for 30 minutes. Open the foil and divide the whiting into six servings.
- Serve on plates with the *fines herbes* sauce garnished with shrimp.

ATLANTIC TOMCOD

Microgadus tomcod (Walbaum) *1792*

Characteristics: The back is brownish, with a greenish or yellowish tint; the abdomen is grayish or yellowish-white. Maximum length is 18 inches (45 cm).

Flesh: Lean

Where & When to Find It: November to March, in abundance

Processed & Sold: Whole

Cooking Method: Fried or poached

Value: A small fish, the Atlantic tomcod is ideal for frying.

$$

Fried Atlantic Tomcod

4 1/2 lbs (2 kg)	Tomcod
As needed	All-purpose flour
To taste	Salt
2	Eggs
2/3 cup (150 mL)	White bread crumbs
As needed	Oil
3/4 cup (50 g)	Fresh parsley
	Lemon wedges

- If the tomcod are small, remove everything but the head and the tail. If larger, cut off the head only. Clean and dry off.
- Dredge the fish in the flour, to which salt has been added. Dip each fish in the mixture of beaten eggs, milk and salt, then dredge the pieces in the bread crumbs.
- Bake the fish in oil at 375°F (190°C). Serve hot with fried parsley. Serve the lemon wedges on the side.

NOTE: White bread crumbs can be made by removing the crusts from white bread and crumbling it in a food processor.

Preparation time: 20 minutes **Cooking time:** 5 minutes
Servings: 6 **Cost:** $$

Photo on page 91

Atlantic Tomcod Fillets with Endive

2 ¼ lbs (1 kg)	Endive
As needed	Butter
2 lbs (900 g)	Atlantic tomcod fillets
1 ½ cups (350 mL)	Milk
To taste	Salt & ground pepper
As needed	Flour and clarified butter

LEMON BUTTER

¾ cup (175 mL)	White wine
¾ cup (175 mL)	Lemon juice
3 Tbsp (30 g)	Shallots, chopped
3 oz (90 mL)	Cream (35%)
1 ⅔ cups (275 g)	Sweet butter
To taste	Salt & pepper
¾ cup (30 g)	Fresh chives, cut with scissors

- Remove the stem end of the endives and cook whole in very little water with a few knobs of butter, and covered with a heavy lid that presses down on the vegetables.
- Fillet the fish, then dip the fillets in the seasoned milk. Flour then cook *à la meunière* with the clarified butter in an oval fish pan. In the same pan, cook the endives, which have been drained and floured, in the *meunière* style. Remove the cooking fat from each fillet, using a paper towel. Arrange the fillets and the endives on a fairly large oval plate. Cover and let simmer until the fish is opaque and flakes easily.
- **Lemon Butter:** In a cast-iron saucepan, reduce the wine, the lemon juice and the shallots by half on high heat, then add the cream and the small pieces of sweet butter and whisk vigorously. Salt and pepper to taste and add the chives. Serve with the butter.

Preparation time: 30 minutes	**Cooking time:** 10 to 15 minutes
Servings: 6	**Cost:** $$$

SALMON, CHAR, TROUT AND OTHERS

Salmonidae

A cook views this family of fish as being of the highest nobility. The beauty of these fish and their color is such that their being prepared in the kitchen is a cause for celebration.

The size of *Salmonidae* varies from moderate to large. Varying also in shape and appearance, these fish generally have a body that is less compressed than that of herring.

Different names have been given to salmon to distinguish the different stages of life. The newly hatched young are referred to as "fry"; after leaving the gravel beds, they are referred to as "fry of less than one year" or "finger fry." Later, these young salmon, who are called "parr," may stay in the rivers for 2 to 3 years until they go down to the sea as silver "smolts." Those who return after one winter at sea are referred to as "first-sea-winter salmon," or "salmon" if they have spent 2 or more years in the ocean. Salmon, like some Arctic char, are anadromous—they live in salt water and reproduce in fresh water.

The freshwater salmon, also known as "ouananiche," is usually smaller than the anadromous salmon. The average weight of a freshwater salmon is 2 to 4 lbs (900 g to 1.9 kg), but some ouananiche can weigh as much as 7 lbs (3.4 kg). In the Atlantic, there is only one salmon species, i.e., "Atlantic salmon," while on the Pacific coast, 4 species are fished: chum, coho, sockeye and chinook salmon.

The recipes in this chapter can be used interchangeably as the flesh of all these fish is equally delicate. Other *Salmonidae* that can be prepared by simply adapting the recipes contained in this chapter include Arctic char, salmon trout, pink salmon, cutthroat trout, lake herring, inconnu and round whitefish.

Arctic char
Atlantic salmon
Sockeye salmon
Coho salmon
Chum salmon
Chinook salmon
Lake trout
Speckled trout
Rainbow trout
Whitefish

ARCTIC CHAR
Salvelinus alpinus (Linnaeus)

Characteristics: With a dark green or green-blue back, silver-blue sides with orange or red spots and a whitish or reddish-orange abdomen, this fish measures, on average, 12 to 18 inches (30 to 45 cm).

Flesh: Fatty

Habitat: Alaska and northern Canada

Where & When to Find It: If farmed, this fish is generally available all year round.

Processed & Sold: Whole, as fillets and steaks

Cooking Method: Roasted whole, *meunière*, stuffed, braised or poached

Value: Of high culinary quality

Comments: Because of its delicate flesh, this fish does not tolerate freezing well. The true Arctic char, a game fish, is found only in the most northerly regions. Obviously, farmed fish are not quite as good as game fish.

$$$

Arctic Char * with Cloudberries

approx. 1 cup (160 g)	Butter
approx. 1 ⅓ cup (80 mL)	Peanut oil
To taste	Salt & pepper
4 × 4 oz (120 g)	Fresh Arctic char fillets
1 ⅓ cups (160 g)	Cloudberries
As needed	Wild leek leaves, cut with scissors

- In a cast-iron skillet, heat half the butter and the oil. Salt and pepper the fillets.
- Cook *à la meunière*, searing the fillets. Once cooked, set the fillets aside and keep warm. Remove the cooking fat.
- Gently melt the remaining butter and braise the cloudberries.
- Arrange the fillets on hot plates and spoon the cloudberries over each fillet. Sprinkle with the wild leek leaves.

NOTE: Cloudberries, a small fruit found on the tundra, have a refined taste which goes well with that of the char.

* Dedicated to my son, Joel, who introduced me to this marvelous northern fish.

Preparation time: 15 minutes	**Cooking time:** 12 minutes
Servings: 4	**Cost:** $$$

Nunavik Arctic Char Savarin *with Smoked Char Sauce*

approx. 1 lb (500 g)	Arctic char flesh
4	Eggs
1 cup (250 mL)	Cream (35%)
To taste	Salt & pepper
1 cup (170 g)	Butter, whipped
approx. 2 oz (50 g)	Arctic char, diced
3 1/2 Tbsp (30 g)	Mushrooms, diced
12	Chives
1/2 cup (125 mL)	Fish fumet (see "Basic Ingredients for Some Recipes")
approx. 3 oz (100 g)	Arctic char, smoked

- In a blender, purée the 1 lb (500 g) of Arctic char. Add the eggs and 2/3 cup (150 mL) of cream. Season, then add 1/3 cup (60 g) of whipped butter. Fold the mousse gently, keeping it very light. With 2 Tbsp (20 g) of butter, grease the *savarin* molds and fill with the mousse. Place the molds in a *bain-marie* and cook at 350°F (180°C).
- Sweat the small pieces of char and the mushrooms in 3 1/2 Tbsp (40 g) of butter. Season with salt and pepper. Add the chives and 3 1/2 oz (100 mL) of cream at the last minute. Garnish the inside of the *savarins* with this ragout.
- Reduce the (unsalted) fish fumet. Purée the smoked Arctic char and combine with 4 1/2 Tbsp (50 g) of butter. Thicken the fumet reduction with this mixture. Add pepper. Cover the *savarins* with this preparation and serve.

Preparation time: 5 minutes	**Cooking time:** 15 minutes
Servings: 6	**Cost:** $$$

ATLANTIC SALMON
Salmo salar

Where & When to Find It: All year round for farmed fish

Processed & Sold: Whole, as fillets and steaks

Cooking Method: Grilled, *meunière*, poached, steamed or braised in the oven

Characteristics: Color varies according to age. The sides and abdomen are generally silver; the back shades of brown, green or blue, with black spots; turns a violet-copper shade with reddish spots when spawning. Weight varies from 3 to 20 lbs (1.4 to 9.2 kg).

Flesh: Fatty

Habitat: Atlantic

Value: The wild Atlantic salmon remains a fish for special occasions.

Comments: Now that Atlantic salmon is farmed, it is generally available. However, the farmed fish is fragile once cooked, as it is sedentary in life. Obviously, nothing compares to the taste of a wild catch.

$$

Smolt in Red Wine, Stuffed with Julienned * *Vegetables*

2 cups (500 mL)	Red wine
2 ¾ Tbsp (25 g)	Shallots, chopped
14 oz (400 mL)	Fish fumet (see "Basic Ingredients …")
¾ cup (100 g)	Butter
⅓ cup (35 g)	Carrot, finely julienned
¾ cup (85 g)	Leek (white part), finely julienned
As needed	Red wine
10 oz (300 g)	Fresh smolt
To taste	Salt & pepper
As needed	White roux (see "Basic Ingredients …")

- Heat the red wine with the chopped shallots and reduce almost completely. Add the fish fumet and cook for 7 to 8 minutes. Set the reduced fumet aside and keep warm.
- Cook the julienned vegetables in the butter until tender. Add a few drops of red wine and braise. Let cool.
- Bone the smolt through the stomach, salt and pepper. Stuff with the julienned vegetables and place on a buttered ovenproof dish. Add the fish fumet.
- Cover with buttered aluminum foil. Bake at 400°F (200°C) for 7 to 10 minutes. Remove from the oven and skin while the fish is still hot. Set the smolt aside and keep warm; keep the cooking liquid. Add to the reduced

Preparation time: 1 hour	**Cooking time:** 7 to 10 minutes
Servings: 2	**Cost:** $$$

fumet, which has been set aside. Bind with a little white roux.

- Arrange the smolt on a hot platter and cover with the red wine sauce (except the head).

Accompaniment: Small *cocotte* potatoes cooked in red wine

* Dedicated to chef Pierre Garcin.

Grilled Atlantic Salmon Steaks

4 × 6 oz (180 g)	Atlantic salmon steaks
To taste	Salt & pepper
As needed	Peanut oil
1	Lemon

- After drying off the salmon steaks, salt, pepper and brush with oil.
- Heat the grill to two different intensities: on the one side, very hot; on the other, moderate heat. Sear and crisscross both sides of the steak on the hot side, then transfer to the moderately warm side and finish cooking.
- Before serving, remove the skin and the backbone. Serve with lemon or béarnaise sauce (see "Basic Ingredients for Some Recipes").

Accompaniment: Steamed *cocotte* potatoes
NOTE: To successfully grill a fish, it is important that the steaks be dried off to prevent steaming.

Preparation time: 20 minutes	**Cooking time:** 12 to 15 minutes
Servings: 4	**Cost:** $$

Atlantic Salmon Wrapped in Cabbage

4	Savoy cabbage leaves
approx. 1 cup (160 g)	Butter
1/2 cup (50 g)	Shallots, chopped
1/2 cup (50 g)	Leek (white part only), sliced thin
1/2 cup (125 mL)	Dry white wine
7 oz (200 mL)	Fish fumet (see "Basic Ingredients for Some Recipes")
As needed	White roux (see "Basic Ingredients ...")
1/2 cup (125 mL)	Cream (35%)
1	Lemon (juice)
To taste	Salt & pepper
1 1/4 cup (160 g)	Mushrooms, chopped
1/2 cup (100 g)	Tomatoes, blanched, peeled, seeded and diced
4 × 5 oz (150 g)	Atlantic salmon fillets, skinned

- Blanch the cabbage leaves in salted water.
- Cook the chopped shallots and minced leek with 4 1/2 Tbsp (50 g) of butter until tender; add the white wine and reduce by 9/10. Add the fish fumet and lightly bind with the white roux. Add the cream and the lemon juice. Season to taste, strain through cheesecloth or a fine mesh strainer. Set aside.
- Sweat the mushrooms in 4 1/2 Tbsp (50 g) of butter until dry, then add the diced tomatoes, salt and pepper. Set aside.
- Lay out the blanched savoy cabbage leaves, then salt and pepper the salmon fillets. Place the mushrooms and the diced tomatoes on the fillets. Fold the cabbage leaves over the salmon fillets.
- Brush an ovenproof dish with 1/3 cup (60 g) of butter and place the cabbage wraps in the dish. Pour the sauce around them and bake at low temperature (185°F or 85°C) for 25 to 40 minutes. Serve as is with white rice, rice Creole or rice pilaf.

NOTE: How do you determine if wrapped fish is done? Ideally, with a thermometer. The temperature should be 175°F (80°C). Otherwise, poke the tip of a knife into the middle of the cabbage wrap and pull out. If the tip is warm to hot, the fish is ready.

Preparation time: 30 minutes	**Cooking time:** 40 minutes		
Servings: 4		**Cost:** $$$	

Photo on facing page →

SOCKEYE SALMON

Oncorhynchus nerka

Incorrect name: Red salmon

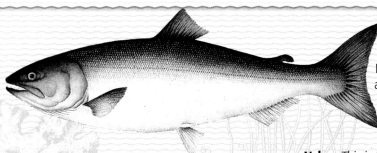

Where & When to Find It: If farmed, available all year round

Processed & Sold: Whole, smoked, as fillets and steaks

Cooking Method: Grilled, *meunière*, poached, steamed or braised in the oven

Value: This is the best of the Pacific salmon, especially the wild species.

Characteristics: Sides are silver and the back is green with black spots. Its weight ranges from 3 to 20 lbs (1.4 to 9.2 kg); its average length is 28 inches (72 cm).

Flesh: Fatty

Habitat: Pacific

Comments: The Pacific salmon (males and females) always die once they have returned to fresh water and spawned. This does not happen to Atlantic salmon. Sockeye salmon is the best-known of the Pacific salmon.

$$$

Escalopes of Salmon Cooked on One Side, with Shrimp Coulis

4 × 4 oz (120 g)	Salmon escalopes
2/3 cup (160 mL)	Shrimp coulis (see "Basic Ingredients for Some Recipes"—for Lobster Coulis)
To taste	Salt & pepper
1/3 cup (60 g)	Butter
12	Chives

- **Essentials**: Buy a whole salmon, boned, skinned, and filleted. Cut (or have cut) into small, scallop-size fillets (1/2 inch or 1 cm each). Lay them out on plastic wrap and freeze. Once frozen, wrap the escalopes and store in the freezer. One salmon should produce approximately 30 escalopes. Moreover, small 1-cup (250-mL) containers of deep-frozen lobster or shrimp sauce should always be kept on hand.

- **To prepare**: Thaw the lobster or shrimp sauce in the microwave oven and keep warm. Take enough salmon escalopes out of the freezer, and spread them out on a non-stick baking sheet. Salt, pepper and drop knobs of butter on the salmon escalopes, then broil in the oven on one side only. Arrange on a very hot plate and pour the sauce around them. From freezer to table in just 20 minutes.

Accompaniment: Rice with chives

NOTE: This recipe can be a lifesaver when unexpected guests arrive at the dinner hour.

Preparation time: Prepared in advance	
Cooking time: 2 minutes	
Servings: 4	**Cost:** $$$

Steamed Salmon Sausage with Lemon Butter

approx. 1 lb (500 g)	**Salmon flesh**
1/2 cup (125 mL)	**Cream (35%)**
5	**Whole eggs**
As needed	**Chopped parsley**
To taste	**Salt & pepper**
As needed	**Grated nutmeg**
1/2	**Lemon (juice)**
1	**Sheep casing (for sausage making)**
As needed	**Court-bouillon (see "Basic Ingredients for Some Recipes")**

LEMON BUTTER

1/3 cup (80 mL)	**Lemon juice**
1 1/2 cups (250 g)	**Sweet butter**
1 Tbsp (15 mL)	**Cream (35%)**
To taste	**Salt & pepper**

- In a blender, purée the salmon, cream, eggs and parsley until a fairly smooth forcemeat is obtained. Season with salt and pepper, then add the grated nutmeg. Adjust the seasoning, if necessary, then add the lemon juice.

- Soak the sheep casing at least 2 hours ahead. Slip the casing onto the end of a funnel and make a knot at the end, then stuff with the salmon forcemeat. Tie off the casing every 4 inches (10 cm).
- *Court-bouillon*: Add a fair amount of salt to the *court-bouillon* and bring to a boil. Lower the heat and add the sausages, cooking them for 10 minutes in the simmering *court-bouillon* (do not boil). Take the sausages out of the *court-bouillon* and set aside. To reheat, place the sausages in the upper section of a couscous kettle and steam for 4 minutes.
- **Lemon butter**: Bring the lemon juice to a boil, then gradually stir in the pieces of hard butter.
- Add the cream to the lemon-butter mixture; season and bring once more to a boil. Remove from the heat and serve.

Preparation time: 1 hour	**Cooking time:** 5 minutes
Servings: 6	**Cost:** $$$

COHO SALMON
Oncorhynchus kisutch

Characteristics: Almost entirely silver with metallic blue-green on the back. Its weight varies from 3 1/2 to 10 lbs (1.6 to 4.5 kg) and its length averages 15 inches (38 cm).

Flesh: Fatty

Habitat: Pacific

Where & When to Find It: If farmed, available all year round

Processed & Sold: Whole, smoked, as fillets and steaks

Cooking Method: Braised, poached, steamed, grilled and *meunière*

Value: Good-quality fish

Comments: Coho salmon is the most common variety and can be found wherever fish is sold.

$$$

Coho Salmon Mousseline *with Smoked Eel Rillettes*

6 slices	Sandwich bread
7 oz (200 mL)	Cream (35%)
approx. 1 lb (500 g)	Coho salmon fillets
5	Egg yolks
5	Egg whites
To taste	Salt & pepper
To taste	Nutmeg
1/3 cup (60 g)	Butter
As needed	Eel rillettes (recipe follows)

- Remove the crusts and soak the bread in cream for 5 minutes. In a blender, combine the coho salmon, the soaked bread and the egg yolks, and purée for 2 to 3 minutes.
- Add the cream and the egg whites. Season with salt and pepper, and grate a little nutmeg; purée for another minute in the blender.
- Generously butter an earthenware dish and fill half-full. Make an "eye" in the middle with the eel rillettes. Cover with the remaining preparation. Cook in a *bain-marie* at 350°F (180°C), covered, for 1 hour. Chill for 12 hours before serving.

Accompaniment: Muscovite sauce (see "Basic Ingredients for Some Recipes")

Preparation time: 1 hour	**Cooking time:** 1 hour
Servings: 10	**Cost:** $$$

Smoked Eel Rillettes

5 oz (150 g)	Smoked eel meat
5 oz (150 g)	White fish flesh
1	Egg white
To taste	Salt & pepper

- In a food processor, roughly purée all the ingredients. Spread out a sheet of plastic wrap and, with the forcemeat, make a small roll of rillettes. Steam for a few minutes and refrigerate. This roulade will serve as the salmon mousseline.

Preparation time: 10 minutes **Cooking time:** 5 minutes
Servings: 12   **Cost:** $$$

Coho Salmon Darioles with Sautéed Oyster Mushrooms and Beurre blanc

1 ½ lbs (650 g)	Coho salmon
1	Egg
1	Egg white
2 cups (500 mL)	Cream (35%)
To taste	Salt & pepper
½ bunch	Watercress
approx. 1 lb (500 g)	Large oyster mushrooms
As needed	Butter
2 ½ cups (600 mL)	Beurre blanc (see "Basic Ingredients for Some Recipes")
10 mL (2 tsp)	Chives, cut with scissors

- In a blender or food processor, purée the salmon. Add the egg and the egg white and blend until a uniform consistency is obtained. Strain through a fine sieve and refrigerate. Return the preparation to the blender and incorporate the cream, which should be very cold. Season and add the watercress leaves. Purée for several minutes or until the leaves are roughly chopped and well incorporated into the mixture. Refrigerate again.
- Grease small *dariole* molds with butter. Transfer the salmon mousseline to the molds using a pastry bag. Cover the mousselines with buttered aluminum foil and cook in a *bain-marie* at 350°F (180°C) for approximately 10 minutes until they are firm.
- After removing the inedible stems, lightly sauté the oyster mushrooms at high heat, constantly rotating the skillet, or steam them for a few minutes.

Presentation: Turn out the hot mousselines onto serving plates and garnish with the oyster mushrooms. Pour a little *beurre blanc* onto the plate. Decorate with the chives and serve immediately.

NOTE: The mousselines can be cooked ahead of time, set aside, then reheated at the last minute.

Preparation time: 30 minutes **Cooking time:** 20 minutes
Servings: 12   **Cost:** $$$

Photo on next page →

CHUM SALMON
Oncorhynchus keta

Characteristics: Silver-colored sides, metallic dark blue back. Weight can vary from 4 to 30 lbs (1.8 to 13.5 kg) Average length is 31 $^1/_2$ inches (80 cm).

Flesh: Fatty

Habitat: Pacific

Where & When to Find It: If farmed, available all year round

Processed & Sold: Whole, as fillets or steaks

Cooking Method: Poached, grilled, steamed or baked

Value: Slightly firm after cooking

Comments: The meat is white to creamy-white. Of all the varieties of salmon, this one has the lowest fat content. This salmon is generally used for canning.

$$$

Smoked Fish Bavarois

approx. $^1/_2$ lb (250 g)	Smoked fish trimmings (trout, salmon, sturgeon, cod, etc.)
2 cups (500 mL)	Milk
6	Egg yolks
3 Tbsp (45 mL)	Lemon juice
4 $^1/_2$ Tbsp (45 g)	Unflavored gelatin
1 cup (250 mL)	Cream (35%)
To taste	Ground pepper
As needed	Oil
approx. 3 oz (100 g)	Smoked salmon, sliced
20 half slices	Lemon
8 sprigs	Dill

- Soak the smoked fish trimmings in the milk for several minutes. Bring to a boil and immediately remove from the heat.
- Beat the egg yolks and add the hot liquid, constantly beating with a whisk. Return the entire mixture to the stove and, at low heat, continue stirring until the preparation has thickened; do not boil. Purée in a blender, then strain through cheesecloth or a fine mesh strainer. Add the lemon juice.
- Allow the gelatin to expand in water and incorporate into the warm smoked-fish preparation.
- Whip the cream until stiff peaks form. Incorporate the whipped cream into the chilled preparation.
- Adjust the seasoning, if necessary. Pour the *bavarois* mixture into a greased earthenware

mold. Let chill and set in the refrigerator for at least 6 hours before serving.

- Turn out of the dish and put one slice per serving on a cold plate; garnish each slice with a smoked salmon rosette, two lemon half-slices and a sprig of dill.

Accompaniment: Toasted baguette slices and butter

Preparation time: 40 minutes **Cooking time:** 5 minutes
Servings: 10 **Cost:** $$$$

Parr Feuillantine *with Spinach*

4	Smolt (parr)
To taste	Salt & pepper
4 1/2 lbs (2 kg)	Spinach leaves & stems
3/4 cup (125 g)	Butter
2 1/4 lbs (1 kg)	Mushrooms
4 1/2 lbs (2 kg)	Puff pastry
1/2 cup (60 g)	Shallots, chopped
14 oz (400 mL)	Cream (35%)
14 oz (400 mL)	Lobster bisque (see "Basic Ingredients for Some Recipes")

- Trim the smolt. Fillet and season. Sear the fillets briefly.
- Sweat half the spinach in half the butter; set the other half aside.
- Peel and chop the mushrooms. Combine the spinach and the mushrooms; season.
- Roll out the puff pastry and divide into two equal portions. Lay the fillets out on one of the rolled-out pastry halves. Spread with the stuffing (spinach and mushrooms). Cover with the other pastry half. Cut out in the shape of a fish and bake at 350°F (180°C) until the pastry turns golden.
- Sweat the leftover spinach with the remaining butter and the shallots. Add the cream and bring to a boil. Reduce and add the lobster bisque. Purée in a blender. Adjust the seasoning. Serve the sauce separately.

NOTE: Parr are rarely found on the market as it is unlawful to catch and sell them. However, there was a time when it was possible to find parr from the United States. On the other hand, this recipe works just as well using rainbow trout or speckled trout (brook trout).

Preparation time: 30 minutes **Cooking time:** 20 minutes
Servings: 4 **Cost:** $$$

Photo page 109

KING, CHINOOK AND SPRING SALMON
Oncorhynchus tshawytscha (Walbaum)

Characteristics: Silver sides and a dark green back with black spots. Average length is 22 inches (56 cm). Weight varies from 3 to 15 lbs (1.4 to 6.8 kg).

Flesh: Fatty

Habitat: Pacific

Where & When to Find It: If farmed, available all year round

Processed & Sold: Whole, smoked, as fillets and steaks

Cooking Method: *Meunière*, oven-grilled, poached, steamed or roasted

$$

Chinook Salmon Ballottines *with Shrimp and Maltese Sauce*

1 ¹/₄ lbs (600 g)	Fresh chinook salmon fillets, cut in ¹/₂-inch (1-cm) slices
To taste	Salt & pepper
2	Nori seaweed sheets
7 oz (200 g)	Raw shrimp
1	Small egg
¹/₄ tsp (1 mL)	Cayenne pepper
¹/₂ tsp (2 mL)	Paprika
3 ¹/₂ oz (100 mL)	Cream (35%)
8 cups (2 L)	Fish fumet (see "Basic Ingredients for Some Recipes")
2 sheets	Gelatin
3 ¹/₂ oz (100 mL)	Warm water
2	Leek leaves
As needed	Water
3 Tbsp (50 mL)	Fish aspic*

- Form a rectangle with the salmon fillets on a sheet of plastic wrap. Season with salt and pepper. Lay the seaweed out on the fillets; press lightly and refrigerate for 1 hour.

- In a food processor, combine the shrimp and the egg. Season with salt and pepper, then add the cayenne pepper and the paprika, and blend into a fine purée. Slowly add the cream while puréeing. Adjust the seasoning and refrigerate the mousse before using. Spread the salmon fillets with the mousse, creating a smooth surface. Roll the fillets up and squeeze lightly. Remove the plastic wrap and roll the fillet in cheese-cloth to form a *ballottine* (cylinder). Tie up with a string; avoid squeezing too hard. Place the *ballottine* in the cold fish fumet, place in the oven at 350°F (180°C) and poach for 30 minutes.

- Allow the gelatin to expand in warm water for 10 minutes. Drain the gelatin and add to the fish fumet containing the *ballottine*. Let cool in the fumet, in the refrigerator, for 24 hours. Take the *ballottine* out of the fumet. Remove the cheesecloth, then wrap the *ballottine* in plastic wrap until ready to use.
- Blanch the leek leaves in boiling, salted water; refresh in cold water and dry. Cut the leek leaves into the shape of thin blades of seaweed and arrange on the plates to resemble moving seaweed. Using a brush and a little fish aspic, "glue" the leek leaves to the plate. Refrigerate for 15 minutes. Cover the bottom of the plate with a thin layer of fish aspic. Slice the *ballottine*, allowing 3 slices per person. Lightly cover the slices with fish aspic and arrange on the plates. Serve with a Maltese sauce (see "Basic Ingredients for Some Recipes").

* Fish aspic is made with fish fumet and gelatin.

Preparation time: 45 minutes	**Cooking time:** 40 minutes
Servings: 15	**Cost:** $$$

Chinook Salmon Tails with Sea Urchin Cream

4 × 6 oz (170 g)	Chinook salmon tails
8	Sea urchins
1/2 cup (120 mL)	Dry white wine
1/3 cup (40 g)	Shallots, chopped
2/3 cup (160 mL)	Brown veal stock (see "Basic Ingredients for Some Recipes")
2/3 cup (160 mL)	Cream (35%)
To taste	Salt & pepper

- Using a steamer, steam the chinook salmon tails in a little bit of salted water. While still hot, remove the skin and bones, then set aside the tails, covering them with a damp cloth.
- Open the sea urchins using scissors, and empty completely. Blend the contents well using a whisk. Set aside.
- Reduce the white wine with the chopped shallots by 9/10. Add the brown veal stock and cook for 10 minutes. Incorporate the cream, then the sea urchin mixture. *Caution:* Do not bring to a boil as the sea urchin components will cause the sauce to turn sour. Remain at 170°F (75°C). Strain through cheesecloth or a fine mesh strainer, season with salt and pepper to taste, and pour over the chinook salmon tails.

Accompaniment: Wild rice

NOTE: Why use the tails? Tails are economical and represent the part of the salmon that "works" the hardest, and therefore contains the least amount of fat and is often the tastiest.

Preparation time: 15 minutes	**Cooking time:** 10 minutes
Servings: 4	**Cost:** $$

Photo on next page →

LAKE TROUT

Salvelinus namaycush
Incorrect name: Gray trout

Characteristics: Color varies from pale green or gray to dark green, brown or almost black, with numerous pale spots. This is one of the largest freshwater fish. Although it can reach 77 lbs (35 kg) in weight, its average weight is 4 1/2 lbs (2 kg) when raised in commercial fisheries.

Flesh: Fatty

Habitat: Deep-water lakes

Where & When to Find It: If farmed, available all year round

Processed & Sold: Whole, as fillets and steaks

Cooking Method: Baked, *meunière*, grilled, steamed or poached

Value: Excellent quality, with a delicate melt-in-your-mouth taste

Comments: This salmon is prized by fishermen and appreciated by many.

$$$

Lake Denain Trout with Wild Herbs *

5 1/2 lbs (2.5 kg)	Lake trout
To taste	Salt & pepper
approx. 1 cup (160 g)	Butter
1 1/2 cup (150 g)	Shallots, chopped
2 bunches (400 g)	Watercress
1/2 cup (100 g)	Wild leek leaves
1/2 cup (100 g)	Purslane
approx. 1/2 lb (250 g)	Whitefish fillet
2	Eggs
2/3 cup (160 mL)	Cream (35%)
1 cup (250 mL)	White wine
2/3 cup (160 mL)	Fish fumet (see "Basic Ingredients for Some Recipes")
2 tsp (20 g)	True watercress, chopped
2 tsp (20 g)	Purslane, chopped
2 tsp (20 g)	Wild leek leaves, chopped

- Remove the lake trout bones through the stomach, season with salt and pepper and set aside.
- In 1/3 cup (60 g) of butter, braise the chopped shallots, then sauté the true watercress, the wild leek and the purslane with the shallots. Drain well to remove as much liquid as possible. Let cool. Season.
- In a food processor, finely chop the whitefish fillet, incorporate the 2 eggs, then the cream and strain the preparation through a sieve. Incorporate the preceding mixture into this preparation and stuff the lake trout.

- Grease an ovenproof dish with $1/3$ cup (60 g) of butter. Lay the stuffed trout in the dish. Pour in the wine and the fish fumet. Cover with aluminum foil and bake at 350°F (180°C). Poke with the tip of a knife to test if cooked. When the knife tip is warm, the forcemeat is hot and the lake trout is cooked. Remove the skin while still hot.
- Pour the cooking liquid into a saucepan.

Bind with the remaining butter, then add the raw wild herbs. Serve hot.

Accompaniment: Cattail hearts cooked in butter

* Dedicated to Renée and Gilbert Godbout, two great chefs.

Preparation time: 1 hour	**Cooking time:** 40 minutes
Servings: 6	**Cost:** $$$

Lake Trout and Vegetable Papillotes *with Port Sauce*

2 $1/4$ lbs (1 kg)	Lake trout
6 Tbsp (70 g)	Butter
$3/4$ cup (85 g)	Carrots, finely minced
$2/3$ cup (60 g)	Leeks (white part only), finely minced
$3/4$ cup (85 g)	Celery, finely minced
4 Tbsp (20 g)	Shallots, finely minced
To taste	Salt & pepper
3 $1/2$ oz (100 mL)	Port
3 $1/2$ oz (100 mL)	White wine
4 $1/2$ Tbsp (50 g)	Butter
$1/2$	Lemon (juice) (Optional)

- Cut open the stomach of the lake trout and remove the backbone. Sweat the minced vegetables in butter; cook until half tender, then remove from the heat and let cool.

Season the inside of the fish with salt and pepper. Stuff the lake trout with the vegetables and close. Season the surface of the fish with salt and pepper.

- Lay the lake trout on a sheet of buttered aluminum foil. Fold in on three sides to form a *papillote*, and pour the port and the wine into it. Completely seal the *papillote* and bake on a baking sheet at 350°F (180°C) for 12 to 15 minutes, depending on the thickness of the fish.
- Open the *papillote* and immediately remove the skin of the lake trout. Lay the fish on a serving dish, set aside and keep warm.
- Thicken the cooking liquid with butter. Add the juice of half a lemon, if so desired.
- Serve the fish very hot with the sauce and any vegetables you like, such as steamed potatoes and fiddleheads.

Preparation time: 40 minutes	**Cooking time:** 12 to 15 minutes
Servings: 3	**Cost:** $$$

BROOK TROUT
Salvelinus fontinalis

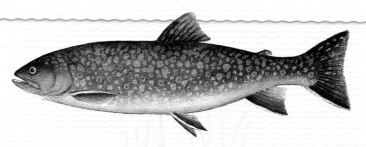

Characteristics: Shades of green and blue with silver jowls and sides, a white stomach and several faint orange spots on the sides. Can attain a weight of approx. 3 1/2 lbs (1.4 kg).

Flesh: Fatty

Habitat: Lakes and rivers

Where & When to Find It: Now possible to find farmed brook trout wherever fish is sold

Processed & Sold: Whole

Cooking Method: *Meunière*

Value: Refined flesh

Comments: Brook trout is a highly prized game fish and one of the most popular in Eastern North America.

$$

Brook Trout and Vegetables en Papillote *with Aniseed*

1 cup (125 g)	Carrot, julienned
1 cup (125 g)	Celery, julienned
1 1/2 cups (125 g)	Leek, julienned
2 1/2 Tbsp (30 g)	Butter
6 × 1/2 lb (220 g)	Brook trout
To taste	Salt & pepper
3 oz (90 mL)	White wine
As needed	Aniseed

Preparation time: 30 minutes **Cooking time:** 20 minutes
Servings: 6   **Cost:** $$

- Sweat the julienned vegetables in butter, ensuring they remain crunchy. Set aside.
- Cut the aluminum foil into sections large enough to wrap the fish. Brush each section with butter. Bone the fish through the back; salt, pepper and stuff with the crunchy vegetables.
- Sprinkle each portion with 1 Tbsp (15 mL) of white wine. Sprinkle with aniseed. Wrap each trout by making a *papillote* with the aluminum foil. Bake at 350°F (180°C) for approximately 20 minutes. Serve as is.

Brook Trout with Hazelnut Milk *

³/4 cup (120 g)	Whipped butter
As needed	Flour
8 small	Brook trout
To taste	Salt & pepper
¹/3 cup (60 g)	Butter
¹/4 cup (60 mL)	Peanut oil
1 ¹/2 Tbsp (25 mL)	Hazelnut milk
1	Lemon (juice)

- The whipped butter should be removed from the refrigerator and allowed to warm to room temperature.
- Flour the fish. Season with salt and pepper. Heat the ¹/3 cup (60 g) of butter and the oil. Sear the brook trout, until nicely golden on each side, then lower the heat. Once cooked, let the fish "rest."
- Heat the hazelnut milk and the lemon juice. Emulsify the mixture with the whipped butter, then apply to the brook trout.

Accompaniment: Buttered parsnips

NOTE: Brook trout is a delicacy with an exceptionally refined taste. The hazelnut milk and the taste of buttered parsnips enhance the flavor of this magnificent fish.

*   Dedicated to my friend, chef Marcel Bouchard.

Preparation time: 20 minutes	**Cooking time:** 7 to 8 minutes
Servings: 4	**Cost:** $$$

RAINBOW TROUT

Salmo gairdneri (Richardson) *1836*

Characteristics: Metallic blue back with black spots and silver sides. Its weight varies from 5 to 6 lbs (2.3 to 2.7 kg).

Flesh: Fatty

Habitat: Almost everywhere in North America

Where & When to Find It: Both a game and a farmed fish

Processed & Sold: Whole and as fillets

Cooking Method: *Meunière* and in a *court-bouillon*

$$

Smoked Rainbow Trout with Maple-Flavored Beurre blanc

4	Smoked rainbow trout fillets, cold
approx. 1/3 cup (80 mL)	Water
approx. 1/3 cup (80 mL)	Wine vinegar
3 1/2 oz (100 g)	Shallots, chopped
3 1/2 oz (100 mL)	Cream (35%)
1 1/2 cups (250 g)	Sweet butter
To taste	Salt & pepper
1/4 cup (60 mL)	Maple syrup
1 1/2 Tbsp (20 g)	Tomato, blanched, peeled and diced
As needed	Chervil

- Cut the smoked trout fillets in four equal parts and reassemble on a lightly oiled baking sheet; set aside.
- Pour the water and the vinegar into a saucepan. Add the shallots and reduce over low heat. Simmer slowly until a marmalade-like consistency is obtained.
- Add the cream to the reduction and simmer for a few minutes. Thicken this sauce with butter; i.e., whisk knobs of cold butter into the sauce until it is a uniform consistency.
- Season the sauce with salt and pepper, then add the maple syrup and reheat at low heat. Heat the trout in the oven at 450°F (230°C) for 1 minute. Pour the sauce into the middle of the plate and arrange the pieces of trout on the sauce so as to reproduce the shape of the whole fish.
- Sprinkle hot diced tomato around the fish. Garnish with a sprig of chervil and serve.

Preparation time: 10 minutes	**Cooking time:** 10 minutes
Servings: 4	**Cost:** $$

Rainbow Trout Fillets with Watercress Sauce

6 × ¹/₂ lb (220 g)	**Rainbow trout fillets**
To taste	**Salt & pepper**
As needed	**All-purpose flour**
²/₃ cup (100 g)	**Sweet butter**
2 bunches	**Watercress**
As needed	**Water**
As needed	**Vinegar**
¹/₄ cup (60 mL)	**Cream (35%)**
4 Tbsp (30 g)	**Chopped shallots**
2 ¹/₂ Tbsp (30 g)	**Butter**
1 cup (250 mL)	**Fish fumet (see "Basic Ingredients for Some Recipes")**
¹/₄ cup (45 g)	**Butter**

- Scale, fillet and trim the trout by removing the bones. Season the fillets with salt and pepper, then lightly flour.
- Cook the fillets in butter. Remove from the saucepan, arrange on a serving dish, set aside and keep warm.
- Remove the stems from the watercress and wash well in a water-and-vinegar solution. Cook with the cream.
- Brown the shallots in butter on low heat for 2 to 3 minutes.
- Add the fish fumet and reduce by half. Add the watercress; purée the preparation in a blender and strain through cheesecloth or a fine mesh strainer.
- Reduce the sauce and thicken with butter; i.e., whisk knobs of cold butter into the sauce until it is a uniform consistency. Cover the trout fillets with the watercress sauce and serve immediately.

Accompaniment: Watercress leaves and celery

Preparation time: 30 minutes **Cooking time:** 5 to 7 minutes
Servings: 6 **Cost:** $$

WHITEFISH
Coregonus clupeaformis (Mitchill) *1818*

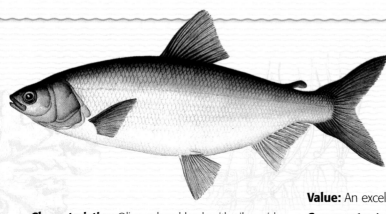

Habitat: North American lakes

Where & When to Find It: Available all year round where fish is sold

Processed & Sold: Whole and as fillets

Cooking Method: Whole, in the oven or *meunière*

Value: An excellent, yet neglected fish

Characteristics: Olive-colored back with silver sides and a white abdomen. Average length is approximately 27 inches (70 cm).

Flesh: White and soft

Comments: Appreciated in Europe for its great culinary qualities

$

Braised Whitefish with Wild Mustard

2 × 2 ³/4–3 ¹/4 lbs (1.2–1.5 kg)	Whitefish
To taste	Salt & pepper
3 ¹/2 Tbsp (40 g)	Wild mustard seeds
¹/2 cup (45 g)	Sliced almonds, toasted
¹/2 cup (50 g)	Shallots, chopped
¹/2 cup (120 mL)	White chicken stock (see "Basic Ingredients for Some Recipes")
2	Lemons (juice)
2 tsp (10 mL)	Fish glaze (see "Basic Ingredients …"— Glazes)
²/3 cup (100 g)	Butter

- Remove the whitefish bones through the stomach; season with salt and pepper. Sprinkle the mustard seeds and the toasted almonds over the fish. Place the whitefish in an ovenproof dish. Sprinkle with the chopped shallots, pour in the white chicken stock and the lemon juice. Cover with aluminum foil.
- Cook for 30 minutes at 350°F (180°C). Pour the cooking juice into a saucepan, add the fish glaze, reduce and thicken with the butter. Adjust the seasoning and serve very hot.

Accompaniment: Potato rounds cooked in fish fumet

Preparation time: 20 minutes	**Cooking time:** 30 to 40 minutes
Servings: 4	**Cost:** $$

Whitefish à la Meunière *with Citrus Butter*

6 × 9–11 oz (250–300 g)	Whitefish fillets
To taste	Salt & pepper
As needed	Flour
1/2 cup (85 g)	Butter
6	Lemon wedges
1/2 cup (30 g)	Fresh parsley, chopped

CITRUS BUTTER

1	Lemon (juice)
1	Orange (juice)
1	Grapefruit (juice)
3/4 cup (120 g)	Whipped butter

- Clean the fish, season and flour, making sure to remove any excess.
- Sauté the fish in butter, 5 to 7 minutes each side.
- Sprinkle the fillets with the chopped parsley, and serve immediately with the lemon wedges and the citrus butter.

Citrus Butter: Mix the fruit juices with the butter, salt and pepper. Store at room temperature.

Preparation time: 15 minutes	**Cooking time:** 10 to 15 minutes
Servings: 6	**Cost:** $$

123

Sea Bass and Other Families

This group includes several families, but all are part of the order *perciformes*, that is, those with spiny rays. First of all, there is the *Serranidae* family, including those fish that resemble perch (striped bass, grouper and white perch). Then there is the *Branchiostegal* family, which can be found primarily in warm seas, with some living in deep water (tilefish). Lastly, there is the *Carangidae* family, a large family of ocean fish (greater amberjack and blue runner). The *Sparidae* family includes the sheepshead.

Almost all of these fish live in the South Atlantic. They are relatively unknown in certain parts of North America and should be better known. Some are of great culinary interest.

Bass Family
Red grouper
White perch or White bass
Striped bass
Sea bass

Other Families
Tilefish
Bluefish
Blue runner
Weakfish
Sheepshead

RED GROUPER
Epinephelus morio (Valenciennes) *1828*

Habitat: Middle and western Atlantic (United States and Caribbean)

Where & When to Find It: Generally available all year round wherever fish is sold

Processed & Sold: Whole and as fillets

Cooking Method: Grilled, steamed, poached, braised or *meunière*

Value: Great culinary qualities

Comments: If possible, do not buy the whole fish, as the head, and therefore the unusable portion, is very large.

$$$$

Characteristics: Generally olive green or brownish-green with touches of red or salmon on the lower parts of the head. Pale olive green spots on the sides and orange spots on the head. Can reach up to 43 inches (110 cm) in length

Flesh: Lean

Grouper with Green Onions

4 2/3 cups (500 g)	Green onions
2/3 cup (100 g)	Butter
7 oz (200 mL)	White wine
1 sprig	Thyme
2 Tbsp (10 g)	Fresh coriander
To taste	Salt & pepper
2 1/4 lbs (1 kg)	Grouper
1 cup (250 mL)	Court-bouillon (see "Basic Ingredients for Some Recipes")
1 cup (250 mL)	Fish fumet (see "Basic Ingredients ...")

- Peel, wash and cut the green onions with scissors. Toss with butter in a high-sided frying pan, cover and cook at low heat. Braise for 10 minutes, occasionally stirring.

Moisten with wine and add the thyme and the coriander seeds. Season with salt and pepper and cook for 20 minutes, removing the lid toward the end to help evaporate the liquid.
- During the cooking, remove the skin from the grouper and cut the fish into escalopes.
- Bring the *court-bouillon* and the fish fumet to a simmering boil. Poach the grouper escalopes for 2 minutes.
- To serve, spread the green onions out on plates and cover with the grouper escalopes.

Accompaniment: Rice pilaf or rice Creole

Preparation time: 30 minutes	**Cooking time:** 15 minutes
Servings: 4	**Cost:** $$$$

Red Grouper with Mushrooms and Mint

4 cups (300 g)	White mushrooms, sliced thin
2 cups (500 mL)	Fish fumet (see "Basic Ingredients for Some Recipes")
approx. 1 cup (160 g)	Sweet butter
1 3/4 lbs (800 g)	Red grouper fillets
2/3 cup (150 mL)	White wine
2	Dried shallots, minced
As needed	Mint leaves

- Braise the mushrooms and keep the juice. Add the fish fumet.
- With 4 1/2 Tbsp (50 g) of butter, generously brush the bottom of an ovenproof dish and place the grouper fillets in the dish.
- Cover with the mushrooms, fish fumet, white wine, shallots and a dozen mint leaves. Cover and bake in the oven at 400°F (200°C) for 6 to 8 minutes, depending on the thickness of the fish. Drain the cooked fillets. Set aside. Drain the mushrooms and the mint leaves using cheesecloth or a fine mesh strainer; set aside.
- Reduce the cooking liquid by 2/3 and thicken with 1/3 cup (60 g) of butter.
- Sauté the mushrooms in butter (4 1/2 Tbsp or 50 g) until all the moisture has evaporated. Add the cooked mushrooms and the mint leaves to the cooking liquid to make a sauce. Pour the sauce over the grouper fillets.
- Garnish with fresh mint leaves. Serve very hot.

Accompaniment: Navy beans

Preparation time: 35 minutes	**Cooking time:** 6 to 8 minutes
Servings: 4	**Cost:** $$$$

WHITE PERCH OR WHITE BASS

Roccus americanus (Gmelin) *1789*

Incorrect names: sea bass and perch

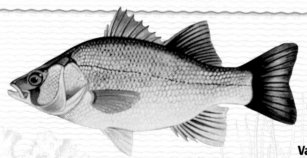

Where & When to Find It: Irregular availability wherever fish is sold

Processed & Sold: Whole and as fillets

Cooking Method: *Meunière*; in the oven, braised and poached

Value: Despite its soft flesh, this fish has a delicate taste.

Characteristics: Olive green and gray back, silver-white abdomen. Can reach 22 inches (56 cm) in length and weigh 5 lbs (2.3 kg); however, the average length is 9 inches (24 cm) and the average weight 1 lb (450 g).

Flesh: Lean

Habitat: North Atlantic

Comments: White perch is anadromous; i.e., it lives in salt water and reproduces in fresh water. However, in many North American waters, this fish behaves like a landlocked fish, that is, a fish that lives in fresh water. White perch is a sea fish and is not to be confused with yellow perch.

$$

White Perch or White Bass in Basil Sauce

BASIL SAUCE

6 sprigs	Basil
1/3 cup (80 mL)	Olive oil
2 3/4 cups (500 g)	Well-ripened tomatoes
1/2	Garlic clove
To taste	Salt & pepper
1 1/4 cup (300 mL)	Fish fumet (see "Basic Ingredients for Some Recipes")
7 oz (200 mL)	Milk

1 1/4 lbs (600 g)	White perch or white bass
4	Basil leaves, cut with scissors

- **Basil Sauce:** Remove the leaves of the basil from the stems and set aside the best leaves. Wash, drain and crush the leaves in a container until a paste is obtained. Slowly pour 3 Tbsp (40 mL) of olive oil, working constantly with the pestle to achieve a uniform mixture. Blanch, peel, seed and mince the tomatoes. In a saucepan, brown the garlic in 3 Tbsp (40 mL) of olive oil at low heat, then cook gently for 7 to 8 minutes. Season with salt and pepper. When the tomato is cold, incorporate it into the basil and oil mixture. Set aside.

Preparation time: 30 minutes	**Cooking time:** 8 to 12 minutes
Servings: 4	**Cost:** $$$

128

- Pour the fish fumet and the milk into a saucepan. Add the pieces of perch fillet. Begin cooking at low heat and allow 8 minutes of simmering without bringing to a boil.
- Turn off the heat, cover and let cool in the liquid.
- Drain the fish carefully, then remove the skin and the bones.

- Reheat the basil sauce and ladle some onto a plate.
- Lay the white perch on the plate. Cover with the remaining sauce and sprinkle with the cut basil.

NOTE: This fish is a sea fish, from the same family as the striped bass. Its flesh is fragile yet bland, making it necessary to add the tomato and the basil.

White Perch or White Bass with Red Peppers and Tomatoes

2 1/2 cups (350 g)	Red peppers, peeled and seeded
3 3/4 cups (700 g)	Tomatoes, blanched, peeled and seeded
3 Tbsp (35 g)	Butter
3/4 cup (100 g)	Onion *brunoise*
1	Garlic clove
7 oz (200 mL)	White wine
7 oz (200 mL)	Fish fumet (see "Basic Ingredients for Some Recipes")
1	Lemon (juice)
1 1/2 lbs (650 g)	White bass fillets
To taste	Salt & pepper
4	Radicchio leaves

- Finely dice the peppers and the tomatoes. Sweat the onion, peppers and garlic in the butter.

- Add the white wine, fish fumet and lemon juice, then cook for approximately 10 to 15 minutes.
- Add the tomatoes and thicken with butter; keep warm.
- Place the bass fillets on a baking sheet; season and drop knobs of butter on top. Broil the fish fillets for 3 to 4 minutes. Pour the pepper and tomato preparation onto hot plates.

Presentation: Arrange the fish fillets on top of this preparation and garnish the plates with the blanched radicchio leaves.

Preparation time: 20 minutes	Cooking time: 10 to 15 minutes
Servings: 4	Cost: $$

Photo on next page →

STRIPED BASS

Roccus saxatilis (Walbaum) *1792*
Incorrect names: Atlantic wolffish, sea bass

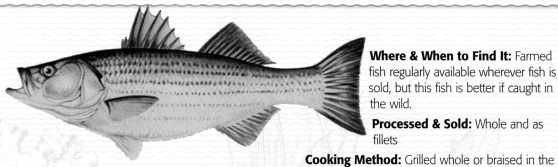

Where & When to Find It: Farmed fish regularly available wherever fish is sold, but this fish is better if caught in the wild.

Processed & Sold: Whole and as fillets

Cooking Method: Grilled whole or braised in the oven

Characteristics: Olive green varying from blue to black on its back, paler on the sides and silver to white on the abdomen. Seven or eight dark horizontal stripes on its sides. Weight varies a lot according to age and can reach as much as 40 lbs (18.4 kg).

Flesh: Lean

Value: High culinary quality, depending on where it came from

Comments: This fish is a first cousin of the European bass, but has lesser culinary quality as it lives in a different environment. It is, however, a fish that deserves to be better known.

$$$$

Striped Bass Steaks with Wild Leeks and Shallots

6 × 5 oz (150 g)	Striped bass steaks
To taste	Salt & pepper
As needed	All-purpose flour
1/4 cup (45 g)	Butter
3 Tbsp (45 mL)	Peanut oil
1 tsp (5 g)	Wild leeks, finely sliced
2 Tbsp (15 g)	Shallots, chopped
1/3 cup (75 mL)	Cream (35%)
3/4 cup (125 g)	Butter, small knobs
4 tsp (20 mL)	Lemon juice

- Have 6 striped bass steaks prepared by the fishmonger. Season with salt and pepper then lightly flour both sides.
- Heat the butter and oil until the mixture begins to bubble. Add the steaks and cook each side for 6 minutes.
- Gently cook the garlic and the shallots in the cream for 2 minutes. Thicken the sauce with butter. Season with salt and pepper and add the lemon juice. Remove the backbone and the skin around the steaks. Arrange the steaks on a plate and cover with sauce.

Accompaniment: Boiled *noisette* potatoes

Preparation time: 15 minutes	**Cooking time:** 12 to 15 minutes
Servings: 6	**Cost:** $$$$

Aniseed-Flavored Striped Bass

1 Tbsp (15 mL)	Olive oil
³/₄ cup (100 g)	Onion, chopped
As needed	Aniseed and fennel seeds, crushed
1 ³/₄ cups (150 g)	Leek (white part only), julienned
4 tsp (20 mL)	Ricard
2 cups (500 mL)	Milk
¹/₂	Garlic clove, minced
To taste	Salt & pepper
As needed	Butter
approx. 1 ¹/₄ cups (600 g)	Striped bass
1 ¹/₄ cups (250 g)	Rice

- Brown the onion, aniseed, fennel seeds and leek in the olive oil. Add the Ricard and flambé. Then, add the milk and the garlic. Season with salt and pepper.
- Brown the striped bass fillets in butter.
- Sweat the rice in butter. Add 1 ¹/₂ cups (350 mL) of the milk preparation and bake covered in the oven at 350°F (180°C) for 18 to 20 minutes. Cover the fish with the rice and bake in the oven at 350°F (180°C) for 5 minutes. Remove from the oven and serve immediately.

Preparation time: 30 minutes **Cooking time:** 20 minutes
Servings: 4 **Cost:** $$$$

SEA BASS

Dicentrarchus labrax
Incorrect names: catfish

Characteristics: Silver with spots and a pale blue band; silver head and white abdomen. This fish can reach a length of 18 inches (45 cm) and a weight of 3 to 4 lbs (1.4 to 1.8 kg). Same characteristics as the striped bass, except that it has no stripes.

Flesh: Lean

Habitat: Atlantic coast of Europe, and the Mediterranean

Where & When to Find It: Irregular availability where imported fish is sold

Processed & Sold: Generally whole

Cooking Method: Grilled whole or braised in the oven

Value: A fish for special occasions

$$$$$

Sea Bass with Coarse Salt

3 sprigs	Parsley
1 sprig	Dill or fennel
2 sprigs	Chervil
3/4 cup (120 g)	Butter
1/3 cup (60 g)	Saltwater cordgrass
To taste	Pepper
2 3/4 lbs (1 kg)	Sea bass
11 to 15 cups (3 to 4 kg)	Coarse salt

- Wash and chop the fresh herbs; using a mixer, combine with the butter and saltwater cordgrass and season with pepper. Stuff the washed fish with this mixture.
- In the bottom of a dish, spread approx. 4 cups (1 kg) of the coarse salt. Lay the sea bass fillets on the salt, in the dish, and completely cover with the remaining salt. Bake in the oven at 400°F (200°C) for 40 minutes.
- To serve, break the block of salt.
- Can be served with lemon butter.

Preparation time: 25 minutes	**Cooking time:** 40 to 60 minutes
Servings: 2	**Cost:** $$$$

Photo on page 131

Grilled Sea Bass with Fennel

2 ¾ lbs (1.2 kg)	**Sea bass**
To taste	**Salt & pepper**
3 Tbsp (50 mL)	**Olive oil**
15 sprigs	**Fennel, dried**

- This recipe requires the use of a grilling basket for fish.
- Season the bass well with salt and pepper, then brush with the olive oil.

- Lay half the fennel sprigs in the bottom of the basket, then the bass, then the remaining fennel sprigs.
- Grill over live coals, turning the fish frequently.
- Serve with unsalted butter warmed to room temperature and steamed potatoes.

Preparation time: 10 minutes **Cooking time:** 40 minutes
Servings: 2 **Cost:** $$$$

135

TILEFISH

Lopholatilus chamaeleonticeps (Goode and Bean) *1879*

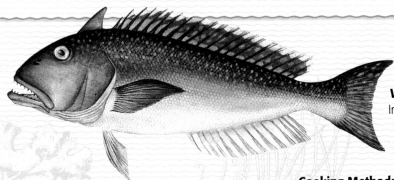

Habitat: South Florida and the Gulf of Mexico

Where & When to Find It: Irregular availability wherever imported fish is sold

Processed & Sold: Whole and as fillets

Characteristics: Can reach 4 ft (1.2 m) and weigh 35 lbs (16 kg). It has a large head. The upper part of the sides and back are colored in shades of blue and green. The lower section of the sides and the abdomen are pink. Yellow spots on the head, with yellow spots and red spots on the sides

Flesh: Lean and soft

Cooking Method: In the oven, steamed, *meunière* and poached

Value: Because of its soft and rather bland flesh, it is usually prepared with many secondary ingredients.

Comments: A lot of wastage if purchased whole, because of its large head.

$$$

Braised Tilefish with Spring Vegetables and Yogurt and Horseradish Sauce

8	Blue potatoes (small)
4	Onions (small)
8	New carrots
4	Small white turnips
4	Yellow pattypan squash
To taste	Salt & pepper
4 × 6–7 oz (180–210 g)	Tilefish fillets
2 1/2 tsp (5 g)	Grated lemon zest

YOGURT AND HORSERADISH SAUCE

1 cup (240 mL)	Plain yogurt
3 Tbsp (10 g)	Fresh dill, chopped
1 Tbsp (10 g)	Horseradish, chopped

- Using a basket steamer, cook the vegetables separately, then set aside in an ovenproof dish.
- Season the tilefish fillets with salt and pepper, then arrange them on top of the vegetables. Pour ¾ inch (2 cm) of water into the bottom of the dish and sprinkle with lemon zest. Seal and bake in the oven at 300°F (150°C) for 8 to 10 minutes. The fish flesh should flake.
- Yogurt and Horseradish Sauce: Combine the yogurt, chopped dill and chopped horseradish. Season with salt and pepper.

Presentation: Arrange the vegetables, then lay the tilefish fillets on a plate. Serve the sauce separately.

Preparation time: 30 minutes	**Cooking time:** 40 minutes
Servings: 4	**Cost:** $$$

Roasted Tilefish with Crispy Rice Sheets

1/3 cup (40 g)	Shallots, chopped
As needed	Olive oil
To taste	Salt & pepper
4 × 6 oz (180 g)	Tilefish steaks
2/3 cup (160 mL)	Clam juice
2/3 cup (160 mL)	Soya milk
As needed	White roux (see "Basic Ingredients for Some Recipes")
1/2	Lemon (juice)
4	Rice sheets

- Brown the chopped shallots in olive oil.
- Season the tilefish steaks with salt and pepper. Sauté with the shallots. When cooked, remove and keep warm.
- In a saucepan, combine the clam juice and the soya milk. Lightly bind with a little white roux. Strain through cheesecloth or a fine mesh strainer. Add the lemon juice. Set aside.
- Drop the rice sheets in hot oil to fry. They should be very crispy.
- On each plate, arrange a tilefish steak, cover with sauce and garnish with a rice sheet.

Preparation time: 20 minutes   **Cooking time:** 7 to 12 minutes
Servings: 4   **Cost:** $$$

137

BLUEFISH
Pomatomus saltatrix (Linnaeus) 1758

Habitat: Warm seas, on the eastern Atlantic coast from Cape Cod to Brazil

Where & When to Find It: Irregular availability wherever fish is sold

Characteristics: Greenish back and silver abdomen with black spots at the base of the pectoral fins. Can reach as much as 50 lbs (22.7 kg) in weight, with an average of 10 to 15 lbs (4.5 to 6.8 kg).

Processed & Sold: Whole and as fillets

Cooking Method: Grilled, *meunière* or braised

Value: The flesh of this fish is unusual; therefore, it will either please or disappoint diners.

Flesh: Semi-fatty and soft

$$

Grilled Marinated Bluefish with Citrus Fruit Sauce

3 oz (90 mL)	Tangerine juice
3 oz (90 mL)	Orange juice
1/2 cup (120 mL)	White vinegar
1/2 cup (120 mL)	Cold water
1/3 cup (80 mL)	Honey
1 pinch	Thyme sprigs
1/2	Bay leaf
10	Black peppercorns
To taste	Salt & pepper
2 × 14 oz (400 g)	Bluefish fillets
7 oz (200 mL)	Peanut oil
2 Tbsp (40 g)	Lemon zest
1 tsp (10 g)	Fresh ginger, chopped
2	Mint leaves

- Bring the tangerine and orange juices as well as the vinegar, water, honey, thyme, bay leaf and pepper to a boil. Season with salt and let cool. Marinate the bluefish fillets in this mixture for 1 hour.
- Drain and let the fillets dry off for at least 30 minutes.
- Reduce the marinade by 9/10, strain through cheesecloth or a fine mesh strainer and let cool. Emulsify with approx. 2/3 cup (150 mL) of the peanut oil and set aside.
- Season the bluefish fillets with salt and pepper. Brush with 3 Tbsp (50 mL) of oil and grill, beginning with the skin side, until slightly crispy, then turn and finish cooking on the grill.
- Serve the fillets on hot plates and pour the emulsion around them. Sprinkle with the lemon zest, ginger and chopped mint leaves.

NOTE: This recipe can be prepared using whole bluefish.

Preparation time: 1 hour	**Cooking time:** 6 to 8 minutes
Servings: 4	**Cost:** $$

Bluefish Fillet Ceviche with Red Onion and Hot Chili

1 ¾ lbs (800 g) Bluefish fillets, skinless

1 Hot green chili, minced

1 Red onion, minced

To taste Salt & pepper

2 Tbsp (30 mL) Tamari sauce

6 to 8 Limes (juice)

10 Fresh mint leaves, finely sliced

- Cut the bluefish fillets into ¾-inch (2-cm) strips.

- In a dish, place the bluefish strips in a single row, sprinkle with the chili and red onion. Season with salt and pepper, and pour the tamari sauce and the lime juice around the strips, ensuring that the liquids spread well. Cover with plastic wrap and chill in the refrigerator for at least 12 hours.

Presentation: Arrange the bluefish strips attractively on a plate. Pour a little of the marinade over the fish and sprinkle with the chopped mint.

Accompaniment: Diced potato salad

Preparation time: 30 minutes
Servings: 4 **Cost:** $$

BLUE RUNNER

Caranx crysos (Mitchill) *1815*
Incorrect names: hard tail and yellow jack

Characteristics: Back in shades of green, lower sides and abdomen gold or silver colored. Can measure 24 inches (60 cm) in length and weigh 4 lbs (1.8 kg).

Flesh: Firm and lean

Habitat: Mid-west Atlantic (United States)

Where & When to Find It: Irregular availability wherever imported fish is sold

Processed & Sold: Whole

Cooking Method: Grilled or poached

Value: Excellent fish for grilling

$$

Grilled Blue Runner Fillets with Passion Fruit and Guava Juice

8 × 2 ³/₄ oz (80 g)	Blue runner fillets
To taste	Salt & pepper
3 ¹/₂ oz (100 mL)	Passionfruit juice
3 ¹/₂ oz (100 mL)	Guava fruit juice
3 ¹/₂ oz (100 mL)	Coconut milk
4 oz (120 g)	Chayote, diced
²/₃ cup (80 g)	Pecans, chopped
²/₃ cup (100 g)	Sweet butter
As needed	Virgin olive oil
8	Small plantains
2 ¹/₂ Tbsp (5 g)	Oregano, chopped

- In a fairly large dish, arrange the blue runner fillets in a single row. Season with salt and pepper, then pour in the passionfruit, guava and coconut juices. Let macerate for at least 1 to 2 hours.
- Drain the blue runner fillets and wrap in a paper towel to remove as much of the liquid as possible. Gently heat the macerating liquid and cook the diced chayote. When cooked, add the chopped pecans, adjust the seasoning, set aside and keep warm.
- Gently cook the small, seasoned plantains in the butter and olive oil.
- Sprinkle the blue runner fillets with oregano and grill until crispy outside and tender inside.

Presentation: Place the plantains, then the chayote and pecans with the fruit juices, on a plate. Arrange the blue runner fillets on top.

Preparation time: 30 minutes	**Cooking time:** 10 to 15 minutes
Servings: 4	**Cost:** $$$

Blue Runner Fillets Stuffed with Nuts and Raisins and Baked in Banana Skins

2 × 1 1/2–1 3/4 lbs (700–800 g)	Blue runners
To taste	Salt & pepper
4 oz (120 g)	Flounder fillets
2	Egg whites
1/2 cup (120 mL)	Cream (35%)
4 1/2 Tbsp (40 g)	Hazelnuts, chopped
5 Tbsp (40 g)	European walnuts, chopped
4 Tbsp (40 g)	Raisins, chopped
1 pinch	Black cumin
1/2 cup (120 mL)	Olive oil
4	Banana leaves
2	Lemons (juice)

- Clean the fish and bone through the stomach. Season with salt and pepper and set aside.

- Chop the flounder fillets in a food processor and season with salt and pepper; add the egg whites, then the cream. Transfer from the food processor to a round metal mixing bowl and incorporate the hazelnuts, walnuts, dried raisins and the black cumin. Adjust the seasoning.
- Stuff the two blue runners with the forcemeat.
- Brown the blue runners in very hot olive oil for several minutes, then wrap in the banana leaves and bake in an ovenproof dish at 400°F (200°C). Remove the fillets from the oven and unwrap. Serve as is, on the banana leaves with lemon juice.

Preparation time: 40 minutes	**Cooking time:** 35 minutes
Servings: 4	**Cost:** $$$

WEAKFISH

Cynoscion regalis (Bloch and Schneider) *1801*

Incorrect names: sea trout

Characteristics: Slimmer than the striped bass and the white perch, this fish has 2 small anal spines. Average weight is approx. 5 lbs (2.2 kg).

Flesh: Soft and semi-fatty

Habitat: East coast of the United States, from Massachusetts Bay to Florida

Where & When to Find It: Irregular availability wherever imported fish is sold

Processed & Sold: Whole

Cooking Method: In the oven or grilled

Value: Delicious with exotic vegetables

Comments: Often sold under the name "Spanish mackerel," this fish is highly prized by residents of the Caribbean.

$$

Tea-Steamed Weakfish with Almond Milk Butter

To taste	Salt & pepper
4 × 5–6 oz	Weakfish fillets
(160–180 g)	
3 1/2 oz (100 mL)	White wine
3 1/2 oz (100 mL)	Fish fumet (see "Basic Ingredients for Some Recipes")
2 Tbsp (30 mL)	Jasmine tea
1 cup (180 g)	Sweet butter, whipped
3 1/2 oz (100 mL)	Almond milk
1	Lemon (juice)
4 Tbsp (15 g)	Chervil, chopped

- Season the weakfish fillets with salt and pepper.
- Place a large basket steamer in a high-sided frying pan and pour in the white wine, fish fumet, then the jasmine tea. Cover and cook for 6 to 8 minutes.
- When cooked, set aside the fillets and keep warm.
- Strain the cooking juice through cheesecloth or a fine mesh strainer and reduce by 9/10. Add the whipped butter, almond milk and lemon juice. Emulsify and finish by adding the chopped chervil. Adjust the seasoning.

Serving: Arrange the weakfish fillets and cover with the almond, butter, tea mixture.

Accompaniment: Small boiled *cocotte* potatoes

Preparation time: 15 minutes	**Cooking time:** 8 to 12 minutes
Servings: 4	**Cost:** $$$

Curried Weakfish

1/2 cup (120 mL)	Olive oil
3/4 cup (100 g)	White onion, chopped
2 cups (400 g)	Tomatoes, blanched, peeled, seeded and diced
2	Garlic cloves, minced
3/4 cup (40 g)	Fresh basil, chopped
To Taste	Salt & pepper
6 cups (400 g)	Eggplant, diced
1/2 cup (80 g)	Whole-wheat flour
2 tsp (40 g)	High-quality curry powder
4 × 5 oz (150 g)	Weakfish fillets
1/3 cup (60 g)	Unsalted butter
1/4 cup (20 g)	Fresh coriander, chopped
1/3 cup (20 g)	Fresh parsley, chopped

- Heat 1/4 cup (60 mL) of olive oil in a large skillet and sauté the chopped onion. Add the diced tomato, garlic, salt and pepper. Let simmer for a few minutes, then add the diced eggplant and cook until tender. Set aside.
- Combine the flour and the curry. Coat the weakfish fillets. Sauté the fillets *à la meunière* in the butter and 1/4 cup (60 mL) of oil until golden.
- Fish *à la meunière* should always have a "rest" once cooked.
- Lay out the fillets on hot plates, then cover with the eggplant, basil, garlic and onion mixture. Sprinkle with coriander and chopped parsley.

Accompaniment: Brown rice and lemon wedges

Preparation time: 20 min	**Cooking time:** 15 min
Servings: 4	**Cost:** $$$

143

SHEEPSHEAD
Archosargus probatocephalus (Walbaum) *1792*

Characteristics: Gray to yellow-green, with 7 vertical bands ranging from brown to black. This fish can reach a length of 35 inches (90 cm) and a weight of 20 lbs (9.2 kg).

Flesh: White and firm

Habitat: Mid-west Atlantic (United States)

Where & When to Find It: Irregular availability wherever imported fish is sold

Processed & Sold: Whole

Cooking Method: Grilled

Value: Excellent when grilled

$$

Sheepshead Fillets with Purslane and Pistachio Sauce

approx. ⅓ cup (80 mL)	Virgin olive oil
14 oz (400 g)	Purslane
1	Garlic glove, minced
1 ¾ cups (200 g)	Potato, diced small
To taste	Salt & pepper
4 × 6 oz (180 g)	Sheepshead fillets
⅔ cup (160 mL)	Lobster coulis (see "Basic Ingredients for Some Recipes")
1 cup (160 g)	Pistachios, shelled and chopped

- Heat the olive oil, and brown the purslane and the chopped garlic. Add the potatoes, season with salt and pepper, and cook gently. When the potatoes are cooked, use a whisk to crush them. The crushed potatoes will bind the juice.
- Place this preparation into an ovenproof dish. Arrange the fish fillets. Season with salt and pepper. Cover with aluminum foil and bake at 400°F (200°C) for 6 to 8 minutes.
- Heat the lobster coulis and add the chopped pistachio nuts.

Presentation: Using a hoop, create a mold in the center of the plate for the purslane and potato mixture. Arrange the sheepshead fillets on top and surround with the pistachio sauce.

Preparation time: 20 to 30 minutes
Cooking time: 6 to 12 minutes
Servings: 4   **Cost:** $$$

Sheepshead Stuffed with Seaweed and Papaya Juice

2 Tbsp (60 g)	Fresh kelp, finely sliced
2 Tbsp (60 g)	Fresh rockweed, finely sliced
3 1/2 oz (100 mL)	Dry white wine
2	Egg whites
2 × 1 1/4 lbs (600 g)	Sheepsheads
7 oz (200 mL)	Papaya juice
1	Lime (juice)
3 1/2 oz (100 g)	Potato, very finely sliced
As needed	Olive oil
3/4 cup (120 g)	Sweet butter, whipped
To taste	Salt & pepper

- Combine the seaweed, white wine and the egg whites. Set aside.

- Remove the bones through the stomach and brush with 1/4 cup (60 mL) of papaya juice. Season with pepper, but do not add salt because of the seaweed. Set aside in the refrigerator for 30 minutes.
- During this time, reduce 2/3 cup (140 mL) of papaya juice and the lime juice by 9/10. Set aside.
- Add the very finely sliced potatoes to the seaweed mixture and stuff the two sheepsheads. Seal and make small incisions on both sides of each fish. Brush with olive oil and "crisscross" the fish on a hot grill. Finish cooking in the oven at 350°F (180°C) for 15 to 20 minutes.
- While the fish are baking, emulsify the papaya juice and the lime juice reduction with the whipped butter. Season to taste.
- Place the sheepsheads on a serving plate and keep them warm. Once the fish is on the diner's plate, pour the butter and papaya emulsion over each piece.

Accompaniment: Diced chayote cooked in papaya juice

NOTE: If the seaweed is too salty, boil first.

Preparation time: 1 hour	**Cooking time:** 30 minutes
Servings: 4	**Cost:** $$$

MACKEREL, TUNA, HERRING AND OTHERS

Scombridae and Clupeidae

All the fish that make up these families share one characteristic: their flesh is relatively fatty.

SCOMBRIDAE FAMILY

These fish are of great commercial value. We will not discuss them all in this chapter; however, it is important to name them all: king mackerel, Atlantic mackerel, chub mackerel, bonito, bluefin tuna, Atlantic albacore, yellowfin tuna and bigeye tuna.

These fish, which live in the deepest areas of the ocean, are generally very fast swimmers. Their bodies are streamlined and recognizable by a deeply notched tail fin. Between the dorsal and the caudal fins, there are several types of small spikes called finlets that can also be found between the anal and the caudal fins.

CLUPEIDAE FAMILY

Bony fish make up the largest group of fish. The caudal fin has two lobes, the skeleton is made of bony tissue and the vertebrae are well developed. The scales are shaped as thin, small bony plates. These fish are relatively primitive and live primarily at great depths. Their bladder is joined to their digestive tract. The order includes 20 families. They live in schools and eat plankton.

Scombridae

Bonito

Atlantic mackerel

Atlantic albacore

Yellowfin tuna

Bluefin tuna

Clupeidae

Atlantic herring

Anchovy

(*Engraulidae* family)

Alewife

American shad

Sardine

ATLANTIC BONITO

Sarda sarda (Bloch) *1793*

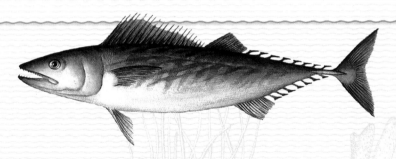

Characteristics: Steel blue back, sliver sides and 7 dark blue lines sweeping forward and downward from the back to the lower front area of the fish

Flesh: Fatty

Habitat: The warmest areas of the Atlantic

Where & When to Find It: Irregular availability wherever imported fish is sold

Processed & Sold: Whole and as fillets

Cooking Method: Braised, grilled, sautéed or raw

Value: This fish is of a lesser quality than tuna, but has some good qualities.

$$

Atlantic Bonito Tartare with Seaweed

¹/₄ cup (20 g)	Dried sea lettuce (ulva)
3 Tbsp (50 mL)	White wine
2 cups (200 g)	Glasswort (brown seaweed)
2	Lemons (juice)
²/₃ cup (160 mL)	Sunflower oil
2 ¹/₂ Tbsp (10 g)	Fresh chervil
approx. 1 lb (500 g)	Bonito flesh
2	Shallots, minced
¹/₄ cup (60 mL)	Clam juice
1/3 cup (80 mL)	Extra virgin olive oil
2	Limes (juice)
2 Tbsp (30 mL)	Papaya juice
To taste	Salt & pepper
¹/₂ cup (30 g)	Parsley, minced

- First of all, it should be noted that the fish used to make tartare must be fresh out of the water.
- Rehydrate the sea lettuce (ulva) with the white wine. Combine the glasswort with the seaweed, lemon juice, sunflower oil and the chervil.
- Mince the bonito, using a knife; incorporate the chopped shallots, the clam juice, extra virgin olive oil as well as the lime and papaya juices. Taste. Season to taste with salt and pepper and, at the last minute, add the parsley. Chill in the refrigerator as the tartare must be eaten cold.

Presentation: Arrange the glasswort salad on the upper part of the plate, below, the tartare.

NOTE: Bind the tartare with a little mayonnaise if necessary. This recipe is even more delicious made with bluefin tuna.

Preparation time: 30 minutes
Servings: 4   **Cost:** $$$

Bonito Fillet with Saffron Butter

1 tsp (4 g)	Saffron threads
¼ cup (60 mL)	White wine
1	Lemon (juice)
approx. 1 cup (160 g)	Unsalted butter
To taste	Salt & pepper
4 × 6 oz (180 g)	Bonito fillet pieces
As needed	Peanut oil

Preparation time: 10 minutes **Cooking time:** 10 to 12 minutes
Servings: 4   **Cost:** $$$

- Rehydrate the saffron with the white wine and the lemon juice for 10 minutes. In a food processor or another container, mix this preparation with the sweet butter, kneaded. Season with salt and pepper, and set aside at room temperature.
- Grill the bonito pieces after brushing them with oil.

NOTE: To cook bonito, begin by quickly cooking (crisscrossing) the fish, then by continuing more slowly on the side of the grill that is not as hot. Bonito should not be overcooked.

ATLANTIC MACKEREL

Scomber scombrus (Linnaeus) *1758*

Characteristics: Dark steel-blue back and body with 23 to 33 undulating dark bands. Abdomen silver-white. Can measure up to 22 inches (56 cm) and weigh 4 1/2 lbs (2 kg).

Flesh: Semi-fatty

Habitat: Continental shelves on both sides of the Atlantic

Where & When to Find It: From June to October, in abundance; frozen, all year round

Processed & Sold: Whole and as fillets

Cooking Method: In the oven, grilled or braised

Value: Underappreciated fish which deserves to be better known

Comments: Mackerel catches have fluctuated greatly from one year to another.

$

Mackerel Ragout with Vegetables and Mustard Sauce

1 cup (125 g)	Carrot, julienned
1 cup (125 g)	Celery, julienned
1 cup (125 g)	Leek, julienned
2 lbs (900 g)	Mackerel fillets, diced
2 cups (500 mL)	Dry white wine
2 cups (500 mL)	Cream (35%)
3 Tbsp (45 mL)	Strong mustard
To taste	Salt & pepper

Preparation time: 10 minutes **Cooking time:** 8 to 10 minutes
Servings: 6 **Cost:** $$

- Cook the vegetables separately in salted water. They should remain crunchy. Set aside.
- Poach the pieces of mackerel in the wine. Set aside the hot pieces of fish with the vegetables. Reduce the cooking liquid by 3/4.
- Add the cream and mustard. Let simmer until the consistency of a sauce is obtained. Remove from the heat. Add the pieces of mackerel to the sauce and let sit for 2 to 3 minutes. Adjust the seasoning. Serve hot with the vegetables.

Mackerel Fillets with Spinach

2 lbs (900 g)	Spinach leaves
As needed	Cream (35%)
As needed	Butter
To taste	Salt and nutmeg
2 lbs (900 g)	Mackerel fillets
6 cups (1.5 L)	*Court-bouillon* (see "Basic Ingredients for Some Recipes")
3	Hard-boiled eggs
4 oz (125 g)	Grated cheese
To taste	Paprika

Preparation time: 15 minutes **Cooking time:** 4 to 6 minutes
Servings: 6   **Cost:** $$

- Boil the spinach leaves in salted water. Drain. Chop the leaves, then add 1/2 cup (125 mL) of cream and mix. Garnish the bottom of a buttered ovenproof dish with this preparation. Season with salt and nutmeg.
- Poach the mackerel fillets in a salty *court-bouillon* for 4 to 6 minutes. Drain and lay on top of the spinach.
- Chop the eggs and garnish the two ends of the dish. Cover with the remaining fresh cream, dust with grated cheese and paprika. Warm in the oven for a few minutes.

Accompaniment: Boiled potatoes

Mackerel Ragout with Vegetables and Mustard Sauce

ALBACORE

Thunnus alalunga (Bonnaterre) *1788*
Incorrect names: tuna and porbeagle

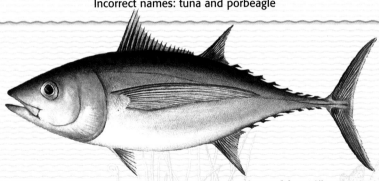

Characteristics: Back and sides the color of blue steel, silver abdomen and dark, metallic fin. Can measure 47 inches (120 cm) in length and weigh between 75 and 80 lbs (34 and 36.3 kg).

Flesh: Firm, dense, white and fatty

Habitat: Tropical Atlantic as well as the Mediterranean

Where & When to Find It: From August to October, in abundance

Processed & Sold: As fillets to cut into pieces

Cooking Method: Grilled or braised

Value: Especially used for canning

Comments: When it comes to canned tuna, albacore is the best. The label should read "albacore tuna." "Tuna" alone denotes other types of tuna.

$$

Grilled Albacore with Citrus Fruit Butter

1 ³/4 lbs (800 g)	Albacore section (cut from the middle of the fish)
To taste	Salt & pepper
6 slices	Smoked pork breast, finely sliced, or 6 bacon slices
¹/4 cup (60 mL)	Extra virgin olive oil
approx. 1 cup (160 g)	Citrus fruit butter (see Lemon Herb Butter, in "Basic Ingredients for Some Recipes")
4	Lemons (wedges)

- Try to remove as many bones as possible from the albacore section, using a pair of food tongs. Season with salt.
- Surround the albacore section with slices of smoked pork breast or bacon. Tie up with a string. Season with pepper only.
- Brush the fish with olive oil. On a fairly hot grill, cook the albacore for approximately 15 minutes each side. Serve immediately with the citrus fruit butter and the lemon wedges.

Preparation time: 10 minutes **Cooking time:** 30 minutes
Servings: 4 **Cost:** $$$

Albacore Fillets with Aromatics

3 Tbsp (50 mL)	Olive oil
³/₄ cup (85 g)	Carrot, sliced into thin coins
²/₃ cup (100 g)	Spanish onion, sliced into thin rounds
¹/₂	Lemon, sliced into fluted rounds
¹/₂	Garlic clove, chopped
2 Tbsp (10 g)	Coriander
To taste	Thyme
1	Bay leaf
¹/₂	Clove
3 ¹/₂ oz (100 mL)	Wine vinegar
³/₄ cup (175 mL)	Dry white wine
To taste	Salt & pepper
10 oz (300 g)	Albacore fillets
4 sprigs	Fresh parsley, chopped

- Heat the olive oil in a skillet and add the vegetables, lemon, garlic, coriander, thyme, bay leaf and clove.
- Brown the vegetables, then deglaze the skillet with vinegar. Reduce by ³/₄ and add the white wine. Season with salt and pepper and cook for 4 to 5 minutes.
- Lay the albacore fillets in an ovenproof dish. Pour the mixture over the fillets. Cover and bake in the oven at 350°F (180°C) for 4 to 5 minutes.
- Remove from the oven and sprinkle with the chopped parsley. Arrange the fillets on a large platter and serve, preferably cold.

NOTE: This recipe can be adapted for use with mackerel, yellowfin tuna, bluefin tuna and alewife, but keep a watchful eye when cooking each type of fish.

Preparation time: 35 minutes **Cooking time:** 4 to 5 minutes
Servings: 2   **Cost:** $$

YELLOWFIN TUNA

Thunnus albacares (Bonnaterre) *1788*

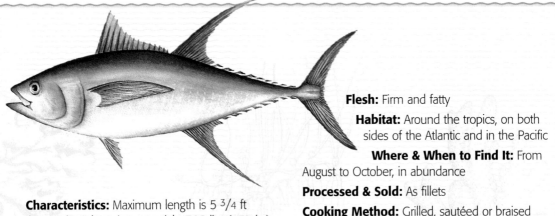

Flesh: Firm and fatty

Habitat: Around the tropics, on both sides of the Atlantic and in the Pacific

Where & When to Find It: From August to October, in abundance

Processed & Sold: As fillets

Cooking Method: Grilled, sautéed or braised

Value: Used especially for canning

$$

Characteristics: Maximum length is 5 ³/₄ ft (1.75 m) and maximum weight 300 lbs (135 kg). Lives in the Atlantic Ocean. Skin color in shades of blue. The abdomen and sides of the head are a metallic white.

Yellowfin Tuna Fillet Steamed in Banana Leaves

2 ³/₄ lbs (1.2 kg)	Yellowfin tuna fillet
To taste	Salt & pepper
¹/₃ cup (80 mL)	Papaya juice
2	Limes (juice)
1 or 2	Banana leaves
3 ¹/₂ oz (100 mL)	Coconut juice
7 oz (200 mL)	Fish *velouté* (see "Basic Ingredients for Some Recipes")
²/₃ cup (100 g)	Butter

- This recipe calls for a three- or four-part steamer, or a large basket steamer.
- Remove as many bones as possible from the fillet. Season with salt and pepper. Brush with papaya and lime juice. Wrap the piece of yellowfin in the banana leaves.
- Pour water into the bottom of the steamer. In the first section, place the piece of yellowfin. Cover and steam for 30 to 40 minutes, depending on the thickness of the fish.
- Combine the coconut juice with the fish *velouté*, then heat. Adjust the seasoning and strain through cheesecloth or a fine mesh strainer. Finish by adding the butter and set aside.

Presentation: Cut the piece of tuna into equal sections. Cover with the sauce and garnish with pieces of chayote sautéed in butter.

Preparation time: 30 minutes	**Cooking time:** 40 to 50 minutes
Servings: 4	**Cost:** $$

Yellowfin Tuna Fillets with Cider

³/₄ cup (85 g)	Carrot rounds
1	Medium onion
1	Golden Delicious apple
To taste	Salt & ground pepper
6 × 3 oz (90 g)	Fresh yellowfin tuna fillets, skin on
As needed	Butter
2 cups (500 mL)	Cider
²/₃ cup (160 mL)	Cider vinegar
1	Bay leaf
As needed	Chives, chopped

- Peel and flute the carrot, then cut into small rounds. Blanch the rounds by cooking in boiling water for a few seconds, then let cool.

Preparation time: 15 minutes **Cooking time:** 10 minutes
Servings: 6   **Cost:** $$

- Slice the onion into fine rounds. Cut the apple into thin wedges.
- Season the inside of the yellowfin with salt and pepper (roughly ground).
- Lightly butter a cooking dish, and place the fruit and vegetables in the bottom. Lay the yellowfin fillets on top, skin side up. Pour in the cider and vinegar. Break the bay leaf in four and place in the liquid.
- Cover with buttered aluminum foil and bake at 400°F (200°C) for 10 minutes. Remove the fish from the oven and let cool in the cooking liquid. Refrigerate the fish for at least 12 hours before serving.
- Arrange the fillets on plates. Garnish with the braised fruit and vegetables, and a little of the marinade, which has become gelatinous. Sprinkle with chopped chives and serve.

BLUEFIN TUNA

Thunnus thynnus (Linnaeus) *1758*

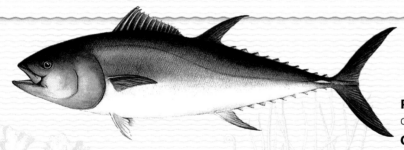

Processed & Sold: As fillets to cut into pieces

Cooking Method: Grilled, sautéed, braised or *meunière*

Characteristics: Dark blue back, grayish abdomen with silver spots, dark dorsal fins and silvery-gray anal fins. A very large fish capable of reaching 16 1/2 ft (5 m) in length and 2000 lbs (909 kg) in weight.

Flesh: Fatty

Habitat: Warm waters of the Atlantic south to the Antilles

Where & When to Find It: In July, August and September, in abundance

Value: Raw, grilled or braised, this fish is fit for a royal feast.

Comments: Prized by the Japanese, bluefin tuna is to them what meat is to North Americans. This is a noble fish.

$$$$

Bluefin Tuna in Sashimi

approx. 1 lb (480 g)	Bluefin tuna of the finest quality
To taste	Salt & pepper
3/4 cup (80 g)	Daikon radish, finely sliced
As needed	Sesame oil, roasted
1	Lime (juice)

GINGER AND SESAME SAUCE

3 1/2 oz (100 mL)	Tamari sauce*
3 Tbsp (40 mL)	Cold water
2 1/4 Tbsp (20 g)	Sesame seeds, roasted
1 tsp (4 g)	Fresh ginger, grated
1/2 Tbsp (10 g)	Honey
3 Tbsp (20 g)	Shallots, minced
1	Lime (juice)

WASABI SAUCE

4 tsp (10 g)	Wasabi powder*
As needed	Cold water
1/4 cup (60 mL)	Tamari sauce

- A very sharp knife that cuts like a razor is absolutely essential. Cut the tuna into very fine slices, and arrange in the shape of a daisy on a large plate, leaving some space in the middle. Season with salt and pepper.
- Combine the finely sliced daikon with a little roasted sesame oil and the lime juice. Arrange in the middle of the plate. Serve the sauces separately in small bowls.

Ginger and Sesame Sauce: Mix all the ingredients together and let sit covered with plastic wrap to ensure no flavor is lost. Set aside.

Wasabi Sauce: Combine the wasabi powder with enough water to make a paste and refrigerate. After 10 minutes, mix the tamari, wasabi and some cold water until the desired consistency is obtained.

* Tamari: Soya sauce that is less salty

* Wasabi: A type of green horseradish generally sold in powder form

Preparation time: 30 minutes
Servings: 4   **Cost:** $$$$

Bluefin Tuna Niçoise

approx. 3 lbs (1.4 kg)	Fresh tomatoes
1/2 lb (250 g)	Black olives (approx. 48)
As needed	Olive oil
3 1/4 cups (450 g)	Onion, chopped
4	Garlic cloves, chopped
To taste	Thyme
1	Bay leaf
2/3 cup (170 g)	Tomato paste
4 cups (1 L)	White wine
3 1/2 lbs (1.6 kg)	Bluefin tuna fillets
To taste	Salt & pepper
As needed	Lettuce leaves (Optional)

- Blanch, peel and seed the tomatoes, then dice. Pit the olives and blanch.
- Brown the tomatoes, onions, garlic, thyme and bay leaf in olive oil. Heat the tomato paste separately to remove any acidity. Add the cooked tomato paste to the vegetable mixture.
- Moisten with the white wine, then add the olives. Cook for 10 minutes.
- Cut the tuna fillets into medallions 3/4 inches (2 cm) thick. Place the medallions in a pan with high sides.
- Season the fish with salt and pepper, then cover with the tomato preparation. Cover and bake in the oven at 350°F (180°C) for between 1 and 1 1/2 hours. Serve in pieces or crumble the cooked fish, and cover with sauce. Serve hot or cold.
- If serving cold, garnish with lettuce leaves.

Preparation time: 1 hour   **Cooking time:** 2 hours
Servings: 8   **Cost:** $$$$

Photo on next page →

ATLANTIC HERRING

Clupea harengus harengus (Linnaeus) *1758*
Incorrect name: sardine

Characteristics: Blackish-blue or greenish-blue in color on its back, silver on its abdomen and sides. Average length is 20 inches (50 cm) and average weight is 1 ¹/2 lbs (675 g)

Flesh: Fatty

Habitat: West of Greenland

Where & When to Find It: From April to September, in abundance; frozen, all year round

Processed & Sold: Whole and as fresh or smoked fillets

Cooking Method: Grilled, in the oven or braised

Value: Winter fish of surprising quality

Comments: The following products are made from herring:

— Buckling: fresh, salted for a few hours; smoked, hot

— Smoked herring (whole or in fillets): salted and smoked

— Kipper: fresh, opened at the back, washed, eviscerated, salted for 1 or 2 hours and lightly smoked

— Rollmops: head removed, eviscerated, salted and marinated in vinegar and aromatics

$$

Marinated and Smoked Herring Fillets

1 ¹/2 lbs (700 g)	Smoked herring fillets
2 cups (500 mL)	Milk
1 ¹/3 cup (200 g)	Spanish onion, sliced fine into rounds
²/3 cup (85 g)	Carrots, sliced thin
3 Tbsp (20 g)	Celery, sliced thin
2	Garlic cloves, sliced fine into rounds
To taste	Thyme
2	Bay leaves
As needed	Pickling spices

To taste	Pepper
¹/2	Clove
2 cups (500 mL)	Peanut oil
2 cups (500 mL)	Olive oil
As needed	Potatoes, unpeeled

- Soak the herring fillets in milk for 12 hours; drain and dry off with a cloth.
- Arrange the fillets in a glass or stoneware container, and combine with the onion, carrot, celery and garlic rounds, the thyme, bay leaves, pickling spices, pepper, clove and the two oils. Let marinate for at least 48 hours.

- Serve the fillets on a bed of warm potatoes with the vegetables from the marinade.

NOTE: The marinated fillets can be stored in a pantry or in the refrigerator for several weeks.

Smoked herring fillets are soaked in milk when they are too salty. However, it is now possible to buy smoked herring fillets that are not too salty and only lightly smoked.

Preparation time: 30 minutes	Marinade: 48 hours
Servings: 10	Cost: $$

Fresh Herring

12 × 2 oz (60 g)	Fresh herring fillets, skin on
1 3/4 cups (250 g)	Flour
To taste	Salt & pepper
1/2 cup (80 g)	Butter
2 Tbsp (30 mL)	Oil
3 1/3 cups (500 g)	Onions, finely sliced
1/2 cup (125 mL)	Fish fumet (see "Basic Ingredients for Some Recipes")
2 Tbsp (30 mL)	Red wine vinegar
2 tsp (5 g)	Dried mustard
4 servings	Cooked green vegetables (Optional)

Preparation time: 20 minutes	Cooking time: 30 minutes
Servings: 4	Cost: $$

- Wash the herring fillets and take care to remove all the scales. Dry off, and dredge in flour to which salt and pepper have been added.
- Heat half the butter in a skillet and fry the fillets until golden, beginning with the meat side. Arrange the fillets in an ovenproof dish and set aside.
- Melt the remaining butter in the same skillet and cook the onions for several minutes without browning.
- Add the fish bouillon, wine vinegar and the mustard. Cook until the liquid has completely evaporated (about 5 to 10 minutes). Arrange the onions on the fillets and bake in the oven at 350°F (180°C) for 15 minutes.
- Serve immediately with green vegetables, if so desired.

Photo on page 159

ANCHOVY

Engraulis encrasicolus (Linnaeus) *1758*
Incorrect name: sardine

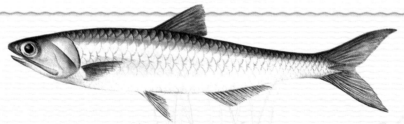

Characteristics: A small fish, at most 8 inches (20 cm) in length, with a very elongated body. Gray with a little green or yellow on the head; the abdomen is metallic silver. Moves in large schools in coastal waters.

Flesh: Thin and a little fatty

Habitat: European Atlantic coast and the Mediterranean

Where & When to Find It: All year round, salted and canned

Processed & Sold: Whole, as fillets and canned

Cooking Method: Grilled

Value: Either you like it or you don't

Comments: The body of the anchovy is much more elongated than that of the sardine, and its eye is larger. Fragile, it does not keep well.

$$

Anchovy Fritters with Lobster Sauce and Capers

20	Fresh anchovies
7 oz (200 mL)	Lobster sauce (see "Basic Ingredients for Some Recipes")
1/2 cup (80 g)	Capers, chopped
As needed	Cooking oil
1 1/4 cup (300 mL)	Batter

BATTER

3	Eggs
2 cups (300 g)	Flour
To taste	Salt & pepper
As needed	Beer

Preparation time: 20 minutes **Cooking time:** 10 minutes
Servings: 4   **Cost:** $$

- Clean the anchovies and wrap in paper towel to absorb as much moisture as possible.
- **Batter:** Separate the egg yolks from the whites. Spoon flour into a bowl and create a well in the center. Season with salt and pepper, and incorporate the beer and the egg yolks until the mixture becomes a liquid paste. Stiffen the egg whites and incorporate into the preparation at the last moment.
- Heat the lobster sauce and add the chopped capers.
- Heat the cooking oil until very hot. Dredge each of the anchovies in the batter and deep fry. When cooked, serve very hot with small individual bowls of sauce.

Anchovies à la portugaise

1 3/4 lbs (800 g)	Fresh anchovies, whole
To taste	Fleur de sel de Guérande
1/2 cup (80 g)	Capers
12	Black olives, pitted
3 1/2 oz (100 mL)	Olive oil
3 tsp (10 g)	Black pepper, crushed
7 oz (200 mL)	White wine
As needed	Tomatoes *provençale*

- Clean and wipe the anchovies. Place in a container and dust with a little Guérande salt. Chill for 2 hours, mixing from time to time.

- Wipe the anchovies, cut off the heads, and bone without separating the fillets.
- In a mortar or in another solid container, make a paste with the capers and the previously minced olives.
- Lay the anchovies on their backs in a well-oiled *au gratin* dish (4 tsp or 20 mL of oil). Sprinkle with the crushed black pepper, white wine and the remaining oil. Stuff with the olive-and-caper paste and close the fish. Cover with aluminum foil and bake in a fairly hot oven for 5 to 6 minutes.
- Serve immediately with *provençale* tomatoes.

Preparation time: 10 minutes **Cooking time:** 5 to 8 minutes
Servings: 4 **Cost:** $$

ALEWIFE

Alosa pseudoharengus (Wilson) *1811*

Incorrect name: herring

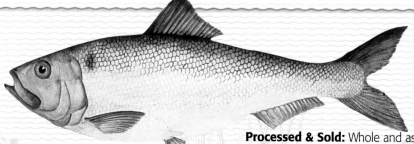

Characteristics: Greenish-gray back and sides; silver abdomen. Approximate length, 9 to 12 inches (24 to 30 cm) and average weight 1/2 lb (22 g)

Flesh: Fatty

Habitat: South Carolina. This species can be found landlocked in Lake Ontario and Lake Erie.

Where & When to Find It: In May and June, in abundance

Processed & Sold: Whole and as fillets

Cooking Method: In the oven or braised

Value: Winter fish of surprising quality

Comments: Alewife fry can be found in lakes; they move farther upstream than shad and easily traverse rapids and climb fish ladders, then they return to the sea.

$$

Alewife in Cider Aspic

6 × 4 oz (120 g)	Alewife fillets
approx. 1/2 cup (60 g)	Carrots, sliced thin
1/3 cup (45 g)	Onions, sliced thin
To taste	Bouquet garni (celery, bay leaf and thyme)
10	Coriander seeds
2 cups (500 mL)	Dry cider
To taste	Salt & pepper
3 sheets	Unflavored gelatin
3 Tbsp (50 mL)	Water
1 Tbsp (15 mL)	Wine vinegar
2 Tbsp (30 mL)	Oil

- Roughly cut the alewife fillets, then place in a saucepan with the vegetables, *bouquet garni*, coriander, cider and seasoning. Gently cook for 10 to 15 minutes.
- Allow the gelatin to expand in water, then incorporate into the cooking bouillon with the vinegar. Place the alewife in an earthenware dish and adjust the seasoning if necessary. Filter the bouillon, then pour over the alewife. Set the vegetables aside.
- Pour in the oil at the very end. Refrigerate for 24 hours before serving. To present, arrange the alewife with the aspic and vegetables.

Preparation time: 15 minutes **Cooking time:** 10 to 18 minutes

Servings: 6   **Cost:** $$

Warm Alewife Salad with Raspberry Vinegar on a Bed of Spinach

4 × 4 oz (120 g)	Alewife fillets
To taste	Salt & pepper
2 cups (500 mL)	Oil
1 cup (250 mL)	Raspberry vinegar
2 packages	Spinach
3 cups (125 g)	Fresh chives, cut with scissors

- Season the alewife, then macerate them in the oil and raspberry vinegar for 24 hours. Drain. Grill.
- Wash the spinach, remove the stems, drain and cut with scissors. Arrange on a plate. Heat the marinade, sprinkle lightly over the fillets and keep the rest for later use.
- Sprinkle with fresh cut chives. Serve warm.

Preparation time: 10 minutes **Cooking time:** 5 to 8 minutes
Servings: 4 **Cost:** $$

AMERICAN SHAD

Alosa sapidissima (Wilson) *1811*

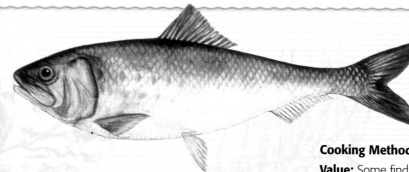

Habitat: Florida

Where & When to Find It: In May and June, in abundance

Processed & Sold: Whole

Cooking Method: In the oven or braised

Value: Some find this fish tasty.

Characteristics: Dark blue on its back and silver-white on the sides and abdomen. May reach 35 inches (90 cm) in length and weigh 8 to 9 lbs (4 kg).

Comments: American shad is an anadromous fish; i.e., it moves into the rivers when still a fry.

$

Flesh: Fatty

Poached American Shad with Aromatic Garden Herb Cream

²/₃ cup (100 g)	Butter
4	Shallots, cut with scissors
¹/₂ cup (20 g)	Chives
8	Sorrel leaves
20	Tarragon leaves
6	Lettuce leaves
1 cup (60 g)	Parsley
¹/₂ cup (25 g)	Chervil
7 oz (200 mL)	Noilly Prat, white
¹/₄ cup (60 mL)	White chicken stock (see "Basic Ingredients for Some Recipes")
To taste	Salt & pepper
4 cups (1 L)	*Court-bouillon* (see "Basic Ingredients …")
4 × 6 oz (180 g)	American shad fillets, boned
7 oz (200 mL)	Cream (35%)

- With the butter, cook the cut shallots until tender, then add the garden herbs, Noilly Prat and the chicken stock. Season with salt and pepper and let simmer for 4 to 5 minutes.
- While this is cooking, heat the *court-bouillon* and poach the American shad fillets for 7 to 10 minutes, depending on thickness.
- While the fish is cooking, emulsify the preceding preparation with an electric mixer and incorporate the hot cream. Adjust the seasoning and keep warm—170°F (85°C) maximum because of the acids.

Presentation: In the middle of each plate, arrange the shad fillets and cover with the aromatic herb sauce.

Accompaniment: Salsify and Jerusalem artichokes

Preparation time: 30 minutes	**Cooking time:** 7 to 15 minutes
Servings: 4	**Cost:** $$

American Shad Fillets with Spice Loaf

approx. 3 oz (100 g)	Honeyed spice loaf
³/4 cup (130 g)	Sweet butter
¹/2 cup (125 mL)	Peanut oil
To taste	Salt & pepper
4 × 5 oz (150 g)	American shad fillets
³/4 cup (80 g)	Shallots, chopped
3 ¹/2 oz (100 mL)	White wine
¹/2 cup (125 mL)	Brown veal stock (see "Basic Ingredients for Some Recipes")

- In a food processor or with a knife, mince the spice loaf.
- Gently heat 4 ¹/2 Tbsp (50 g) of butter and 3 Tbsp (50 mL) of oil. Season the shad fillets with salt and pepper, then marinate in the butter and oil, and coat with chopped spice loaf. Set aside in the refrigerator at least 30 minutes. This step allows the spice loaf to adhere to the fish by cooling the fats.
- Heat the remaining butter and oil, and cook the shad fillets à la meunière. Set aside.
- Deglaze the skillet with the shallots and wine. Reduce and incorporate the brown veal stock.
- Arrange each American shad fillet on a plate and surround with the sauce.

Accompaniment: Boiled cocotte potatoes

Note: This fish has very thin and delicate flesh, containing many bones.

Preparation time: 25 minutes	**Cooking time:** 15 minutes
Servings: 4	**Cost:** $$

167

SARDINE
Sardina pilchardus (Walbaum) *1792*

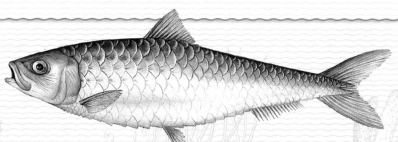

Characteristics: A small fish of the open sea, the sardine lives in compact schools. It has blue tones on its back, with some gold highlights and a silver abdomen. It also has large scales, which can be removed easily.

Flesh: Fatty

Habitat: South Atlantic

Where & When to Find It: Irregular availability wherever imported fish is sold

Processed & Sold: Whole

Cooking Method: Grilled

Value: Excellent when grilled, but grill outdoors since it gives off a strong smell.

$$

Sardine Fillets with Dill

16	**Fairly large sardines**
To taste	**Pepper**
To taste	**Coarse sea salt**
As needed	**Fennel or dill sprigs**
3 Tbsp (50 mL)	**Extra virgin olive oil**

- Clean the sardines by cutting the head 2/3 of the length from the back to the throat without completely severing. Pulling on the head will cause the guts to come out. Slide the thumb along the backbone, dividing the body in half to the tail, which will be saved, and pull out the backbone. The sardine is opened flat and the skin saved. It forms a *portefeuille*. With a knife, remove the large side bones and pull out the vertebrae. (See "How to" photographs—"How to bone a fish through the stomach").

- Season with coarse sea salt, then sprinkle each sardine with sprigs of dill or fennel. Pass a small, lightly oiled brush over the fish and let chill for 2 hours.

- When ready to serve, heat a non-stick skillet containing a few drops of oil. Fold each sardine over the dill, after having added some to each side, and cook at moderate heat for one minute per side.

- Serve immediately with small sautéed potatoes.

Preparation time: 10 minutes	
Cooking time: 2 to 4 minutes	
Servings: 4	**Cost:** $$

Sardine Escabèche

24	Sardines (24 to 26 per kilo)
As needed	Flour
approx. 2/3 cup (150 mL)	Olive oil
12	Small white onions
1	White onion, chopped
2	Carrots, sliced into thin rounds
4	Garlic cloves
7 oz (200 mL)	White wine vinegar
14 oz (400 mL)	Water
1	Bay leaf
1 pinch	Thyme sprigs
1 pinch	Saffron, chopped
1 hint	Cayenne pepper
To taste	Salt & pepper

- Clean the sardines and wipe, then dredge in flour and shake by the tail to remove any excess.
- Heat half the oil and fry quickly for one minute on each side. Place the sardines on a paper towel and lay head to tail in an appropriately sized dish.
- Heat the remaining oil and brown the small white onions, carrots and garlic, then cook at low heat for 7 to 8 minutes. Add the vinegar, water, bay leaf, thyme, saffron and cayenne pepper. Season with salt and pepper and let simmer for 15 minutes.
- Pour this hot preparation over the sardines. Let cool and refrigerate at least 24 hours. Serve chilled.

Accompaniment: Potato salad

Preparation time: 25 minutes	**Cooking time:** 15 minutes
Servings: 4	**Cost:** $$

SMELT, GOATFISH, SEA BREAM AND OTHERS

Miscellaneous Families

This group is composed of several species from different families that are commercially available. Some of these fish are already well known, others deserve to be discovered.

Ocean pout
Cunner
Capelin
American smelt
Spiny dogfish
Monkfish
American conger eel
Redfish
Goatfish
Dory and John Dory
Sea bream
Northern searobin
Atlantic wolffish
Red Snapper
Swordfish

OCEAN POUT

Macrozoarces americanus (Bloch and Schneider) *1801*

Characteristics: Can reach 3 3/4 ft (1.15 m) in length and 12 lbs (5.5 kg) in weight, but generally examples of this fish larger than 31 1/2 inches (80 cm) are rare. Its color varies from yellowish to reddish-brown, sprinkled with gray or olive-green spots.

Flesh: Lean

Habitat: Western part of the North Atlantic, south to Delaware and New Jersey

Where & When to Find It: Currently, it is possible to order directly from fishers.

Processed & Sold: As deep-frozen fillets (new on the market)

Cooking Method: *Meunière*, poached or steamed

Value: Excellent fish; its flesh, when cooked, resembles that of sole.

Comments: This fish resembles the Atlantic wolf-fish, but its body is more spindly and its lips bigger.

$$

Ocean Pout en Papillote *with Spinach*

10 oz (300 g)	Spinach leaves
To taste	Salt & pepper
1 3/4 lbs (800 g)	Ocean pout fillets
approx. 3/4 cup (150 g)	Butter
1	Lemon, diced
1 cup (250 mL)	Dry white wine
As needed	Fish fumet (see "Basic Ingredients for Some Recipes")
14 oz (400 g)	Rhubarb (stalks)
2 cups (200 g)	Leek, julienned
1 3/4 cups (200 g)	Carrot, julienned
As needed	Sugar

Preparation time: 30 minutes	**Cooking time:** 10 to 15 minutes
Servings: 4	**Cost:** $$

approx. 2/3 cup (150 mL) Cream (35%)

- Blanch the spinach leaves in salted water and chill with ice water.
- Season the ocean pout fillets with salt and pepper, place on each spinach leaf, add 4 1/2 Tbsp (50 g) of butter on each fillet and a few lemon cubes. Wrap the fish in the spinach leaves and tie with a string.
- Brush an ovenproof dish with 4 1/2 Tbsp (50 g) of butter and lay the ocean pout fillets wrapped in spinach in the dish. Moisten with the white wine and fish fumet, then cover with aluminum foil and bake at 400°F (200°C) for about 10 minutes.
- During this time, peel and thinly slice the rhubarb. With the remaining butter, sauté the rhubarb, then add the leeks and carrots.

Braise until cooked. Taste and, if the mixture is too acid, add a little sugar.

- After the ocean pout is cooked, pour the cooking juice into a saucepan and reduce by $9/10$. Add the cream and reduce by $1/2$, then pour into the saucepan holding the vegetables.

Presentation: Ladle the vegetable sauce preparation onto the plates, then arrange the ocean pout on top, in rows, after carefully removing the string.

Ocean Pout Fillets with Bay Mussels

$1/2$ cup (80 g)	Saltwater cordgrass
4 × 5 oz (150 g)	Ocean pout fillets
To taste	Salt & pepper
$1/2$ cup (60 g)	Shallots, chopped
$2/3$ cup (160 mL)	Mussel juice
$1/2$ cup (120 mL)	Brown chicken stock (see "Basic Ingredients for Some Recipes)
6 Tbsp (70 g)	Sweet butter, whipped
approx. 5 oz (160 g)	Bay mussels, shelled
$1/2$ cup (20 g)	Chives, cut with scissors

- Blanch the saltwater cordgrass; i.e., place it in cold water and, as soon as it boils, quickly drain.
- Lay the seasoned ocean pout fillets in an ovenproof dish, sprinkle with the chopped shallots, then pour in the mussel juice. Cover with aluminum foil and bake at 400°F (200°C) until small white droplets escape from the fish. Set aside.
- Reduce the cooking juice by $9/10$, add the chicken stock and reduce by $1/2$. Thicken this sauce with the whipped butter.
- A few minutes before serving, add the shelled mussels and the saltwater cordgrass. Let simmer a few minutes before serving.
- Arrange the fillets in the middle of the plate, pour the sauce over the fish and sprinkle with the cut chives.

Accompaniment: Boiled rice

NOTE: This fish is not used very often. It deserves to be better known as it is excellent and has the texture of sole.

Preparation time: 30 minutes	**Cooking time:** 10 minutes
Servings: 4	**Cost:** $$

Photo on next page →

CUNNER

Tautogolabrus adspersus (Walbaum) *1792*
Incorrect names: tench, perch, tilefish

Flesh: Semi-fatty

Habitat: Atlantic coast of North America

Where & When to Find It: Rarely requested; can be custom ordered directly from fishermen.

Processed & Sold: As deep-frozen fillets

Characteristics: Can measure up to 20 inches (50 cm) in length and weigh 3 1/2 lbs (1.6 kg) Its color varies according to its surroundings. It can sport red, brown or blue spots, with one of these colors being dominant.

Cooking Method: *Meunière*, poached, steamed or grilled

Value: An interesting flavor that is an acquired taste.

$

Cunner Fillets in a Spicy Croûte

2 Tbsp (20 g)	Shallots, finely sliced
3 1/2 oz (100 mL)	Olive oil
8	Tomatoes, blanched, peeled, seeded and diced
1	Garlic clove, minced
To taste	Salt & pepper
2/3 cup (150 mL)	Brown chicken stock (see "Basic Ingredients for Some Recipes")
2/3 cup (30 g)	Sweet basil, cut with scissors
1 3/4 tsp (5 g)	Paprika
1 pinch	Cayenne pepper
To taste	Black pepper, ground
1 pinch	Thyme sprigs

2 tsp (3 g)	Dried onion, ground
1/2 tsp (2 g)	Black cumin, ground
1 tsp (2 g)	Ginger, ground
1/2 tsp (2 g)	Celery seed, ground
4 × 6 oz (180 g)	Cunner fillets
2/3 cup (100 g)	Sweet butter
10 oz (300 g)	Rapini

- In a saucepan, sweat the shallot in 3 Tbsp (50 mL) of olive oil, add the diced tomatoes and garlic, season with salt and pepper. Let simmer for a few minutes, and add the chicken stock and the cut basil. Cook for 20 minutes and set aside.
- Combine all the spices.
- Cut the cunner fillets into pieces of equal size.

- Season the fillets with salt and pepper. Coat in the spice mixture and sear in a non-stick skillet without any fat to lightly brown the spices, then put small knobs of butter (1/3 cup or 60 g) on each fillet to finish cooking. Set aside.

- At the same time, quickly sauté the rapini at high heat in 3 Tbsp (50 mL) of butter and 3 Tbsp (40 g) of olive oil. Season.

Presentation: Ladle the sauce into the bottom of the plate, then arrange the cunner fillets on top. Place the sautéed rapini on top of the fillets.

Preparation time: 20 minutes	Cooking time: 5 to 10 minutes
Servings: 4	Cost: $$

Cunner with Lovage

3 1/2 lbs (1.6 kg)	Cunner
To taste	Salt & pepper
1/4 cup (60 mL)	Olive oil
1 cup (120 g)	Shallots, chopped
1	Garlic clove, chopped
2/3 cup (160 g)	Celery leaves
2/3 cup (160 g)	Lovage leaves
2/3 cup (100 g)	Butter
1/2 cup (120 mL)	White wine
3 1/2 oz (100 mL)	Brown veal stock (see "Basic Ingredients for Some Recipes")

- Bone the cunner through the stomach, season with salt and pepper and set aside.
- Heat the olive oil and cook half the chopped shallots with the garlic until tender, then add the celery and lovage leaves. Cook for 10 minutes or until all the moisture has evaporated. Season and refrigerate for about 12 minutes.
- Stuff the cunner with the preceding mixture. With 1/3 cup (60 g) of butter, grease an oven-proof dish and sprinkle with the remaining shallots. Place the fish in the dish and pour in the white wine. Cover with aluminum foil and bake at 400°F (200°C) for 20 minutes.
- Transfer the cooking stock to a saucepan, reduce by 9/10 and add the brown veal stock. Thicken the sauce with the remaining butter.
- Place a piece of cunner in the middle of each plate, garnish and pour the sauce over the fish.

Accompaniment: Boiled potatoes

NOTE: This fish, which is the principal predator of lobster, has considerable culinary qualities.

Preparation time: 30 minutes	Cooking time: 20 to 30 minutes
Servings: 4	Cost: $$

Photo on page 175

177

CAPELIN

Mallotus villosus (Müller) *1777*

Characteristics: Green back, white abdomen and silver sides under the lateral line. Can reach 10 inches (26 cm) in length.

Flesh: Lean

Where & When to Find It: In June and July, in abundance

Processed & Sold: Whole

Cooking Method: Fried, baked or *meunière*

Value: Delicate taste

Comments: Capelin is a fish of the high seas that goes to the coastal areas to spawn on the sand and gravel beaches. Large numbers of capelin spawn right where the waves break on the beach.

$$

Capelin Marinated in White Wine

1 1/4 lbs (600 g)	Fresh capelin (small)
1/2 cup (125 g)	Coarse salt
1/2 cup (125 mL)	Olive oil
1/2 cup (125 mL)	Peanut oil
2/3 cup (90 g)	Onions, sliced thin
3 cups (350 g)	Fennel, sliced thin
1 Tbsp (30 g)	Dill, chopped
1/2 cup (30 g)	Chinese parsley, chopped
1/2 tsp (5 g)	Salt
1 tsp (5 g)	Chili peppers, ground
3 cups (750 mL)	White wine
1 cup (250 mL)	Vinegar

- Clean the capelin. Cover with coarse salt and leave for 2 hours. Wipe well and sauté in the mixture of smoking oils. Drain and dry off to remove any trace of fat. Combine the capelin with the onions, fennel, dill, Chinese parsley, salt and crushed chili pepper.
- Moisten with the white wine and vinegar. Marinate for 24 hours.

Accompaniment: Warm, boiled potato slices

Preparation time: 30 minutes	**Cooking time:** 5 to 8 minutes
Servings: 6	**Cost:** $$

Capelin Charlevoix

3 ½ oz (100 mL)	Peanut oil
1 ¼ lbs (600 g)	Capelin
10 oz (300 g)	Bacon
To taste	Salt and paprika
6	Lemon wedges
As needed	Parsley, chopped

- Brush a mold with about 2 oz (50 mL) of oil. Weave the capelin and bacon slices together (as if weaving a basket) and place in the mold. Season with salt and brush with the remaining oil. Dust with paprika. Bake in the oven at 400°F (200°C) for 10 to 15 minutes, until the top turns golden in color.
- Serve with the lemon wedges and garnish with the chopped parsley.

Preparation time: 30 minutes **Cooking time:** 10 to 15 minutes
Servings: 6   **Cost:** $$

AMERICAN SMELT

Osmerus mordax (Mitchill) *1815*

Characteristics: Green back, lighter sides with a silver stripe and silver abdomen. The entire body is sprinkled with black dots. Length ranges from 5 to 8 inches (13 to 20 cm).

Flesh: Lean

Habitat: The entire Atlantic coast of North America

Where & When to Find It: In October and November, in abundance

Processed & Sold: Whole

Cooking Method: Grilled, in the oven, *meunière* or fried

Value: Small smelt are excellent when lightly fried. Larger fish should be baked in the oven.

Comments: Smelt live in coastal waters, migrating upstream to spawn.

$$

American Smelt Stuffed with Sea Urchin Mousse

8	Small sea urchins
3 oz (85 g)	Flounder fillet
1	Egg white
1/2 cup (130 mL)	Cream (35%)
To taste	Salt & pepper
16	American smelt, medium-sized
1/2 cup (125 mL)	White wine
1 tsp (20 g)	Dried shallot, chopped
7 oz (200 mL)	Fish fumet (see "Basic Ingredients for Some Recipes")
1	Fresh lemon
As needed	Small vegetable garnish (Optional)

- Open the sea urchins and completely empty; set the liquid, flesh (gonads) and the shells aside separately. In a food processor, chop the flounder flesh, then add the sea urchin flesh and chop. Incorporate the egg white and 3 Tbsp (50 mL) of the cream. Season with salt and pepper, set aside and chill. Later, stuff the sea urchin shells, which have been washed and the spines removed beforehand, with the preceding mixture.

- Remove the backbone from the smelt, then season with salt and pepper. Stuff the smelt with the remaining forcemeat and set aside. In a *bain-marie*, poach the sea urchin shells in the oven at 400°F (200°C) for 10 to 12 minutes.

- Heat the white wine. Add the shallots and the smelt and bake in the oven at 375°F (190°C) for 2 to 3 minutes. Dry off the smelt with a cloth. Reduce the cooking liquid from the smelts and the fish fumet by 3/4. Add the remaining cream and reduce again until the sauce is smooth. Add the sea urchin liquid and the lemon juice. Strain this sauce through cheesecloth or a fine mesh strainer, set aside and keep warm.

Preparation time: 45 minutes **Cooking time:** 2 to 8 minutes
Servings: 4   **Cost:** $$$

- With the American smelt, form the shape of a star on each hot plate. Cover with the sauce. Place two stuffed sea urchins on each plate. Serve with small, shaped vegetables, if so desired.

American Smelt Fritters in Buckwheat Flour

3 dozen	**American smelt**
To taste	**Salt & pepper**
1/2 cup (100 g)	**Buckwheat flour**
1/2 tsp (3 g)	**Baking powder**
1/3 cup (45 g)	**Corn starch**
2 Tbsp (65 g)	**Dehydrated onion**
1	**Egg**
2/3 cup (150 mL)	**Milk**
As needed	**Cooking oil**
2	**Lemons**

- Extract the backbone from the smelt using a paring knife, snipping the back, from the head to the tail. Season the fish and set aside.
- Sift the dry ingredients together and mix. Add the egg. Combine by gradually adding the milk. Let the batter sit for 20 minutes.
- Heat the oil to 300°F (150°C). Dip each smelt in the batter and fry for about 3 minutes. Serve the fish hot with lemon wedges.

Preparation time: 20 minutes **Cooking time:** 5 minutes
Servings: 6   **Cost:** $$

SPINY DOGFISH

Squalus acanthias (Linnaeus) *1758*

Comments: North American waters teem with this fish that deserves to be better known. Other sharks are available and are becoming increasingly popular in restaurants.

• mako (*Isurus oxyrinchus*) Rafinesque 1810: A deep-water species, its flesh resembles that of swordfish.

Characteristics: Its back is sometimes grayish-brown and the abdomen varies from pale gray to white. This fish can reach 53 inches (135 cm) in length and 20 lbs (9.2 kg) in weight.

Flesh: Semi-fatty

Habitat: Both sides of the North Atlantic, particularly in temperate and sub-Arctic waters

Where & When to Find It: June to October

Processed & Sold: Whole, skinned* and as fillets

Cooking Method: Braised, in the oven or steamed

Value: Surprising, despite its texture

• spotted dogfish (*Scyliorhinus canicula*) Linnaeus 1758: cousin of the spine shark

• tope (*Galeorhinus galeus*) Linnaeus 1758

* As in the case of eel, the fish is skinned by holding on to the head and pulling on the skin.

$$

Spiny Dogfish with Seaweed and Pears

3	Pears for cooking
7 oz (200 mL)	Fish fumet (see "Basic Ingredients for Some Recipes")
2/3 cup (150 mL)	Dry white wine
1 tsp (30 g)	Dried shallot, chopped
As needed	Black seaweed, dried
1/2 cup (120 mL)	Cream (35%)
To taste	Salt & pepper
1 3/4 lbs (800 g)	Spiny dogfish, skinned*

1	Lemon (juice)
4 1/2 Tbsp (50 g)	Butter
As needed	Chives, chopped
2 cups (200 g)	Green beans, sliced extra fine

• Peel the pears, cook in the fish fumet and keep 4 pear halves for garnishing. Finely dice the remaining pear.

• Heat the white wine with the shallots and reduce by 9/10. Add the seaweed and the diced pear. Add the fish fumet and reduce by half. Let the vegetables cool. Heat the cream and reduce by half; add to the seaweed sauce. Season with salt and pepper.

- In an ovenproof dish, place the fish, previously cut into sections 4 to 5 inches (10 to 12 cm) long. Pour the sauce over the fish and bake at 400°F (200°C) for 10 to 12 minutes, depending on the thickness of the sections. Place the fish in the plates. Add the lemon juice, butter, salt and pepper to the sauce, and pour over the fish. Garnish each plate with half a pear and sprinkle with the chopped chives. Serve with the green beans, boiled in salted water.

* Skinned: As in the case of the eel, the fish is skinned by holding on to the head and pulling the skin.

Preparation time: 35 minutes	Cooking time: 10 to 12 minutes
Servings: 4	Cost: $$

Photo on next page →

Spiny Dogfish Sections with Cocoa Fragrance

4	Cobs of corn
1	Spanish onion, chopped
1/2	Garlic clove, minced
5	Tomatoes, blanched, peeled, seeded and diced
10	Fresh coriander leaves
2/3 cup (30 g)	Chives, cut with scissors
1/2 Tbsp (5 g)	Green chili, diced
2	Limes (juice)
To taste	Salt & pepper
7 oz (200 mL)	Brown chicken stock (see "Basic Ingredients for Some Recipes")
2/3 cup (60 g)	Unsweetened cocoa
4 × 6 oz (180 g)	Spiny dogfish, skinned and sectioned

- Cook the corn in salted water. When cooked, remove the kernels and keep warm.
- In a bowl, place the onion, chopped garlic, diced tomatoes, coriander leaves, diced green chili and the lime juice. Season with salt and pepper and macerate for at least 1 hour.
- Heat the brown chicken stock with the unsweetened cocoa, and poach the spiny dogfish sections for 8 to 12 minutes, depending on the thickness of the sections. Taste and adjust the seasoning as needed.

Presentation: In the middle of the plate, place the macerated vegetables, then a dogfish section on top. Cover with sauce. Surround with corn.

Preparation time: 20 minutes	Cooking time: 8 to 15 minutes
Servings: 4	Cost: $$

183

MONKFISH

Lophius americanus (Valenciennes) *1837*

Incorrect names: shorthorn sculpin, burbot

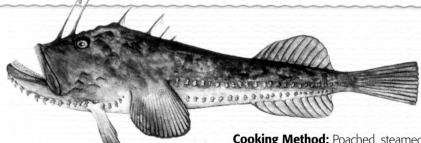

Characteristics: Brownish with dark spots and a whitish abdomen, this fish can reach 55 inches (140 cm) in length and 50 to 60 lbs (22.7 to 27.2 kg) in weight.

Flesh: Lean and firm

Habitat: East coast of North America, south to North Carolina

Where & When to Find It: From June to August, in abundance

Processed & Sold: Whole and as fillets

Cooking Method: Poached, steamed, baked, braised or roasted

Value: This fish is ideal for someone just starting to eat fish. Without any particular taste or smell, it goes well with all sauces.

Comments: Monkfish is referred to as "burbot" when the head has been removed. Why? This fish is so ugly that, by changing its name to burbot, we forget its ugliness. Monkfish is highly appreciated by those who do not like fish with a lot of bones, as this one has only a large backbone.

$$

Monkfish Medallions with Two Sauces

1 ¹/₂ lbs (700 g)	Monkfish fillets
To taste	Salt & pepper
As needed	Butter

TOMATO AND MUSSEL SAUCE

7 oz (200 mL)	White wine
³/₄ cup (80 g)	Shallots, minced
3 Tbsp (50 g)	Tomato paste
7 oz (200 mL)	Mussel juice
7 oz (200 mL)	Fish fumet (see "Basic Ingredients for Some Recipes")
As needed	White roux (see "Basic Ingredients …")

ASPARAGUS SAUCE

7 oz (200 g)	Fresh asparagus
²/₃ cup (150 mL)	Cream (35%)

- Cut the monkfish fillets into medallions and lay in an ovenproof dish. Season with salt and pepper, then sprinkle with knobs of butter. Broil or bake at 450°F (230°C) for a few minutes, depending on the thickness of the medallions. Pour the tomato sauce onto one half of each of the preheated plates, then pour the asparagus sauce onto the other half. Arrange the monkfish medallions on top of the sauces and serve immediately with a garnish of choice.

- **Tomato and Mussel Sauce**: Heat the white wine with half of the shallots and reduce completely. Add the tomato paste and cook well to remove any acidity. Add half the mussel juice and half the fish fumet. Cook for 10 to 15 minutes. Bind the sauce with the white roux. Season with salt and pepper, then thicken with butter. Strain through cheesecloth or a fine mesh strainer. Set aside and keep warm.
- **Asparagus Sauce**: Boil the asparagus in salted water; drain and purée in a blender. Incorporate the cold cream, then season with salt and pepper. Heat the white wine with the remaining shallots and reduce by $9/10$. Add the remaining mussel juice and fish fumet and cook for 10 minutes. Gradually incorporate the asparagus mixture. Season with salt and pepper and strain through cheesecloth or a fine mesh strainer, then thicken with butter. Set the sauce aside, near the heat.

Preparation time: 1 hour	**Cooking time:** 10 to 15 minutes
Servings: 4	**Cost:** $$$

Monkfish Curry Ragout

2 1/4 lbs (1 kg)	Monkfish fillets, trimmed
1 cup (165 g)	Onions, chopped
1/2 cup (60 g)	Shallots, chopped
3 1/2 Tbsp (40 g)	Butter
To taste	Salt & pepper
3 1/2 oz (100 mL)	Cognac
2 cups (200 g)	Tomato, blanched, peeled, seeded and diced
1	Garlic clove, chopped
2 Tbsp (60 g)	Curry powder
7 oz (200 mL)	Cream (35%)
1 hint	Cayenne pepper
As needed	Parsley, chopped

- Cut the monkfish into pieces.
- In a fairly large, high-sided frying pan, cook the chopped onions and shallots in butter until a light golden shade. Season the monkfish with salt and pepper, and add to the onion mixture. Sear at high heat. Sprinkle with cognac and flambé. Add the tomato, garlic and curry powder. Cook covered at low heat for 7 to 8 minutes. Remove the pieces of monkfish from the frying pan and drain. Strain the sauce through cheesecloth or a fine mesh strainer and return to the heat. Add the cream and cook for a few minutes. Check the seasoning and add a hint of cayenne pepper. Return the monkfish to the sauce. Let simmer for a few minutes.
- Arrange the meal in a dish, sprinkle with parsley and serve immediately. Can be served with the cooked vegetables.

Preparation time: 30 minutes	**Cooking time:** 15 minutes
Servings: 6	**Cost:** $$$

Photo on page 185

AMERICAN CONGER EEL

Conger oceanicus (Mitchill) *1818*
Incorrect name: king snake eel

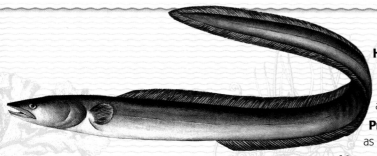

Habitat: Continental shelf off the eastern coast of the North Atlantic

Where & When to Find It: Irregular availability where fish is sold

Processed & Sold: Whole, in pieces and as fillets

Characteristics: The eel can measure 7 ft. (2.1 m) and weigh 22 lbs (10 kg). Generally gray in color, with a whitish abdomen; the tips of the dorsal and anal fins are black.

Flesh: Very compact, neutral in taste

Cooking Method: Poached, steamed, baked or braised.

Value: A fish that, due to its texture and numerous bones, will please only the converted. It is a mandatory ingredient in a Marseille bouillabaisse.

$$

Braised American Conger Eel with Sorrel

¼ cup (60 mL)	Olive oil
4 × 6 oz (180 g)	Conger eel pieces, skinned[*]
approx. ½ lb (250 g)	Fresh sorrel
⅓ cup (60 g)	Butter
1	White onion *brunoise*
1	Carrot *brunoise*
To taste	Salt & pepper
1	Garlic clove, chopped
½ cup (120 mL)	Lobster juice

- Heat the oil and brown the eel pieces. Set aside on a paper towel. Then, in the same oil, quickly sauté the sorrel leaves and drain in a strainer.

- Heat the butter, and cook the onion and carrot *brunoise* until tender. Season the pieces of eel, place on the *brunoise*, then sprinkle the chopped garlic and the sorrel leaves on and around the fish pieces. Pour in the lobster liquid and bake at low temperature (160°F or 70°C) for at least 40 minutes.
- Remove from the oven, sprinkle with small knobs of butter and serve as is.

Accompaniment: Rice Creole or steamed potatoes

[*] As in the case of eel, the skin is removed by holding on to the head and pulling the skin.

Preparation time: 30 minutes	**Cooking time:** 15 minutes
Servings: 4	**Cost:** $$

American Eel with Pesto on a Bed of Chick Peas

16 oz (350 g)	Chick peas
1	Onion, cut with scissors
2/3 cup (100 g)	Butter
3 cups (400 g)	Carrot and celery macédoine
1 1/2 cups (350 mL)	Brown veal stock (see "Basic Ingredients for Some Recipes")
1	Bouquet garni
To taste	Salt & pepper

PESTO

1/3 cup (50 g)	Pine nuts
2 cups (100 g)	Sweet basil leaves
4 1/2 Tbsp (50 g)	Flat-leafed parsley
1/2 cup (50 g)	Parmesan, grated
2/3 cup (150 mL)	Olive oil
4 × 7 oz (200 g)	Eel sections
To taste	Salt & pepper

- Soak the chick peas in cold water for about 12 hours, then cook, starting with cold, unsalted water.
- In a saucepan, cook the onion in 4 1/2 Tbsp (50 g) of butter until tender, then add the carrot and celery *macédoine*, veal stock and *bouquet garni* and let simmer gently, then add the chick peas. Adjust the seasoning, set aside and keep warm.
- Pesto: Roast the pine nuts in a non-stick skillet, then, in a blender, combine the sweet basil, flat-leafed parsley, Parmesan, olive oil and pine nuts.
- Coat each piece of skinned American conger eel with the pesto, and steam, using a basket steamer. When cooked, season with salt and pepper.

Presentation: Place the chick peas on a plate, then the pieces of eel.

Preparation time: 30 minutes	**Cooking time:** 15 to 20 minutes
Servings: 4	**Cost:** $$

189

REDFISH

Sebastes marinus (Linnaeus) *1758*
Incorrect names: ocean perch, goldfish, golden redfish

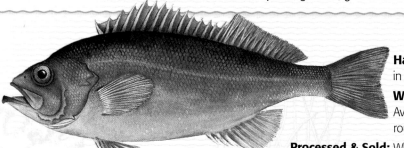

Habitat: North Atlantic coasts, in cold water

Where & When to Find It: Available generally all year round wherever fish is sold

Processed & Sold: Whole or as fillets

Cooking Method: Whole in the oven, braised, *meunière* or grilled

Characteristics: Body color varies from gold to bright red; has black eyes. Length varies from 8 to 16 inches (20 to 41 cm); average weight is approx. 1 lb (500 g).

Value: Although fragile, this fish is very fine.

Comments: There is only one species of redfish off the Atlantic coast, while there are 6 off the Pacific coast.

Flesh: Delicate flavor and fragile

$$

Redfish en Papillote *with Chervil*

2 ¼ lbs (1 kg)	Redfish
To taste	Salt & pepper
10 oz (300 g)	Potatoes, diced small
1 cup (125 g)	Onion *brunoise*
½	Garlic clove, chopped
¼ cup (40 g)	Celery *brunoise*
2 ¾ cups (500 g)	Fresh tomatoes, blanched, peeled, seeded and diced
4 stems	Parsley, chopped
2 ½ Tbsp (10 g)	Chervil, chopped
3 ½ oz (100 mL)	Dry white wine
⅔ cup (100 g)	Sweet butter, melted
2 Tbsp (30 mL)	Olive oil
2 ½ Tbsp (10 g)	Chervil, chopped
1	Lemon

- Scrape the redfish to remove the scales. Cut through the stomach to remove the backbone. Season with salt and pepper, then set aside.
- Cook the potatoes in salted water until ¾ done, then let cool. Stuff the fish with the potatoes. Place the fish on a sheet of aluminum foil; close at the top, leaving half the foil open. Place the onion, garlic, celery, tomatoes, parsley and chervil on the fish and pour the white wine, butter and olive oil into the *papillote*. Season with salt and pepper.
- Seal the *papillote* and bake at 350°F (180°C) for 30 to 40 minutes, depending on the thickness of the fish. Remove the fish from the oven and open the *papillote* immediately.

Divide the fish into servings and place each one on a very hot plate. Cover with the cooking juice and garnish with the potatoes.

Sprinkle with the chervil and serve immediately with lemon wedges.

Preparation time: 40 minutes	**Cooking time:** 30 to 40 minutes
Servings: 4	**Cost:** $$

Redfish Fillets Doria *

8 × 6 oz (60 g)	Redfish fillets, skin on
1 cup (125 g)	Flour
1	Egg
1 cup (125 g)	White bread crumbs
2 Tbsp (30 mL)	Peanut oil
¾ cup (120 g)	Butter
3	Cucumbers
To taste	Salt & pepper
½ cup (30 g)	Parsley, chopped
1	Garlic clove, chopped
3 Tbsp (40 mL)	Meat glaze (see "Basic Ingredients for Some Recipes")

- Wash the fillets and carefully wipe, using a paper towel. Put the flour, the egg wash and the bread crumbs on three different plates. In turn, dredge each fillet in the flour, egg and bread crumbs.
- In a skillet, heat half the oil and half the butter. Cook the fillets at high heat. Once golden on one side, turn with a spatula and cook the other side. The flesh of the fish is tender and cooks quickly.
- Peel the cucumbers, then cut into sections 2 inches (5 cm) long; divide into 4 pieces. In a skillet, put the remaining butter and the cucumber pieces, season with salt and pepper and cook slowly uncovered to evaporate the water from the cucumbers. Turn from time to time so that the pieces are cooked on each side. Drain the cooking fat. Combine the cucumbers with the parsley and chopped garlic. Place in the bottom of a flat dish, then lay the fish in the dish. On each side, create a cordon of hot meat glaze.

Accompaniment: Boiled potatoes shaped like olives

* In memory of my spiritual chef in Quebec, Abel Benguet.

Preparation time: 15 minutes	**Cooking time:** 5 to 6 minutes
Servings: 4	**Cost:** $$$

Photo on next page →

GOATFISH

Mullus barbatus (Linnaeus) *1758*
Incorrect names: red gurnard, red gurnet

Characteristics: A pink back and paler pink stomach. A small fish rarely exceeding 14 oz (400 g). A ground fish recognizable by its barbels under the chin

Flesh: Firm and white; delicate flavor

Habitat: Warm seas

Where & When to Find It: Irregular availability wherever imported fish is sold

Processed & Sold: Whole

Cooking Method: Grilled or *meunière*

Value: Enormous culinary value, a luxury
$$$$$

Goatfish Pie with Fines Herbes *and Crunchy Vegetables*

8	Goatfish fillets
14 oz (400 g)	Flaky pastry
4	Carrots, cut into tagliatelle (long, narrow strands)
1	Leek (white part only), cut into tagliatelle
1 cup (120 g)	Celery stalks, cut into tagliatelle
2/3 cup (120 g)	Zucchini, cut into tagliatelle
4	Tomatoes, cut into rounds
4	Artichoke bottoms, cut into fine strips
To taste	Salt & pepper

4	Swiss chard leaves, cut with scissors
1/2 cup (25 g)	Fresh sweet basil, cut with scissors
3/4 cup (50 g)	Fresh parsley, cut with scissors
1/2 cup (25 g)	Fresh chives, cut with scissors
approx. 1 cup (25 g)	Tarragon leaves
1 3/4 Tbsp (10 g)	Small thyme sprigs
approx. 1/3 cup (70 mL)	Olive oil

- Dry off the goatfish fillets. Be sure to keep the scaled skin on. Store in the refrigerator.
- Roll out the flaky pastry and make circles 3 inches (8 cm) in diameter. Refrigerate for

about 30 minutes, then bake the rolled-out pieces of flaky pastry in the oven at 400°F (200°C) for 4 to 5 minutes. Set aside.

- At this point, heat the salted water to cook the tagliatelle one by one, then drain and dry with a cloth.
- On each piece of half-baked rolled-out pastry, place the tomatoes, artichokes, and the well-seasoned vegetable tagliatelle, then sprinkle with the cut Swiss chard leaves, basil, parsley, chives, tarragon and thyme.
- On each piece of pastry, lay the goatfish fillets head to tail. Bake in the oven for 15 to 20 minutes at 375°F (190°C). Remove from the oven and sprinkle with olive oil.

Preparation time: 40 minutes	**Cooking time:** 15 to 30 minutes
Servings: 4	**Cost:** $$$$

Goatfish with Champagne

4 × 5–7 oz (160–200 g)	Surmullets
1 cup (250 mL)	Champagne
2/3 cup (160 mL)	Fish *velouté* (see "Basic Ingredients for Some Recipes")
16	Asparagus tips
24	Fresh fiddleheads
To taste	Salt & pepper
As needed	Peanut oil
1/2 cup (80 g)	Butter
1/2 package	Enoki mushrooms

- Scale and fillet the surmullets, then quickly wash and wipe the fillets. Set aside.
- Reduce the champagne by 7/10, then add the fish *velouté*. Set aside.
- Cook the asparagus and fiddleheads separately in salted water. Drain and set aside.
- Season the surmullets with salt and pepper, brush with oil, then grill. Always start with the hot side, then finish cooking on the cooler side of the grill.
- Heat the sauce, thicken with the butter, then adjust the seasoning. Reheat the vegetables in a double boiler.
- At the bottom of the dish, lay the goatfish fillets one on top of the other. Delicately arrange the vegetables around the fish, and finish with the raw mushrooms.

Preparation time: 25 minutes	**Cooking time:** 5 minutes
Servings: 4	**Cost:** $$$$

Photo on page 193

JOHN DORY

Zeus fibre (Linnaeus) *1758*

Flesh: Very thin, very white and firm. One of the best fish, but wastage is 65 to 70% (due to the large head).

Habitat: The Atlantic near the European coastline

Where & When to Find It: Irregular availability wherever imported fish is sold

Processed & Sold: Whole and as fillets

Cooking Method: Steamed, *meunière*, grilled or in the oven

Value: Highly appreciated in gastronomic circles

Comments: The flesh of the John Dory has a taste similar to that of crab or lobster.

$$$$$

Characteristics: Gray-blue fish with two large black spots on its sides. Weight varies from 1 ¹/₂ to 6 lbs (675 g to 2.7 kg).

John Dory with Caviar Cream

5 oz (150 g)	Salsify, finely sliced
As needed	Milk
³/₄ cup (120 g)	Fresh green peas
To taste	Salt & pepper
4 × 2 oz (60 g)	John Dory fillets
³/₄ cup (140 g)	Sweet butter
1 ¹/₄ cup (300 mL)	Champagne
1 cup (240 mL)	Shrimp or crayfish bisque (see "Basic Ingredients for Some Recipes")
approx. ¹/₃ cup (80 mL)	Sour cream
2 ³/₄ oz (80 g)	Sturgeon caviar

- Cook the chopped salsify in salted milk. When done, leave in the milk.
- Cook the peas in salted water.

- Season the John Dory fillets with salt and pepper, then with 2 ¹/₂ Tbsp (30 g) of butter, brush an ovenproof dish and place the fillets in the dish. Pour in the champagne and sprinkle with 6 Tbsp (70 g) of knobs of butter. Cover with aluminum foil and bake at 400°F (200°C), keeping a watchful eye on the fillets, ensuring they stay soft.
- When cooked, pour the cooking stock in a saucepan and reduce by half. Add the shrimp or crayfish bisque, let simmer for several minutes, then incorporate the sour cream, whisking vigorously.
- Drain the salsify and the peas, then sauté with the remaining butter. Season to taste.
- Just before serving, incorporate the sturgeon caviar into the sauce.

Presentation: Place the salsify and the green peas around the upper part of the plate, then arrange the John Dory fillets and cover with caviar sauce.

Preparation time: 30 minutes **Cooking time:** 10 to 15 minutes
Servings: 4   **Cost:** $$$$$

Pistachio-Flavored John Dory Fillets

approx. 5 oz (160 g)	Chinese artichoke
1 1/2 cups (160 g)	**Extra-thin green beans**
3/4 cup (180 g)	**Pistachio butter**
4 × 4–5 oz (130–150 g)	**John Dory fillets**
1/3 cup (40 g)	**Shallot, minced**
1/2 cup (120 mL)	**Dry white wine**
1/2 cup (120 mL)	**Fish fumet (see "Basic Ingredients for Some Recipes")**
To taste	**Salt & pepper**
As needed	**Chervil leaves, peeled**

- Cook the Chinese artichokes and the extra-thin green beans in salted water. Set aside.
- Brush an appropriately sized ovenproof dish with 1/3 cup (80 g) of pistachio butter, place the John Dory fillets and the shallots in the dish, then pour in the white wine and the fish fumet. Cover with aluminum foil and bake in the oven at 400°F (200°C).
- *Caution*: This fish is very delicate and should not be overcooked. As it is very thin, 4 to 5 minutes should suffice.
- Remove the fillets from the dish and set aside where they will stay warm. Reduce the cooking juice by 4/5.
- Pour the boiling, reduced juice into a blender and incorporate the remaining pistachio butter. This will bind the mixture.
- Reheat the vegetables in a *bain-marie*, i.e., in a fine mesh strainer sitting in boiling water.
- Arrange the John Dory fillets in the middle of each plate, cover with pistachio sauce and place the seasoned vegetables around the fillets as well as the chervil leaves.

Preparation time: 25 minutes **Cooking time:** 4 to 8 minutes
Servings: 4   **Cost:** $$$$$

Photo on next page →

SEA BREAM

Spondyliesama cantharus (Linnaeus) *1758*
Incorrect names: Atlantic pomfret, gilthead bream

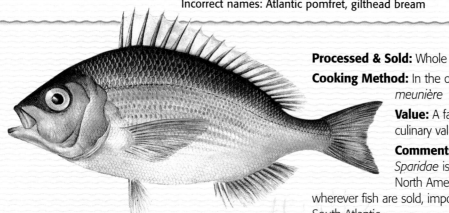

Processed & Sold: Whole

Cooking Method: In the oven, braised, grilled or *meunière*

Value: A family of fish with a high culinary value

Comments: This family of *Sparidae* is not generally found in North America. It is widely available wherever fish are sold, imported from Europe or the South Atlantic.

Characteristics: This fish has a compressed body 20 inches (50 cm) in length and 4 1/2 lbs (2 kg) in weight. Scales are deeply imbedded, gray to silver in color with golden highlights.

Flesh: Very thin, white and tasty

Habitat: South Atlantic (Europe) and the Mediterranean

Where & When to Find It: Generally available all year round where fish is sold, depending on the species and class of sea bream

Gilthead sea bream (*Sparus aurata*)

Blue-spotted sea bream (*Sparus pagrus*)

Red sea bream (*Pagellus centrodontus*)

Red sea bream (*Pagellus bogareveo*)

Common pandora (*Pagellus erythrinus*)

Bogue (*Boops, boops*)

Sargo bream (*Diplodus sargus*)

Common dentex (*Dentex, dentex*)

$$$$

Baked Sea Bream

2 × 1 1/4–2 lbs (600–900 g)	Sea bream
To taste	Salt & pepper
2	Lemons, wedges
2	Garlic cloves
1 cup (125 g)	White bread crumbs
1 1/2 Tbsp (10 g)	Paprika
1/2 cup (30 g)	Fresh parsley, chopped
5	Medium-sized potatoes
1 cup (250 mL)	Water
1/2 cup (125 mL)	Olive oil
1 cup (40 g)	Fresh chives, cut with scissors

• Scale and wash the fish, then season with salt and pepper. Make three parallel cuts across the fish about 1/2 inch (1 cm) deep and 1 1/4 inch (3.5 cm) apart. Put a piece of lemon in each cut, rind facing outwards.

- Mince the garlic. Combine the bread crumbs, garlic, paprika and parsley.
- Slice the potatoes into fine rounds. Place the potato rounds in an ovenproof dish. Add water, then season.
- Place the fish on top of the potatoes and coat with oil. Sprinkle with the bread crumbs. Bake in the middle of the oven at 350°F (180°C) for about 20 minutes or until the meat and the potatoes are cooked. Sprinkle the fish with the cut chives and serve immediately.

Preparation time: 30 minutes **Cooking time:** 20 minutes
Servings: 4   **Cost:** $$$$

Photo on next page →

Black Sea Bream Fillets with Oyster Mushrooms and Lobster Butter

1 cup (180 g)	Sweet butter
To taste	Salt & pepper
3 1/4 cups (200 g)	Oyster mushrooms
1/2 cup (60 g)	Shallots, minced
3 1/2 oz (100 mL)	Peanut oil
4 × 5–6 oz (160–180 g)	Black sea bream fillets
4 oz (120 g)	Lobster butter
3/4 cup (80 g)	Tomatoes, blanched, peeled, seeded and diced

- Heat 2/3 cup (100 g) of butter, season the oyster mushrooms with salt and pepper, then cook gently. When half-cooked, sprinkle the oyster mushrooms with the chopped shallots.
- In a skillet, with the remaining butter and peanut oil, sear the previously seasoned black bream fillets so that the skin becomes crispy.
- Gently heat the lobster butter.
- Arrange the oyster mushrooms attractively on the plate, then place the black sea bream fillets, skin side up. Arrange the raw diced tomatoes on top of the oyster mushrooms and, with a small spoon, sprinkle lobster butter over everything.

Accompaniment: Wild rice

Preparation time: 30 minutes **Cooking time:** 15 minutes
Servings: 4   **Cost:** $$$$

NORTHERN SEAROBIN

Prionotus carolinus (Linnaeus) *1771*
Incorrect name: goatfish

Where & When to Find It:
Rarely found on the market as there is not much demand for it

Processed & Sold: Whole

Cooking Method: Whole in the oven or braised

Characteristics: Can reach 18 inches (45 cm) in length and weigh approx. 2 lbs (850 g); gray or reddish-brown on the upper body and white or pale yellow underneath. It also has about five dark bands along the back.

Flesh: Lean

Habitat: Along the coastal waters of the eastern United States, to South Carolina

Value: Great culinary quality and highly prized in Europe

Comments: The northern searobin is a member of the *Triglidae* family and related to the golden redfish and the sculpin. Sculpin, found off the Atlantic coast of North America, are cooked like the northern searobin.

$$

Northern Searobin with Lavender and Grapefruit

4 × 9–10 oz (250–300 g)	Northern searobins
³/4 cup (120 g)	Butter
2	Shallots, cut with scissors
²/3 cup (150 mL)	White wine
2 1/3 cups (200 g)	Leek, julienned
1 3/4 cups (200 g)	Carrot, julienned
2	Grapefruit (juice)
14 oz (400 mL)	Fish fumet (see "Basic Ingredients for Some Recipes")
1 cup (200 g)	Potato, julienned
1 oz (30 g)	Lavender, chopped
To taste	Salt & pepper
3 1/2 oz (100 mL)	Cream (35%)
1/2 bunch	Chives, cut with scissors
1 1/2 Tbsp (20 g)	Grapefruit zest

- Clean the northern searobins, retaining the heads. Remove all the fins. Refrigerate.
- With the butter, cook the shallots until tender, then add the white wine. Cook to eliminate any acidity from the wine, then incorporate the leek and the carrots. Pour in the grapefruit juice and fish fumet. Cook for 3 to 4 minutes, then add the julienned potato and the chopped lavender. Let simmer for a few minutes.
- Select an ovenproof dish in which the northern searobins, laid head to tail, will have enough room. Season with salt and pepper.

Pour the preceding preparation on top, cover with aluminum foil and bake at 400°F (200°C) for about 20 to 25 minutes.

- Remove from the oven, take out the northern searobins and pour the cooking liquid into a saucepan. Vigorously whisk the mixture, adjust the seasoning and incorporate the cream and the chives.

- On each plate, place one searobin, pour the preceding preparation over each fish and sprinkle with grapefruit zest.
- This fish is always served whole to preserve its shape. The bones can be removed easily.

Preparation time: 25 minutes	**Cooking time:** 20 to 30 minutes
Servings: 4	**Cost:** $$$

Braised Northern Searobin with Apple Juice

4 × 9–10 oz (250–300 g)	**Northern searobins**
To taste	**Salt & pepper**
1 1/3 cup (200 g)	**Spanish onions, finely sliced**
3/4 cup (100 g)	**Carrot** *brunoise*
2/3 cup (100 g)	**Sweet butter**
7 oz (200 mL)	**Apple juice**
1/2 cup (120 mL)	**Brown chicken stock, bound (see "Basic Ingredients for Some Recipes")**
As needed	**Coriander leaves**

- Scale the fish and cut off the larger fins. Do not remove the head. Wash the fish and dry it. Season with salt and pepper, set aside.

- Gently cook the onions and the carrots in butter until tender, add the apple juice and gently cook for 12 to 15 minutes. Add the brown chicken stock, adjust the seasoning and set aside.
- Place the northern searobins in an oven-proof dish, head to tail, and pour in the braising stock. Cover with aluminum foil and bake in the oven at 300°F (150°C) for 25 to 35 minutes.
- On each plate, serve a whole fish, cover with the braising stock and sprinkle with coriander leaves.

NOTE: This recipe can also be prepared using searobin fillets, as shown in the photograph.

Preparation time: 30 minutes	**Cooking time:** 25 to 35 minutes
Servings: 4	**Cost:** $$$

Photo on page 199

ATLANTIC WOLFFISH

Anarhichas lupus (Linnaeus) *1758*

Characteristics: Varying in color from blue to green, the Atlantic wolffish is caught in coastal, pre-coastal and offshore waters. It can measure as much as 33 inches (85 cm) in length and weigh 2 1/4 to 22 lbs (1 to 10 kg).

Flesh: Moderately fatty and white

Habitat: Both sides of the North Atlantic south to Cape Cod

Where & When to Find It: Not currently available on the market; may be custom ordered directly from fishers

Processed & Sold: As fillets

Cooking Method: Poached, steamed, grilled or braised

Value: Deserves to be known

$$

Honey-glazed Atlantic Wolffish with Crunchy Cabbage

approx. 1/2 cup (75 g)	Butter
4 × 5 oz (160 g)	Atlantic wolffish fillets
1/3 cup (70 mL)	Honey
1	Lemon (juice)
1	Clove, chopped
1 pinch	Cinnamon powder
3 1/2 oz (100 mL)	Soya sauce
As needed	Sesame oil, roasted
1	Onion, thinly sliced
1 1/4 lbs (600 g)	Chinese cabbage, thinly sliced
To taste	Salt & pepper
1 1/4 Tbsp (10 g)	Corn starch

- Heat the oven to 300°F (150°C).
- Select an ovenproof dish or pan large enough to leave space between the fillets.
- Butter the pan. With a small brush, coat the fillets in honey, pour 7 oz (200 mL) of water and lemon juice around them, then add the clove and cinnamon. Bake at 400°F (200°C), then broil for a few minutes so that the honey caramelizes. Surround this preparation with the soya sauce.
- With the roasted sesame oil, cook the finely sliced onion until tender, then sauté the Chinese cabbage until crunchy. Season with salt and pepper and set aside.
- Pour the cooking liquid into a saucepan and bind with the corn starch, diluted with a little water. Adjust the seasoning.

Presentation: In the bottom of the plate, create a bed of crunchy Chinese cabbage, then lay the wolffish fillets on top and pour the honey and soya sauce over the fillets.

Preparation time: 20 to 30 minutes	
Cooking time: 10 to 12 minutes	
Servings: 4	**Cost:** $$

Atlantic Wolffish with Lobster Sauce

2/3 cup (60 g)	Leek (white part only), sliced thin
1/4 cup (60 mL)	Olive oil
2/3 cup (100 g)	Sweet butter
1/2 cup (60 g)	White onion, chopped
4 × 5 oz (150 g)	Atlantic wolffish fillets
To taste	Salt & pepper
1/2 cup (120 mL)	Dry white wine
approx. 2/3 cup (160 mL)	Lobster sauce (see "Basic Ingredients for Some Recipes")

- Gently heat the olive oil and half the butter.
- Gently braise the sliced leeks and the chopped onions. When they have absorbed the fat, lay the seasoned wolffish fillets on top. Pour in the white wine and reduce to half in order to remove any acidity, then pour in the lobster sauce.
- Cook covered for 5 to 8 minutes, depending on the thickness of the fillets. Remove and drain. Reduce the sauce until the desired consistency has been obtained and finish with the remaining butter.
- Lay the fillets in the middle of the plate and cover each fillet with sauce. Serve with white rice.

Preparation time: 10 to 15 minutes
Cooking time: 8 to 12 minutes
Servings: 4   **Cost:** $$$

RED SNAPPER

Lutjanus campechanus
Incorrect names: sea bream, redfish, goatfish

Characteristics: A beautiful shade of red, this fish has an average length of 10 inches (25 cm) and a weight that varies from 1 ³/4 to 4 ¹/2 lbs (800 g to 1.2 kg).

Flesh: Semi-fatty

Habitat: South Atlantic and the Caribbean

Where & When to Find It: An imported fish generally available all year round

Processed & Sold: Whole or as fillets

Cooking Method: Braised, *meunière*, grilled or poached

Value: A delicacy, this fish is, however, fragile.

$$$

Red Snapper Stuffed with Filberts and Currants

3	Green onions, sliced thin
3 Tbsp (40 mL)	Pistachio oil
approx. ³/4 cup (150 g)	Sweet butter
3 ¹/2 Tbsp (30 g)	Filberts (hazelnuts), chopped
4 Tbsp (30 g)	Roasted almonds, chopped
3 Tbsp (30 g)	Pistachios, chopped
3 ¹/2 Tbsp (30 g)	Currants
¹/2	Garlic clove, chopped
2 × 2 ¹/4–2 ³/4 lbs (1–1.2 kg)	Red snapper
To taste	Salt & pepper
3 ¹/2 oz (100 mL)	Peanut oil
¹/2 cup (120 mL)	Brown veal stock (see "Basic Ingredients for Some Recipes")

- Heat the pistachio oil and 4 ¹/2 Tbsp (50 g) of the butter, incorporate the green onions, hazelnuts, roasted almonds, pistachios and currants. Braise for about 12 minutes. Add the chopped garlic and set aside.
- Remove the red snapper bones through the stomach; season with salt and pepper; and stuff with the preceding preparation. Close the fish.
- In a heavy-bottomed skillet, heat the peanut oil and the remaining butter. Sear the red snapper, then baste often with the cooking fat. Depending on the thickness of the fish, bake in the oven for 12 to 15 minutes.
- Serve immediately with the hot veal stock in a separate sauce boat.

Preparation time: 30 minutes	**Cooking time:** 12 to 15 minutes
Servings: 4	**Cost:** $$$

Photo on page 210

Red Snapper Fillets with Mushroom Risotto and Curry-Flavored Fumet

1	Shallot, cut with scissors
1	Garlic clove, minced
3/4 cup (140 g)	Sweet butter
3 1/2 cups (300 g)	Firm white mushrooms, diced
2 cups (400 g)	Rice for risotto
2 1/2 cups (600 mL)	White chicken stock (see "Basic Ingredients for Some Recipes")
7 oz (200 mL)	Fish fumet (see "Basic Ingredients …")
1 sprig	Fresh thyme
1/2	Bay leaf
1/3 cup (75 mL)	Cream (35%)
To taste	Salt & pepper
3 tsp (25 g)	Curry powder
3 Tbsp (50 mL)	Olive oil
4 × 5–6 oz (150–170 g)	Red snapper fillets
1 2/3 cups (150 g)	Grated Parmesan
3/4 cup (150 g)	Tomato, blanched, peeled, seeded and diced

- Cook the shallot and garlic in 4 1/2 Tbsp (50 g) of sweet butter until tender, add the mushrooms and the rice. Mix well and cook by gradually adding the chicken stock. This rice is generally cooked in 20 minutes.
- At the same time, heat the fumet with the thyme and bay leaf. Add the cream, season, and incorporate the curry. Set aside.
- In a cast-iron frying pan, quickly sauté the previously seasoned red snapper fillets in the olive oil; then let sit in the pan to allow the flesh to relax.
- Just before serving, mix the Parmesan in with the rice and adjust the seasoning.
- Incorporate the remaining butter into the curry liquid. The liquid should bind slightly.

Presentation: In the bottom of the plate, with a hoop, mold the risotto, place the fillets on top and around the rice, and pour the curry sauce around the fillets. Sprinkle with the diced tomato.

Preparation time: 30 minutes	**Cooking time:** 30 minutes
Servings: 4	**Cost:** $$$

SWORDFISH
Xiphias gladius (Linnaeus) *1758*

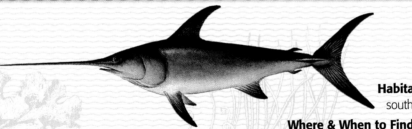

Habitat: Along the Atlantic coast, south to Argentina

Where & When to Find It: In summer and early autumn, in abundance

Characteristics: Swordfish usually swim close to the surface in water at least 60°F (15°C) warm. The upper part of the body is metallic violet, and the lower part, black. Swordfish can reach an enormous size.

Flesh: Fatty and very firm

Processed & Sold: As fillets or in pieces

Cooking Method: Grilled

Value: Very tasty

$$$$

Swordfish with Peanut and Sesame Seed Chips and Mushroom Vinaigrette

14 oz (400 g)	White turnip
approx. 3 oz (100 g)	Potato
2/3 cup (100 g)	Butter
To taste	Salt & pepper
approx. 4 cups (300 g)	Firm white mushrooms
1 1/4 cup (300 mL)	Brown veal stock (see "Basic Ingredients for Some Recipes")
3 Tbsp (50 mL)	Peanut oil
1/2 cup (125 mL)	Olive oil
1/4 cup (60 mL)	Sherry vinegar
2/3 cup (100 g)	Peanuts, crushed
3/4 cup (100 g)	Sesame seeds
1/3 cup (50 g)	Red pepper *brunoise*
1/3 cup (50 g)	Green pepper *brunoise*
1	Egg white
4 × 6 oz (180 g)	Swordfish slices

- To purée, first cook the white turnip with the potato in salted water, then grind in a vegetable mill, add the butter, adjust the seasoning and keep warm.
- Wash the mushrooms and poach in the brown veal stock. Using a skimmer, remove half the mushrooms and keep warm.
- In a blender, purée the brown stock with the remaining mushrooms, peanut oil, olive oil and sherry vinegar. Adjust the seasoning (salt and pepper) as needed and keep warm.
- Make a paste with the peanuts, sesame seeds, and red and green peppers by adding the egg white.

- Season the swordfish slices with salt and pepper, then coat with the preceding mixture on one side only. Place the fish skin side up into a dish and bake in the oven at 400°F (200°C) for 5 to 6 minutes with the heat from below, then 6 to 8 minutes with the heat from above (broiler).

Presentation: Along the upper part of the plate, lay the puréed turnip and potato dumplings. Pour the mushroom vinaigrette onto the plate and arrange the swordfish slices, then sprinkle with the remaining mushrooms.

Preparation time: 1 hour	**Cooking time:** 10 to 15 minutes
Servings: 4	**Cost:** $$$$

Swordfish with Three Sauces

4 × 6 oz (180 g)	Swordfish pieces
To taste	Salt & pepper
3 Tbsp (40 mL)	Peanut oil
3 1/2 oz (100 mL)	Choron sauce (see "Basic Ingredients for Some Recipes")
3 1/2 oz (100 mL)	Lobster sauce (see "Basic Ingredients …")
3 1/2 oz (100 mL)	Lemon butter (see "Basic Ingredients …")

- The best method for cooking this fish is to grill it.
- Season the swordfish with salt and pepper, brush with the peanut oil and begin grilling on the hotter side of the grill. When the fish is "crisscrossed," finish cooking on the cooler side. Allow the fish to rest after cooking.
- The sauces should be served hot in separate sauce boats. Accompany with steamed potatoes.

Preparation time: 10 minutes + 30 minutes for the sauces	
Cooking time: depends on the thickness	
Servings: 4	**Cost:** $$$$

Photo on page 211

213

Freshwater Fish

North America's freshwater fish include numerous exotic species that have been introduced and maintained, 4 of which—sea trout, carp, goldfish and cunner—are discussed in this book.

From the fisher's point of view, quality has replaced quantity. We have already devoted one chapter to the *Salmonidae*, fish of tremendous quality which exist in large numbers. The other freshwater fish are also important and it is these that we discuss in this chapter.

Sturgeon Family

These fish have existed since the late Cretaceous period. They can live as long as 50 to 80 years, depending on their gender, the females living much longer than the males.

These magnificent fish are often eaten smoked, but most people also know them from sturgeon caviar from Russia or Iran. Sturgeon are easily damaged by pollution, but it is still possible to enjoy those which have not been affected. The quality of the caviar is excellent. As for the meat of this fish, it is important that we learn to appreciate it once again.

Perch Family (*Percidae*)

Yellow perch is a member of the same family as the yellow walleye or the sauger. These fish share the same basic structure and are generally cooked in the same way.

From a culinary standpoint, the best-known fish of this family are the pickerel and the yellow perch. On the other hand, this family also includes many species of dace that have relatively little merit in the kitchen.

Atlantic sturgeon

Yellow perch

Walleye

Sauger

Northern pike

American eel

Brown bullhead

Catfish

Smallmouth bass

Pumpkinseed

Carp

Goldeye

Burbot

ATLANTIC STURGEON

Acipenser oxyrhynchus (Mitchill) *1815*
Incorrect name: lake sturgeon

Characteristics: The lower part of the body is in shades of blue, and the underside of the fish is white. This fish is the same size as the yellow sturgeon.

Flesh: Semi-fatty and yellow

Habitat: Lakes and rivers Louisiana

Where & When to Find It: From May to October, in abundance; the rest of the year, farmed fish is available.

Processed & Sold: Whole, as fillets and smoked

Cooking Method: Roasted, *meunière*, poached or steamed

Value: In the 19th century, this fish was considered of great quality. It should be used more today.

Comments: The order *Acipenseriformes* includes the fossil family and two families that exist today. North America is rich in this fish whose eggs are the only ones that can truly be called "caviar," but whose production is not really developed. The species in North America include: Atlantic sturgeon (*Acipenser oxyrhynchus*), green sturgeon (*Acipenser medirostris*), lake sturgeon (*Acipenser fulvescens*) and shortnose sturgeon (*Acipenser breviorstrum*). An Atlantic sturgeon, 60 years old, can measure 8 3/4 ft (2.7 m) and weigh 352 lbs (160 kg).

$$

Marinated Sturgeon and Salmon with Spinach and Endive Salad

3/4 cup (180 mL)	Olive oil
1 1/3 cup (200 g)	Onions, finely sliced
3/4 cup (85 g)	Carrots, sliced thin
1	Garlic clove, chopped
7 oz (200 mL)	White wine
2	Lemons (juice)
3 1/2 oz (100 mL)	White vinegar
To taste	Thyme
1/2	Bay leaf
7 oz (200 mL)	Water
To taste	Salt & pepper

10 oz (300 g)	Fresh salmon
10 oz (300 g)	Fresh sturgeon
approx. 1/2 lb (250 g)	Spinach
approx. 1/2 lb (250 g)	Endive

- In 3 1/2 oz (100 mL) of olive oil, brown the onions, carrots and the garlic. Deglaze the skillet with the white wine. Add the lemon juice, vinegar, thyme, bay leaf and water. Season with salt and pepper, then cook for 12 to 15 minutes.
- Adjust the seasoning and let the marinade cool. Submerge the salmon and the sturgeon in the marinade for at least 36 hours. Wash the spinach and drain. Cut the endives into

Preparation time: 15 minutes	**Marinade:** 36 hours
Servings: 4	**Cost:** $$$

strips without having washed them. Combine the two vegetables and sprinkle the lemon juice and the remaining olive oil on top. Season with salt and pepper and set aside.

- Slice the salmon and the sturgeon into very fine strips. Arrange the salad in the center of the plate. Alternate strips of sturgeon and salmon around the salad to form a crown.
- Serve chilled.

Turret of Roast Sturgeon*

7 oz (200 g)	American plaice
To taste	Salt & pepper
1	Egg white
3 1/2 oz (100 mL)	Cream (35%)
1/3 cup (20 g)	Parsley, chopped
approx. 3 lbs (1.4 kg)	Sturgeon
5 oz (150 g)	Bacon fat in strips (bards)
2 tsp (10 mL)	Oil
1/3 cup (40 g)	Celery *mirepoix*
3/4 cup (85 g)	Carrot *mirepoix*
1 1/3 cup (200 g)	Onion *mirepoix*
3 1/2 oz (100 mL)	White wine
6 Tbsp (70 g)	Butter

- Chop the plaice fillets in a food processor. Season with salt and pepper and add the egg white. Blend in the food processor to obtain an emulsion, and incorporate the cream, blending well. Set the forcemeat aside in the refrigerator and add the parsley just before using.
- Select a small sturgeon; bone from the inside, then season with salt and pepper. Garnish the inside of the fish with the forcemeat.
- Seal the sturgeon and roll up the roast with the bards on the outside; tie up with a string. Brown the sturgeon in the oil. Bake in the oven at 200°C (400°F) for 20 minutes. Add the celery, carrot and onion *mirepoix* and bake for another 20 to 25 minutes. Degrease the cooking pan and moisten with the white wine. Let cook for 5 minutes. Remove the roast from the pan and strain the cooking stock through cheesecloth or a fine mesh strainer. Thicken with the butter.
- Serve a slice of stuffed roast sturgeon with the sauce and roasted *cocotte* potatoes.

* Dedicated to my friend, chef Renaud Cyr.

Preparation time: 45 minutes	**Cooking time:** 1 hour
Servings: 8	**Cost:** $$$

Photo on next page →

YELLOW PERCH

Perca flavescens
Incorrect name: perch

Characteristics: Shades of green and golden brown, with seven stripes in decreasing size located on the abdomen. Average length is 8 inches (20 cm) and average weight is approximately 3 oz (100 g).

Flesh: Lean and white

Habitat: Southern Alabama

Where & When to Find It: During fishing season; generally a game fish

Processed & Sold: Whole and as fillets

Cooking Method: Whole in the oven, *meunière* or steamed

Value: Excellent, especially in the spring

Comments: All fish that are members of the *Percidae* family are prepared in the same manner.

$

Yellow Perch à la provençale *(For Large Pieces)*

3 ¹/₂ oz (100 mL)	Olive oil
²/₃ cup (80 g)	Leek (white part only), cut with scissors
¹/₂ cup (80 g)	Spanish onion, chopped
1 cup (200 g)	Tomato, blanched, peeled, seeded and diced
To taste	Salt & pepper
2	Garlic cloves
1 pinch	Marjoram, chopped
1 pinch	Rosemary, chopped
²/₃ cup (60 g)	Fennel leaves, chopped
1 ¹/₃ cup (80 g)	Fresh parsley, roughly chopped
2	Large yellow perch
7 oz (200 mL)	Dry white wine
3 ¹/₂ oz (100 mL)	Fish fumet (see "Basic Ingredients for Some Recipes")

- Heat the olive oil and cook the leek and onion until tender, then add the tomato and cook for 10 minutes. Season with salt and pepper, and add the garlic, marjoram, rosemary, fennel and parsley. Combine well. Let cool and set aside.
- Remove the yellow perch bones through the stomach; season with salt and pepper and stuff with the preceding preparation.
- In an ovenproof dish, place the stuffed yellow perch, pour in the white wine and fish fumet. Cover with aluminum foil and bake in the oven for 10 to 20 minutes at 400°F (200°C). Recover the cooking liquid from the dish and reduce by half. Pour over the perch and serve immediately.

Accompaniment: White rice or boiled potatoes

Preparation time: 40 minutes	Cooking time: 20 to 30 minutes
Servings: 4	Cost: $

Pan-Roasted Spring Yellow Perch with Citrus Fruit Butter

4 × 4 oz (120 g)	Yellow perch fillets
To taste	Salt & pepper
As needed	Flour
As needed	Oil
1/2 cup (80 g)	Sweet butter
3/4 cup (120 g)	Citrus fruit butter

CITRUS FRUIT BUTTER

1	Lime (juice)
1	Lemon (juice)
1/2	Orange (juice)
1/3 cup (20 g)	Parsley, chopped
1 1/4 cup (200 g)	Sweet butter, kneaded
To taste	Salt & pepper

- Dry off the yellow perch fillets, season with salt and pepper, and flour.
- Heat the oil and the butter, then cook the yellow perch fillets until golden on each side. Serve immediately with small knobs of citrus fruit butter on each fillet.
- **Citrus Fruit Butter**: Combine the lime, lemon and orange juices with the chopped parsley and the kneaded sweet butter. Season with salt and pepper and store at room temperature.

Accompaniment: Small potatoes sautéed in butter

Preparation time: 30 minutes **Cooking time:** 5 to 9 minutes
Servings: 4 **Cost:** $

PICKEREL, WALLEYE AND YELLOW WALLEYE

Stizostedion vitreum
Incorrect name: pike-perch (Europe)

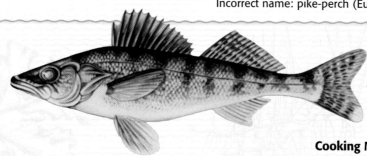

Flesh: White and lean

Habitat: Alabama and Mississippi

Where & When to Find It: Available all year round wherever fish is sold

Processed & Sold: Whole or as fillets

Cooking Method: *Meunière*, grilled, braised, whole, roasted, poached or steamed

Value: One of the culinary stars

$$$

Characteristics: Shades of brown and yellow, with a white abdomen. Can weigh from 10 to 12 lbs (4.5 to 5.5 kg).

Yellow Walleye Fillets en Feuillantine

1 ¼ lbs (600 g)	Puff pastry
1	Whole egg, beaten
1 cup (160 g)	Sweet butter
½ cup (80 g)	Shallots, chopped
1 cup (120 g)	White mushrooms, chopped
4 oz (120 g)	Walleye trimmings (part of the stomach and the tail)
½ cup (120 mL)	Apple wine
⅔ cup (160 mL)	Cream (35%)
4 oz (120 g)	Pink shrimp
To taste	Salt & pepper
5 oz (4 x 150 g)	Yellow walleye fillets
⅓ cup (80 mL)	Peanut oil
As needed	Chervil leaves, peeled

Preparation time: 40 minutes **Cooking time:** 25 minutes
Servings: 4   **Cost:** $$$

- Roll out the puff pastry; using the tip of a knife, cut out 8 small fish that can be placed in the middle of a plate. Lay them on a baking sheet and refrigerate for about 12 minutes. Brush with the egg and bake in the oven at 400°F (200°C). Set aside.
- **Sauces**: Using half the butter, sauté the chopped shallots and mushrooms, then add the walleye trimmings, let simmer for 1 minute, pour in the apple wine and simmer another 3 to 5 minutes. In another saucepan, strain the liquid, using cheesecloth or a fine mesh strainer; add the cream, and reduce until a sauce-like consistency is obtained. Add the shrimp. Season, set aside and keep warm.
- Season the walleye fillets with salt and pepper. Heat the remaining butter and the peanut oil. Sear the walleye fillets until golden. Set aside.

222

- Serve with boiled potatoes and add the chervil leaves.

Presentation: Place one pastry fish and one walleye fillet on each plate, then the sauce and the shrimp. Cover with another pastry fish.

Grilled Walleye Fillets with Mousseline Sauce

2 cups (240 g)	Potatoes, diced
2/3 cup (100 g)	Butter
As needed	Peanut oil
To taste	Salt & pepper
3 1/2 oz (100 mL)	Maple syrup
4 × 5–6 oz (150–180 g)	Walleye fillets, with the skin
7 oz (200 mL)	Mousseline sauce (see "Basic Ingredients for Some Recipes")

- Blanch, then sauté the potatoes in the peanut oil and 3 Tbsp (40 mL) of butter. Season with salt and pepper. Bake in the oven and finish by adding the maple syrup.
- Brush the walleye fillets with a little peanut oil. Season with salt and pepper; grill, beginning with intense heat, then finishing more slowly.
- Ladle the mousseline sauce into small, individual bowls.

Presentation: Arrange the potatoes with maple syrup around the upper part of the plate, and the walleye fillets in the bottom of the plate.

Preparation time: 15 minutes **Cooking time:** 8 to 12 minutes
Servings: 4   **Cost:** $$$

SAND PICKEREL AND SAUGER

Stizostedion canadense
Incorrect name: pike-perch (Europe)

Characteristics: Sand or brown-colored with dark brown spots and a milky white abdomen. Can reach 13 lbs (5.8 kg) in weight.

Flesh: White and lean

Habitat: South to Tennessee

Where & When to Find It: Available all year round wherever fish is sold

Processed & Sold: Whole or as fillets

Cooking Method: *Meunière*, grilled, braised whole, roasted, poached or steamed

Value: Just like the yellow walleye, another culinary star

$$$

Sand Pickerel Stuffed with Milkweed and Braised in Cloudberry Juice

2 × 2–2 ³/4 lbs (900 g to 1.2 kg)	Sand pickerel
To taste	Salt & pepper
7 oz (200 g)	Flounder fillets
1	Egg
3 ¹/2 oz (100 mL)	Cream (35%)
approx. 5 oz (160 g)	Milkweed buds
³/4 cup (120 g)	Butter
7 oz (200 mL)	Cloudberry juice
²/3 cup (150 mL)	White wine
³/4 cup (100 g)	Carrot *brunoise*
³/4 cup (100 g)	Celery *brunoise*

- Scale the fillets, cut off the fins and remove the bones through the stomach (see "How to" photographs). Season with salt and pepper and set aside.
- In a food processor, emulsify the flounder fillets, season with salt and pepper, then add the egg and the very cold cream. Strain through a sieve and refrigerate for about 30 minutes. Following this, gently mix the milkweed buds and stuff the sand pickerel fillets.
- With ¹/3 cup (60 g) of butter, brush an oven-proof dish and lay the fillets in the dish. Pour in the cloudberry juice, white wine, carrot and celery *brunoise*, then cover with aluminum foil and bake at 350°F (180°C) for 30 to 40 minutes.
- Transfer the cooking liquid to a saucepan and reduce slowly.
- Skin the fillets while still hot and divide evenly among the plates. Thicken the sauce with the remaining butter and pour over the fish.

Accompaniment: Boiled white rice

NOTE: If the fish has been scaled well, the skin can be kept on.

Preparation time: 1 hour	Cooking time: 1 hour
Servings: 4	Cost: $$$

Sand Pickerel Fillets and Lemon Corn Purée

1 lb (480 g)	Corn, fresh or canned
4 oz (120 mL)	Cream (35%)
3/4 cup (140 g)	Butter
To taste	Salt & pepper
1 1/2 lbs (720 g)	Sand pickerel fillets
approx. 1 cup (120 g)	Shallots, chopped and cooked
2/3 cup (150 mL)	Noilly Prat, white
1 cup (240 mL)	Lobster sauce (see "Basic Ingredients for Some Recipes")
1 1/4 cup (160 g)	Mushrooms, chopped
1 1/3 cup (80 g)	Parsley, chopped

- If the corn is fresh, cook in salted water. Then transfer to a food mill or a food processor to purée, then add the hot cream and 1/3 cup (60 g) of butter. Season, set aside and keep warm.
- Brush an ovenproof dish with 3 1/2 Tbsp (40 g) of butter. Place the fillets in the dish, sprinkle with the shallots and pour in the Noilly Prat. Cover with aluminum foil and bake at 350°F (180°C) for 8 to 10 minutes. When cooked, remove the fillets and keep warm. Reduce the cooking juice by 9/10, add the lobster sauce and finish off by adding the remaining butter. Just before serving, add the cooked, chopped mushrooms.

Presentation: Using a cookie cutter, create a puréed corn round. Place the sand pickerel fillets on top and pour the Noilly Prat sauce around the fillets. Sprinkle with the chopped parsley.

Preparation time: 25 minutes	**Cooking time:** 8 to 12 minutes
Servings: 4	**Cost:** $$$

Photo on next page →

NORTHERN PIKE, CHAIN PICKEREL AND LAKE PICKEREL

Esox lucius, Esox niger
Incorrect name: muskellunge

Characteristics: The upper part of the head is green to brown in color; the body is sprinkled with pale spots. This fish can reach 27 to 39 inches (70 to 100 cm) in length and weigh 4 1/2 to 16 1/2 lbs (2.0 to 7.5 kg) within 7 years.

Flesh: Pale and fatty

Habitat: From Alaska to Missouri

Where & When to Find It: Available all year round wherever fish is sold

Processed & Sold: Whole and as fillets

Cooking Method: As dumplings, in mousseline, poached, braised or *meunière*

Value: This fish has a lot of bones; although not well known, this fish represents a wonderful gastronomical adventure.

Comments: All these species are cooked in the same way: pike family (*Esocidae*), muskellunge (*Esox masquinongy*), northern pike (*Esox lucius*), chain pickerel (*Esox niger*), redfin pickerel (*Esox americanus*), grass pickerel (*Esox vermiculatus*).

$$

Pike Back with Chablis

4 × 1 1/4 lbs (600 g)	Small pike
To taste	Salt & pepper
3/4 cup (120 g)	Unsalted butter
approx. 1 cup (120 g)	Shallots, chopped
14 oz (400 mL)	Chablis
1 cup (250 mL)	Fish *velouté* (see "Basic Ingredients for Some Recipes")
1 cup (60 g)	Chervil leaves

- Scale the small pike, cut off the head and the tail, then bone through the stomach. Season with salt and pepper. Set aside.
- Brush an ovenproof dish with 1/3 cup (60 g) of butter. In the dish, place the chopped shallots, the pike back, pour in the Chablis, cover with aluminum foil and bake at 350°F (180°C) for 8 to 10 minutes.
- Remove the pike backs and keep warm. Reduce the cooking juice by 4/5, then add the fish *velouté*. Let simmer for several minutes and thicken the sauce with butter. Adjust the seasoning.

Presentation: On each plate, place one pike back, cover with sauce and sprinkle with the chervil leaves. Serve with boiled potatoes.

Preparation time: 25 minutes	**Cooking time:** 8 to 15 minutes
Servings: 4	**Cost:** $$$

Photo page 227

Pike or Muskellunge Dumplings

2 1/4 lbs (1 kg)	Pike or muskellunge flesh, deveined
To taste	Salt & ground white pepper
5	Egg whites
14 oz (400 g)	Panada for fish (see "Basic Ingredients for Some Recipes")
6 cups (1.5 L)	Cream (35%)
To taste	Nutmeg
As needed	Fish fumet (see "Basic Ingredients ...") or salted water
1 1/3 cup (320 mL)	Lobster sauce (see "Basic Ingredients ...")

- Chop the pike in a food processor. Season with salt and pepper and gradually incorporate the egg whites. Using a plastic spatula, add panada a little at a time. Strain the preparation through a sieve and reserve in a covered container. Smooth out with a wooden spoon, then store in the refrigerator for at least 1 hour. Mix frequently. Add 1/3 of the cream and a little nutmeg, then incorporate the remaining 2/3 of cream, half whipped. Once the cream has been added, the forcemeat should be very white, smooth and creamy. Chill in the refrigerator, at least 1 hour.

- Using two large serving spoons, shape the dumplings and poach in the fish fumet or salted water for about 7 to 10 minutes, depending on their size. Refresh in ice water, drain and store in the refrigerator.

- Given the large amount of forcemeat, the dumplings can be frozen. They will keep several days in the refrigerator.

Presentation: Reheat (without boiling) the dumplings. Place the dumplings in an oven-proof dish, cover with hot lobster sauce and put the dish in the oven at 200°C (400°F). The dumplings should double in size. Serve immediately with rice or boiled potatoes.

NOTE: We have chosen two recipes where the bones are completely removed from the pike. This is to better appreciate the taste of the fish. However, there are a number of ways to prepare this fish, leaving it whole.

Preparation time: 80 minutes	**Cooking time:** 10 to 20 minutes
Servings: 30 dumplings	**Cost:** $$$

AMERICAN EEL AND COMMON EEL

Anguilla rostrata (Le Sueur) *1817*

Habitat: Caribbean

Where & When to Find It: From August to November, in abundance

Processed & Sold: Whole and skinned (without the skin)

Cooking Method: *Meunière*, braised, sautéed or steamed

Characteristics: Black or brown back, yellow sides and yellowish-white abdomen. Average length is 27 to 39 inches (70 to 100 cm) and average weight is 2 1/2 to 3 1/2 lbs (1.1 to 1.6 kg).

Flesh: Dark and fatty

Value: This fish is not fully appreciated, largely due to its appearance.

$

Eel au vert

2/3 cup (100 g)	Butter
5 oz (150 g)	Sorrel leaves, peeled
2 1/2 oz (75 g)	New nettle leaves
6 Tbsp (25 g)	Curly parsley
1 tsp (10 g)	Burnet
2 tsp (5 g)	Green sage
2 Tbsp (5 g)	Summer savory
1/3 cup (10 g)	Tarragon
4 tsp (5 g)	Chervil
1 pinch	Thyme
8 × 2 inch (5 cm)	Eel sections
2 cups (500 mL)	White wine
To taste	Salt & pepper
4	Egg yolks
1	Lemon (juice)

Photo on page 219

- Heat the butter and cook the sorrel and nettle leaves, the parsley, burnet, sage, summer savory, tarragon and chervil until tender. Add a pinch of thyme, then dredge the pieces of eel in this mixture. Moisten with the white wine, season with salt and pepper and cook for about 10 minutes. Remove the pieces of eel and set aside.

- Beat the egg yolks, then bind the cooking stock with the yolks. Finish off with the lemon juice. Replace the eel pieces in the sauce. Set aside in an earthenware dish.

- These pieces of eel are generally served cold. NOTE: This recipe is a specialty of Belgium. It can also be eaten warm. The egg yolk binding is difficult and requires some care. Never let the mixture boil.

Preparation time: 30 minutes	**Cooking time:** 10 to 12 minutes
Servings: 4	**Cost:** $$

Eel Ballottines *Stuffed with Rabbit, with Puréed Potato, Goat Cheese and Flat-Leafed Parsley*

2 1/4 lbs (1 kg)	Skinned eel
To taste	Salt & pepper
As needed	Flat sausage
7 oz (200 g)	Potatoes
4 cups (240 g)	Flat-leafed parsley, stems removed

FORCEMEAT

approx. 3/4 cup (150 g)	Butter
3/4 cup (100 g)	Shallots, chopped
1	Garlic clove, chopped
7 oz (200 g)	Rabbit meat (thighs)
To taste	Salt & pepper
2	Eggs
3/4 cup (120 mL)	Cream (35%)
3 1/2 oz (100 mL)	Red wine
1/2 cup (300 mL)	Brown veal stock (see "Basic Ingredients for Some Recipes")
3 Tbsp (50 mL)	Milk
approx. 3 oz (100 g)	Fresh goat cheese

- Bone the eel through the stomach (see "How to" photographs). Season with salt and pepper. Roll out the flat sausage, roll the eel out on top of the sausage and set aside.
- Cook the potatoes, unpeeled, in salted water.
- Blanch the flat-leafed parsley, refrigerate immediately in ice water, drain and dry off.
- Forcemeat: With a little butter, cook the shallots and the chopped garlic in a saucepan until tender. Slice the rabbit thighs into thin strips and sauté in a non-stick skillet. Once they are cooked, transfer the rabbit strips, the shallots and the garlic to a food processor. Season with salt and pepper, and incorporate the egg yolks. Set aside in the refrigerator.
- Beat the egg whites until stiff. Gently mix the egg whites with the rabbit forcemeat, then add 3 1/2 oz (100 mL) of cream. Adjust the seasoning.
- Stuff the eel with this forcemeat, then encase it in the flat sausage.
- In a sauté pan, with half the butter, brown the eel slowly until golden. Deglaze with the red wine, reduce, moisten with the brown veal stock and braise slowly for 20 to 25 minutes. Baste often during cooking.
- While the eel is cooking, peel the potatoes, transfer to a potato ricer, then add the remaining sweet butter. Add the milk and the cream, both hot. Incorporate the goat cheese and adjust the seasoning.
- With a knob of butter, sauté the flat-leafed parsley. Season to taste.

Presentation: Arrange the puréed potato with the goat cheese on the upper part of the plate, then sprinkle with the parsley. Cut the stuffed eel in large rounds, then arrange the pieces in the bottom of the plate. Cover with sauce.

Preparation time: 1 hour	**Cooking time:** 20 to 35 minutes
Servings: 4	**Cost:** $$$

CATFISH, BROWN BULLHEAD AND COMMON CATFISH
Ictalurus nebulosus

Characteristics: Green to brown body. Average length is 8 to 12 inches (20 to 30 cm) and average weight is 12 oz (350 g).

Flesh: Fatty and dark

Habitat: East of the Rockies, south to Central America

Where & When to Find It: From May to October, in abundance

Processed & Sold: Rarely available commercially

Cooking Method: *Meunière* or fried

Value: Has its supporters

$

Brown Bullhead in Curry Sauce with Yellow Couscous

1 ¾ Tbsp (15 g)	Turmeric
3 cups (750 mL)	Vegetable bouillon or *court-bouillon* (see "Basic Ingredients for Some Recipes")
250 g (1 ½ cups)	Couscous
To taste	Salt & pepper
approx. ⅔ cup (120 g)	Zucchinis, shaped like olives
approx. 1 cup (120 g)	Carrots, shaped like olives
1	Red pepper, diced
1 Tbsp (15 g)	Curry powder
As needed	White roux (see "Basic Ingredients …")
¾ cup (140 g)	Butter
1 ¾ lbs (800 g)	Small catfish, skinned
As needed	Flour
approx. ⅔ cup (70 mL)	Peanut oil
16	Coriander leaves

- Mince the turmeric. Heat half the vegetable bouillon or the *court-bouillon*, combine the couscous and the turmeric, season with salt and pepper, cover and cook slowly.
- In the remaining vegetable bouillon or *court-bouillon*, cook the zucchinis, carrots and pepper. Drain the vegetables, set aside and keep warm.
- Reduce the bouillon, incorporating the curry, then lightly bind with a little white roux.
- Strain through cheesecloth or a fine mesh strainer, thicken with half the butter and set aside.
- Season the catfish with salt and pepper, flour and cook *à la meunière* in the remaining butter and the peanut oil.
- In a deep dish, place the couscous, then the vegetables; arrange the catfish on top and surround with the curry sauce. Sprinkle with the coriander leaves.

Preparation time: 35 minutes		**Cooking time:** 12 to 15 minutes	
Servings: 4		**Cost:** $$	

Fried Brown Bullhead with Cornmeal

FRITTERS

As needed	Corn oil
1 cup (150 g)	Whole wheat flour
1 3/4 cups (350 g)	Cornmeal, stone ground
4 tsp (20 g)	Baking powder
2 1/4 tsp (10 g)	Baking soda
To taste	Salt & pepper
1	Egg, beaten
4 oz (120 mL)	Beer
4 oz (120 mL)	Sweet butter, melted
1	Onion *brunoise*

CATFISH

16	Small whole catfish, skinned
To taste	Salt & pepper
1 1/4 cups (250 g)	Cornmeal, stone ground, cooked
As needed	Corn oil for frying

- **Fritters**: Heat the cooking oil (corn oil).
- Sift the whole wheat flour; add the cornmeal, baking powder and baking soda, and season with salt and pepper.
- Beat the egg, incorporate the beer and the melted sweet butter. In a round metal mixing bowl, combine all the dry ingredients. Create a hole in the center and slowly combine the egg-beer-butter mixture with the flour, to form a creamy paste. Incorporate the onion *brunoise* and let sit for at least 30 minutes in the refrigerator.
- Drop the pastry into the oil using a soup spoon, and fry 4 to 5 fritters at a time to keep the oil hot. They will float to the surface once golden and cooked. Drain on a paper towel and keep warm in the oven.
- **Catfish**: Wipe the catfish, season with salt and pepper and coat in cornmeal. Keep in the refrigerator for about 30 minutes.
- Heat the corn oil to fry the fish. Fry the catfish four at a time in order to keep the oil hot. Serve immediately with the fritters.

Preparation time: 40 minutes   **Cooking time:** 20 minutes
Servings: 4   **Cost:** $$

Photo on next page →

CATFISH AND CHANNEL CATFISH

Ictalurus punctatus

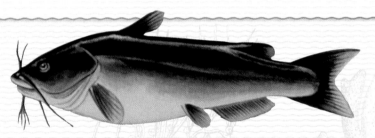

Characteristics: Coloring varies greatly, depending on age. Length can measure 20 inches (50 cm) and weight can reach 3 1/4 lbs (1.5 kg) at 20 years of age.

Flesh: Dark and fatty

Habitat: Central United States

Where & When to Find It: From March to October

Processed & Sold: Game fish

Cooking Method: Fried, poached or braised

Value: Highly prized by some supporters

Catfish Poached in Vegetable Essence

2 cups (500 mL)	Vegetable essence (see "Basic Ingredients for Some Recipes")
1 tsp (2 g)	Thyme sprigs
1/2	Bay leaf
2 1/2 oz (4 x 70 g)	Leeks (white part only)
1 1/2 cups (160 g)	Carrot sticks
1 1/4 cups (160 g)	Celery sticks
1 1/3 cups (200 g)	Potato sticks
4 × 5 oz (150 g)	Catfish fillets
1	Lemon (juice)
1/4 cup (60 mL)	White wine
To taste	Salt & pepper
As needed	Coarse salt
16	Fresh tarragon leaves

- Heat the vegetable essence, add the thyme and the bay leaf. Cook, in the following order: leeks, carrots, then the celery and, when these are half done, add the potatoes. When 3/4 cooked, add the catfish fillets, the lemon juice and the white wine. Adjust the seasoning and keep warm.
- In a soup dish, place all the vegetables, then the catfish fillets. Sprinkle with coarse salt and the fresh tarragon leaves.
- The cooking liquid can also be served as a fish consommé.

NOTE: This recipe is also sometimes called a fish "pot-au-feu," but we prefer to keep this name for "boiled beef."

Preparation time: 30 minutes	**Cooking time:** 40 minutes
Servings: 4	**Cost:** $

Catfish Fillets with Red Wine

4 oz (120 g)	Smoked bacon
³/₄ cup (120 g)	Small white onions
2 cups (150 g)	Firm, white mushrooms, diced
1 ¹/₂ cup (350 mL)	Robust red wine
3 ¹/₂ oz (100 mL)	Fish fumet (see "Basic Ingredients for Some Recipes")
As needed	White roux (see "Basic Ingredients …")
To taste	Salt & pepper
4 × 5 oz (150 g)	Catfish fillets
¹/₂ cup (80 g)	Sweet butter
8 oz (240 g)	Potato *cocottes*

- Brown the finely diced bacon with the onions and the mushrooms, until all the liquid has evaporated, then add the wine and the fish fumet. Cook for about 15 minutes, then strain through cheesecloth or a fine mesh strainer. Set aside the onion, bacon and mushroom garnish. Bind the juice with a little white roux until the desired consistency is reached, then season with salt and pepper to taste, strain through cheesecloth and add the garnish. Simmer for a few minutes.
- In an ovenproof dish, place the catfish fillets, then pour the wine sauce on top. Sprinkle with knobs of butter, cover with aluminum foil and bake in the oven at 400°F (200°C) for 10 to 15 minutes.
- Cook the *cocotte* potatoes in salted water. Serve the catfish fillets immediately with the *cocotte* potatoes.

Preparation time: 25 minutes **Cooking time:** 15 to 20 minutes
Servings: 4   **Cost:** $$

SMALLMOUTH BASS

Micropterus dolomievi
Incorrect name: largemouth bass

Processed & Sold: Whole

Cooking Method: *Meunière*, fried or steamed

Value: With its delicate meat, this fish deserves to be better known.

Comments: The panfish family (*Centrarchidae*) includes:

- Rock bass (*Ambloplites rupestris*)
- Largemouth bass (*Micropterus salmoides*)
- Pumpkinseed (*Lepomis gibbosus*)
- Bluegill (*Lepomis macrochirus*)
- Redbreast sunfish (*Lepomis auritus*)
- Sockbass (*Lepomis cyanellus*)
- Longears sunfish (*Lepomis megalotis*)

Characteristics: In North America, most of these fish measure from 8 to 15 inches (20 to 38 cm) and generally weight from 8 to 20 lbs (240 to 560 g). The back is colored in shades of brown or green with small gold spots. The abdomen varies from cream to milky white.

Flesh: White and flaky

Habitat: New York to Minnesota and south to Oklahoma

Where & When to Find It: Solely a game fish

Steamed Smallmouth Bass with Balm or Lemon grass

12	Small new carrots (in season) or small, shaped carrots
1 1/4 cups (250 g)	Uncooked white rice
14 oz (400 mL)	*Court-bouillon* (see "Basic Ingredients for Some Recipes")
3 1/2 oz (100 g)	Balm or lemongrass
1 3/4 lbs (800 g)	Smallmouth bass fillets
As needed	White roux (see "Basic Ingredients …")
7 oz (200 mL)	Cream (15%)
1/3 cup (75 g)	Soft white cheese
To taste	Salt & pepper
1 tsp (10 g)	Fleur de sel de Guérande

- Cook the carrots and the rice in salted water, drain, set aside and keep warm.
- In a three-part steamer (with lid), pour the *court-bouillon* in the bottom and place 2 3/4 oz (80 g) of balm or lemongrass in the second part. Cover and boil for several minutes to soften and extract the flavor of the balm or the lemongrass. Next, in the third part of the steamer, add the smallmouth bass fillets; then steam. They should remain soft. Keep warm.
- Reduce the *court-bouillon* by 4/5. Infuse for about 12 minutes. Strain through cheese-

cloth or a fine mesh strainer. Very lightly bind with a little white roux, finish the sauce by adding the cream and the soft white cheese. Adjust the seasoning and keep warm.

Presentation: Mold the hot rice in a ramekin, place on the upper part of the plate, pour a little balm or lemongrass sauce into the plate and place the smallmouth bass fillets on top. Sprinkle with the remaining balm or lemongrass, arrange the new carrots around the plate and sprinkle with Guérande salt.

Preparation time: 30 minutes **Cooking time:** 10 minutes
Servings: 4   **Cost:** $$

Breaded Smallmouth Bass with Wild Rice

1 cup (150 g)	Wild rice
1 cup (80 g)	White bread crumbs
1 1/4 tsp (3 g)	Oregano, dried
1/2 tsp (1 g)	Thyme, dried
To taste	Salt & pepper
approx. 1 cup (200 g)	Fiddleheads
1	Egg
As needed	Flour
1 1/4 lbs (600 g)	Smallmouth bass fillets
3/4 cup (120 g)	Sweet butter
7 oz (200 mL)	Brown veal stock, bound (see "Basic Ingredients for Some Recipes")

• In a coffee mill, pulverize the wild rice. Combine the wild rice powder, white bread crumbs, oregano and thyme. Season with salt and pepper and set aside.
• Cook the fiddleheads in salted water and drain.
• Beat the egg. Flour the smallmouth bass fillets, dredge in the beaten egg, then the wild rice and bread crumb mixture, and cook *à la meunière* with the sweet butter, which should not be too hot so that the breading absorbs the butter and creates a crust. Season with salt and pepper.
• In the bottom of the plate, pour the hot brown veal stock, then the breaded smallmouth bass fillets and surround with the fiddleheads.

Preparation time: 15 minutes **Cooking time:** 7 to 8 minutes
Servings: 4   **Cost:** $$

Photo on page 235

PUMPKINSEED

Lepomis gibbosus
Incorrect names: rock bass, black crappie

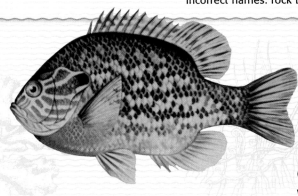

Flesh: White and firm

Habitat: Great Lakes system and upper Mississippi River

Where & When to Find It: From March to October, in abundance; game fish

Processed & Sold: Not available commercially

Cooking Method: *Meunière*, fried or grilled

Value: Deserves to be better known

Characteristics: Golden-brown body tending to olive green. Average length 6 to 8 inches (15 to 20 cm) and average weight 7 oz (200 g).

Comments: Childhood memories surface: who hasn't caught a pumpkinseed in his or her youth?

Small Pumpkinseeds Fried with Spices and Lemon Sauce

3 1/2 cups (300 g)	White bread crumbs
1 tsp (5 g)	Cumin, dried
1 tsp (5 g)	Sesame seeds, dried
1 tsp (5 g)	Fennel, dried
approx. 1 lb (480 g)	Small pumpkinseeds
2	Eggs
1/4 cup (60 mL)	Oil
1/2 cup (80 g)	Sweet butter
To taste	Salt & pepper
7 oz (200 mL)	Fish *velouté* (see "Basic Ingredients for Some Recipes")
2	Lemons (juice)
2 1/2 Tbsp (10 g)	Chervil, chopped

- To prepare the white bread crumbs, remove the crusts from sliced white bread, and pulverize in a food processor. Add the dried cumin, sesame seeds and fennel and set aside.
- Clean, scale, cut off the head of the pumpkinseed and wipe.
- Beat the eggs.
- Heat the oil and the butter in a thick skillet.
- Season the fish with salt and pepper, dip in the beaten eggs, then in the seasoned bread crumbs. Cook the pumpkinseeds in the skillet.
- Heat the fish *velouté* and, at the last moment, add the lemon juice.
- Stack the pumpkinseed fillets in the middle of the plate and sprinkle with the chervil. Serve the sauce separately in small individual bowls.

Preparation time: 10 to 15 minutes	
Cooking time: 5 to 7 minutes	
Servings: 4	**Cost:** $

Sautéed Pumpkinseed Fillets with Garlic Cream

approx. 1 lb (480 g)	**Small pumpkinseed fillets**
To taste	**Salt & pepper**
1 ¼ cups (300 mL)	**Peanut oil**
7 oz (200 mL)	**Garlic cream (see "Basic Ingredients for Some Recipes")**

• Dry off the fillets, then season with salt and pepper. Heat the peanut oil in a fairly high saucepan.

• Sear the fillets in hot oil. To do this, cook in small quantities. The fillets should be crispy on the outside and soft on the inside. Keep them warm on paper towels in the oven until all the fillets are cooked.

• Heat the garlic cream and create dips for the small pumpkinseed fillets.

NOTE: Using garlic with fish is not recommended as it can mask the true taste of the fish. On the other hand, some cheaper fish can have their flavor enlivened by garlic.

Preparation time: 15 minutes **Cooking time:** 5 to 8 minutes
Servings: 4   **Cost:** $

CARP

Cyprinus carpio
Incorrect names: German carp, leather carp, mirror carp

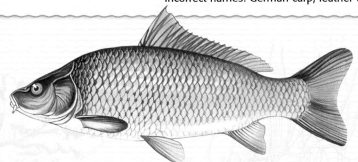

Habitat: Lakes and rivers of United States and Mexico

Where & When to Find It: From March to September, in abundance; if farmed, all year round

Processed & Sold: Whole, often live

Cooking Method: Braised whole, *meunière* or fried

Characteristics: Olive-green back and yellowish abdomen. This fish can reach 8 inches (20 cm) in length and weigh 10 to 15 lbs (4.5 to 6.8 kg).

Flesh: Very fatty and brown

Value: Appreciated by some

$

Carp with Mango on a Bed of Spinach

2	Mangoes
1/2 cup (80 g)	Butter
4 × 6 oz (180 g)	Carp fillets
3 1/2 oz (100 mL)	Dry white wine
7 oz (200 mL)	Fish fumet (see "Basic Ingredients for Some Recipes")
To taste	Salt & pepper
1/3 cup (50 g)	Shallots, cut with scissors
1 3/4 lbs (800 g)	Fresh spinach leaves
approx. 3 oz (100 g)	Dried tomatoes, sliced thin
1	Lime (juice)
3 1/2 oz (100 mL)	Cream (35%)

- Peel the mangoes and cut into slices.
- Brush an ovenproof dish with 2 1/2 Tbsp (30 g) of butter and place the carp fillets in the dish. (Make sure to cut small incisions into each fillet to allow the mango sugars to better penetrate the fish.)
- Place the mango slices on the fillets. Pour the white wine and fish fumet around the fillets, season with salt and pepper. Cover with aluminum foil and bake at 400°F (200°C) for 12 to 15 minutes, being sure to baste the fish from time to time.
- While the fish is cooking, sweat the shallots in the remaining butter, add the spinach and the tomatoes, season with salt and pepper and cook gently. When cooked, drain the vegetables in a strainer and keep warm.
- When the fish is cooked, remove half the mango slices and put them in a blender with the cooking juice and the lime juice. Emulsify quickly, then incorporate the cream. Keep this mixture warm.

Presentation: Create a bed of spinach on the bottom of each plate, then lay the carp fillets with the mango slices on top and cover with the sauce. Can be accompanied by Jerusalem artichokes or tagliatelle pasta.

Preparation time: 25 minutes   **Cooking time:** 15 to 30 minutes
Servings: 4   **Cost:** $$

Carp in Beer

approx. 1 cup (160 g)	Sweet butter
1 cup (150 g)	White onions, sliced thin
2/3 cup (70 g)	Celery, sliced thin
4 × 6 oz (180 g)	Carp steaks, boned
To taste	Salt & pepper
2 oz (60 g)	Spice loaf, diced
14 oz (400 mL)	Beer
1	*Bouquet garni*

- Braise the onions and the finely sliced celery in butter (4 1/2 Tbsp or 50 g). Add the carp steaks, season, then cover with the diced spice loaf, beer and the *bouquet garni*. Braise covered, in the oven, at 400°F (200°C).
- Depending on the thickness of the steaks, the cooking time should be 15 to 20 minutes.
- Remove from the oven, extract the cooking liquid and thicken with 2/3 cup (110 g) of butter. Pour over the steaks and spice loaf garnish.

Accompaniment: Boiled *parisienne* chayotes

Preparation time: 20 minutes   **Cooking time:** 20 to 25 minutes
Servings: 4   **Cost:** $$

GOLDEYE
Hiodon alosoides

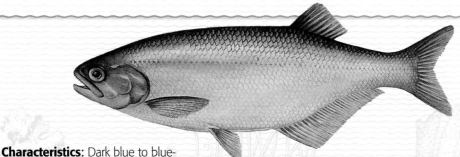

Characteristics: Dark blue to blue-green back and white abdomen. This fish generally measures 12 to 15 inches (30 to 38 cm).

Flesh: Soft and gray

Habitat: Mississippi River system south to Louisiana

Where & When to Find It: From April to October, in abundance

Processed & Sold: Whole, as fillets and smoked

Cooking Method: *Meunière*, poached or steamed

Value: In the 1930s, this fish was considered a luxury.

$

Grilled Goldeye Fillets with Orange Saffron Sauce and Pearl Barley

1 cup (200 g)	Pearl barley
4 × 6 oz (180 g)	Goldeye fillets
or 8 × 3 oz (90 g)	
3	Oranges (juice)
1	Lemon (juice)
¹/₂ tsp (2 g)	Saffron threads
3 ¹/₂ oz (100 mL)	Extra virgin olive oil
7 oz (200 mL)	Fish *velouté* (see "Basic Ingredients for Some Recipes")
To taste	Salt & pepper
As needed	Roasted sesame oil

- Cook the pearl barley in salted water. Keep warm in the water once cooked.
- In a dish, place the goldeye fillets. Pour the orange and lemon juice, saffron threads and olive oil on top. Marinate for 2 to 3 hours. After this, drain the fillets on paper towel. Recover the marinade and heat with the fish *velouté*. Adjust the seasoning, strain through cheesecloth or a fine mesh strainer, set aside and keep warm.
- Drain the pearl barley and sauté with a little sesame oil.
- Grill the goldeye fillets in two stages (very hot to begin, then finish cooking at moderate heat).

Presentation: Make a circle with the barley, lay the grilled goldeye fillets on top, then pour the sauce around the fillets.

Preparation time: 30 minutes	**Cooking time:** 12 minutes
Servings: 4	**Cost:** $$

Goldeye Fillets à la Meunière *with Cattail Hearts*

approx. 5 oz (150 g)	Cattail hearts
To taste	Salt & pepper
4 × 5 oz (150 g)	Goldeye fillets
2/3 cup (150 mL)	Roasted sesame oil
1/2 cup (120 mL)	Noilly Prat, dry
4	Wild leek leaves, cut with scissors

Preparation time: 5 to 8 minutes **Cooking time:** 5 to 7 minutes
Servings: 4   **Cost:** $$

- Cook the cattail hearts in salted water. Let cool, drain and set aside.
- Season the goldeye fillets with salt and pepper, and cook quickly in a thick skillet with the roasted sesame oil. When cooked, remove the cooking fat and deglaze with the Noilly Prat. Reheat the cattail hearts in the same skillet.
- In the middle of the plate, arrange the goldeye fillets and the cattail hearts around the fillets and sprinkle with the wild leek leaves.

BURBOT
Lota lota (Linnaeus)

commercially available

Characteristics: Color varies from yellow to brown; average length is 22 inches (55 cm) and average weight is 2 to 3 lbs (950 to 1.3 kg).

Flesh: White and flaky

Habitat: Most freshwater lakes and rivers in Alaska, and south to Ohio and Missouri drainage basins

Where & When to Find It: Game fish only; not

Processed & Sold: Whole and as fillets

Cooking Method: Steamed, *meunière* or poached

Value: Cooks like cod

Comments: Monkfish, which we call burbot, is not really a burbot. The true burbot is a member of the *Gadidae* (cod, pollock, etc.) family and lives in fresh water.

Braised Burbot on a Bed of Green Puy Lentils with Red Wine Sauce

approx. 2 cups (300 g)	Green Puy lentils
1 1/4 cups (200 g)	Butter
approx. 2 oz (50 g)	Bacon, unsalted, diced
1/2 cup (25 g)	Shallots, cut with scissors
2 cups (500 mL)	White chicken stock (see "Basic Ingredients for Some Recipes")
1	*Bouquet garni*
To taste	Salt & pepper
2/3 cup (100 g)	Carrot *brunoise*
1 3/4 to 2 1/4 lbs (800 g to 1 kg)	Fairly large burbot
12 slices	Bacon
1 1/4 cups (300 mL)	Dry red wine
7 oz (200 mL)	Brown veal stock (see "Basic Ingredients …")

- Wash the lentils.
- Use 4 1/2 Tbsp (50 g) of butter to brown the bacon; add the shallots, then simmer for a few minutes. Add the lentils, the veal stock and the *bouquet garni*. Season and cook gently at low heat. Ten minutes after cooking is finished, add the carrot *brunoise*. Set aside.
- Bone the burbot through the stomach; season with salt and pepper. Wrap the fish with the bacon slices and tie with a string like a roast. Brown until a nice color is obtained, pour in the red wine and reduce by half with the braised fish, add the brown stock and bake in the oven at 350°F (180°C), basting often.
- After checking the temperature (160°F or 72°C), remove the braised fish. Reduce the cooking stock, adjust the seasoning and thicken with the remaining butter. Remove the string.

Presentation: Squeeze the lentils in a round hoop, slice the fish and cover with the wine sauce.

Preparation time: 20 minutes	**Cooking time:** 15 to 20 minutes
Servings: 4	**Cost:** $$

Burbot Fillets with Chanterelles and Wild Watercress

³/4 cup (140 g)	Sweet butter
1 tbsp (40 g)	Shallots, chopped
7 oz (200 mL)	Pineau de Charentes
¹/2	Garlic clove, minced
¹/3 cup (20 g)	Curly parsley, finely sliced
²/3 cup (150 mL)	Peanut oil
5 oz (160 g)	Chanterelle mushrooms
To taste	Salt & pepper
10 oz (300 g)	Wild watercress
7 oz (200 mL)	Cream (35%)
³/4 cup (180 mL)	Fish *velouté* (see "Basic Ingredients for Some Recipes")
4 × 6 oz (180 g)	Burbot fillets
As needed	Flour

- Sauté the shallots in ²/3 cup (100 g) of hot butter until tender, then add the Pineau des Charentes and reduce by ⁹/10. Stir in the chopped garlic and the parsley. Set aside.

- Sauté the chanterelles in 3 Tbsp (50 mL) of hot peanut oil, season with salt and pepper, then drain on a paper towel. Set aside.
- In a blender, purée the wild watercress and add the cream. Add the salt, pepper and the fish *velouté* and heat gently, never reaching 200°F (100°C)—if the sauce is too hot, the acid will turn it. Keep warm.
- Heat the peanut oil and the remaining butter in a heavy-bottomed skillet. Season the burbot fillets with salt and pepper, flour and sauté *à la meunière*.
- Combine and reheat the chanterelles and the Pineau des Charentes preparation. Season to taste.
- Put wild watercress sauce onto a plate. Place the burbot fillets in the center and cover with the chanterelles.

Accompaniment: *Noisette* potatoes prepared in butter

Preparation time: 25 minutes	**Cooking time:** 10 minutes
Servings: 4	**Cost:** $$$

Classification of Seafood and Seaweed

Mollusks and crustaceans are among the most sought-after products from the sea and, although they are caught in only limited numbers, they represent a major part of the income earned by fishers.

Mollusks and crustaceans are invertebrate aquatic animals whose soft body is usually encased in a protective shell. Some, like the lobster and the crab, have a hard yet articulated and flexible shell. They belong to the crustacean class. Others, such as the oyster and the clam, are members of the mollusk class. The term "mollusk," from the Latin, means "soft body." Some mollusks, such as the octopus and the squid, do not have an external shell, but a small internal one.

PURCHASE, FRESHNESS AND STORAGE

1. Crustaceans

Lobster

Famous for its tasty meat, the lobster is really the king of crustaceans. Its color varies from blue-green to red-brown. The size of commercial lobsters varies from 7 to 12 inches (18 to 30 cm) in length and from $1/2$ to 2 lbs (230 to 900 g) in weight, although lobsters can weigh more than 44 lbs (20 kg). To ensure the best possible quality, lobster must be bought live. Live lobsters are fairly heavy. A dead uncooked lobster loses an enormous amount of weight, almost the instant it is

killed. Lobsters can also be bought cooked. Generally, they are cooked in sea water directly on the boats, which has the advantage of certainty about the lobster's freshness. On the other hand, sea water, which is high in salt, will slightly toughen the meat. Apply the same standards when buying shrimp, scampi and crab.

Pink Shrimp

Pink shrimp are often sold cooked, having been cooked in sea water on board ship. It is easy to tell if a shrimp is fresh when the tail is folded up, which indicates that it was not already dead or dying when it was processed. Moreover, check for firmness since, as shrimp get older, they become soft. If they are frozen, or were frozen, and they are being sold thawed, this fact should be clearly indicated on the packaging. A frozen unshelled shrimp will be more difficult to peel after. Raw shrimp, frozen in bulk without the head, should be thawed slowly.

Crab

When you grab a crab from behind to avoid coming in contact with the claws, its legs should fold up quickly. If they remain dangling, swinging aimlessly, this means that death is imminent. Also, the heavier a crab is, the more meat it has. Female crabs are sometimes more sought after for their meat than males, except if the female is carrying eggs. A female is recognized by the size of the tongue which folds up on its abdomen. Among females, the tongue, which serves to protect the eggs, is larger. When buying cooked crab, you will have to depend on the word of the fishmonger.

2. Shellfish

No shellfish can be eaten if it has not been cooked live. In the case of a bivalve shellfish, it is alive if the shell remains closed or, if a little open at room temperature, it suddenly snaps shut at the slightest touch. Whatever its nature, it should be considered unfit for consumption if its shell is pierced or broken. If the mollusk peaks out from its shell or if the shellfish moves (as in the case of a univalve shellfish), this proves that the shellfish is moving inside. A little foam may appear when opened.

3. Invertebrates

Invertebrates, such as squid, octopus and cuttlefish, are never sold live. The absence of any smell indicates freshness, along with firmness and a healthy appearance. They are usually sold washed, ready for use.

4. Seaweed

The Atlantic coast is rich in seaweed, a product that is increasingly popular with consumers due to the influence of Asian cooking. Care should be taken when choosing seaweed, since not all can be eaten. Nevertheless, whether steamed or boiled, seaweed from North American waters rivals dried, imported seaweed.

METHODS AND COOKING TIMES FOR CRUSTACEANS

1. Live crustaceans

Steaming

Steaming is best suited for live crustaceans. A basket steamer or, as in some restaurants, commercial steamers can be used. To cook with steam, an excellent *court-bouillon* (see "Basic Ingredients for Some Recipes") should be used. When using a basket steamer, add enough *court-bouillon* so that the crustacean can be seared by the steam. In the case of small pieces, for example, a small lobster, it is recommended that it be put to sleep by holding its head down for several minutes. This will prevent it from reacting when it comes in contact with the basket steamer and the steam, and greatly reduce the risk of losing the meat.

It should be noted that a crustacean bought live that later dies in the refrigerator is of no culinary interest, since the flesh changes into liquid after death. This is why you find only live crustaceans (lobsters, spiny lobster, scampi, shrimp or crabs) or raw or cooked products sold deep-frozen.

Cooking in a *court-bouillon*

As in the case of steaming, it is important to prepare an excellent *court-bouillon* (see "Basic Ingredients ...") to cook crustaceans. To prevent crustaceans from emptying out of their shells, a large quantity of *court-bouillon* is necessary to cook a minimum number of crustaceans at a time. For example, when you are cooking three or four lobsters in a small amount of liquid, the liquid may cool as the

250

live, raw lobsters are dropped in. The lobsters will have had the time to empty before the court-bouillon has once again come to a boil.

Crayfish are even more fragile than lobster when it comes to being cooked live. Once they are dead, they give off an unpleasant odor. Crayfish cooked in a *court-bouillon* are delicious and sought after by gourmet cooks.

2. Deep-frozen Crustaceans

Problems inherent in cooking live crustaceans and the necessary precautions do not, obviously, apply to deep-frozen crustaceans, whether raw or cooked. It should be noted that cooking shrimp that are sold deep-frozen, cooked or raw is a delicate operation. First of all, a good *court-bouillon* (see "Basic Ingredients …") needs to be prepared and all the shrimp dropped in it at once. The shrimp should be removed from the liquid once it has come to a boil, and they should be plunged into ice water. Next, the *court-bouillon* should be allowed to cool, and the shrimp placed in it again and left for several hours so that they absorb the flavor of the *court-bouillon*.

3. Cooking times

The cooking times for crustaceans are approximate and vary, depending on whether the cooking method is steam or a *court-bouillon*. Care must be taken not to overcook the crustaceans as prolonged cooking may cause the meat to become tough. It should also be noted that lobster, spiny lobster and scampi can be grilled, and that shrimp can be fried. In these cases, the cooking times will depend on the size of the product.

Moreover, it should also be noted that all crustaceans can be eaten cold after being steamed or cooked in a *court-bouillon*. They can also be eaten with an accompanying sauce.

- **Lobster, live**: 5 minutes per lb + 1 minute for each additional 1/4 lb
- **Lobster, deep-frozen raw, thawed before cooking**: 7 minutes per lb + 1 minute for each additional 1/4 lb
- **Lobster, deep-frozen raw, cooked deep-frozen**: 11 minutes per lb + 2 minutes for each additional 1/4 lb
- **Crab, live**: 15 to 20 minutes, at a simmering boil, depending on the size.
- **Crayfish, live**: 2 to 3 minutes, in a *court-bouillon*.

Crustaceans

SOME WALK, OTHERS SWIM

Did you know that a lobster weighing 1 1/2 lbs (725 g) might be 7 years old and that, by this time, it will have changed its shell 22 times? The lobster is a royal dish and most of the flavor can be found in its claws. Often, we do not know how to eat a lobster; in order to extract the meat, we must use our hands, and we must suck out the morsels that can be found in the small legs.

Like the lobster, the scampi is a walker with claws; the spiny lobster and the slipper lobster are walkers, but without claws. Shrimp are swimmers, whereas crabs are walkers with atrophied tails.

Crustaceans are animals that are covered with a horny substance called "chitin" that forms the shell and that hardens more or less, depending on the species. Since the shell does not expand, crustaceans are occasionally forced to abandon it. This is referred to as the molt: they are naked but for a new layer of chitin that began forming beneath the old shell, yet which is still soft. It should be noted that all crustaceans, whatever their natural color, have an insoluble red pigment; the other pigments disappear with cooking. This explains why they turn red when cooked.

Rock crab

Dungeness crab

Snow crab

Glass shrimp

Sculptured shrimp

Common shrimp

Pink shrimp

Arctic argid

Crayfish

Lobster

Spiny lobster

Scampi

ROCK CRAB

Cancer irroratus

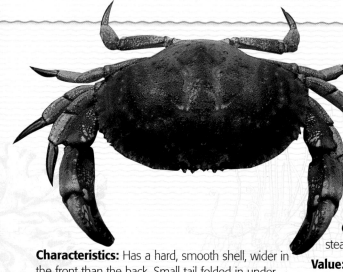

Habitat: North Atlantic

Where & When to Find It: From June to October, in abundance; sometimes available live where fish is sold

Processed & Sold: Always live with its shell; or shelled and deep-frozen

Cooking Method: In a *court-bouillon* or steamed

Value: Excellent meat with a delicate taste

Comments: This high-quality crab has one flaw: it is difficult to extract the meat.

$$$$

Characteristics: Has a hard, smooth shell, wider in the front than the back. Small tail folded in under the shell. Five pairs of flat legs, all longer than the width of the shell, the first pair equipped with strong claws.

Rock Crab Sauté

As needed	*Court-bouillon* (see "Basic Ingredients for Some Recipes")
4 × 1 ¾–2 lbs (800–900 g)	Rock crabs
¹/₃ cup (60 g)	Sweet butter
1	Spanish onion, white, chopped
¹/₂ cup (60 g)	Shallots, chopped
3 cups (250 g)	White mushrooms, diced
4	Tomatoes, blanched, peeled, seeded and cut into large dice
7 oz (200 mL)	Cream (35%)
To taste	Salt & pepper
1 Pinch	Cayenne pepper
3 Tbsp (40 mL)	Calvados
¹/₂ cup (30 g)	*Fines herbes*, minced (flat-leafed parsley, chives and tarragon)

- In a robust *court-bouillon*, cook the crabs for about 20 minutes.
- Let cool in the *court-bouillon*. This step can be done the night before. Drain, shell and recover the creamy parts and the coral from the shell.
- In a skillet with the butter, cook the onions and shallots until tender; do not let them brown. Add the diced mushrooms and tomatoes, and cook until all the liquid has evaporated. Add the shelled crab as well as the coral and the creamy parts. Pour in the cream and gently mix. Season with salt, pep-

per and cayenne pepper. Add the calvados and the *fines herbes*, then serve very hot.

Accompaniment: Sautéed glasswort and boiled white rice

Preparation time: 45 minutes **Cooking time:** 30 minutes
Servings: 4 **Cost:** $$$$

Rock Crab with Potato and Seaweed Salad

1/3 cup (30 g)	**Dried sea lettuce (ulva)**
4 × 1 3/4–2 lbs (800–900 g)	**Rock crabs**
As needed	**Court-bouillon (see "Basic Ingredients for Some Recipes")**
4	**Medium-sized potatoes**
To taste	**Salt & pepper**
As needed	**Wine vinegar**
2	**Lemons (juice)**
2/3 cup (160 mL)	**Sunflower oil**

- Rehydrate the sea lettuce with water.
- Cook the rock crabs for 20 minutes in a *court-bouillon*, then let cool in the *court-bouillon* in the refrigerator.

- Cook the potatoes, unpeeled, in salted water. Drain and refrigerate. These three steps can be performed the night before.
- Shell and remove the crab meat, including the coral. Season with the vinegar, lemon juice and 1/4 cup (60 mL) of sunflower oil. Season with salt and pepper to taste.
- Peel the potatoes and cut into fairly thick rounds. Season with salt and pepper, and flavor with the wine vinegar, the juice of the other lemon and the remaining sunflower oil.
- Arrange the potatoes, flat, on each plate, in the shape of a crown; sprinkle with the drained sea lettuce and place a rock crab in the middle.

NOTE: A mayonnaise sauce may be served separately, if so desired.

Preparation time: 45 minutes **Cooking time:** 30 to 40 minutes
Servings: 4 **Cost:** $$$$

Photo on next page →

DUNGENESS CRAB

Cancer magister

Incorrect name: rock crab

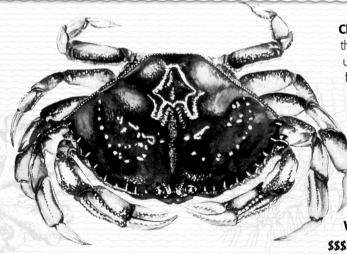

Characteristics: Hard shell, wider in the front than the back, with spines. Small tail, folded in under the shell. Five pairs of short legs, the first set equipped with strong claws

Habitat: Pacific Ocean

Where & When to Find It: From July to November, in abundance

Processed & Sold: Deep-frozen or canned

Cooking Method: Steamed, poached in a *court-bouillon*, or in a sauce

Value: Excellent meat with a delicate taste

$$$$

Stuffed Dungeness Crab Gratin

1 cup (250 mL)	Dry white wine
As needed	*Court-bouillon* (see "Basic Ingredients for Some Recipes")
4 × 1 1/4–2 lbs (600–950 g)	Dungeness crabs
1 cup (180 g)	Sweet butter
3 1/2 cups (300 g)	Firm white mushrooms, diced
1 1/2 cups (180 g)	Potatoes, diced
As needed	White roux (see "Basic Ingredients …")
To taste	Salt & pepper
7 oz (200 mL)	Cream (35%)
2/3 cup (80 g)	White bread crumbs

- Add the white wine to the seasoned *court-bouillon*, add the crabs and cook for 20 to 25 minutes.
- Let cool, drain and extract all the meat, including the coral. Keep the crab shells, wash and keep dry.
- With 1/3 of the butter, cook the mushrooms until all the moisture has evaporated. Set aside and keep warm.
- **Sauce:** Strain 4 cups (1 L) of the *court-bouillon* through cheesecloth or a fine mesh strainer, cook the diced potatoes, then, with a wire skimmer, remove them, set aside and keep warm.
- Add the white roux to the *court-bouillon* until the desired consistency is obtained, season

to taste, add the cream and finish with the second $1/3$ of the butter. Strain through cheesecloth or a fine mesh strainer.

- Gently combine the crab, mushrooms and potatoes with the sauce. Adjust the seasoning and pour into the empty crab shells.

Sprinkle the shells with the white bread crumbs and a few knobs of butter.
- Put in the oven at 400°F (200°C) for 18 to 20 minutes to allow the breading to brown.
- Serve immediately.

Preparation time: 50 minutes	**Cooking time:** 40 minutes
Servings: 4	**Cost:** $$$$

Photo on page 257

Dungeness Crab à l'américaine

$2/3$ cup (100 g)	Sweet butter
$1/2$ cup (60 g)	Shallots, chopped
approx. $1/2$ cup (60 g)	Celery *brunoise*
approx. $1/2$ cup (60 g)	Carrot *brunoise*
1 Pinch	Thyme
$1/2$	Bay leaf
4 × 1 $1/4$–2 lbs (600–900 g)	Dungeness crabs, live
As needed	Peanut oil
3 Tbsp (50 mL)	Cognac
$1/4$ cup (50 g)	Tomato paste, cooked
7 oz (200 mL)	Dry white wine
1 $1/4$ cups (300 mL)	Fish fumet (see "Basic Ingredients for Some Recipes")
To taste	Salt & pepper

- In a large enough saucepan, heat the butter and cook the shallots, celery and carrots, thyme and bay leaf until tender.

- Cut the crabs quickly (remove the claws, cut the body in four and remove the coral and the creamy parts).
- During this step, heat the peanut oil in a large skillet, then sauté the crab.
- When the pieces of crab are sautéed, arrange them on the vegetables and flambé with the cognac, then add the tomato paste, the white wine and the fish fumet. Season and cook for 12 to 15 minutes. Remove the pieces of crab and reduce the sauce until the desired consistency is obtained. Return the crab to the sauce and reheat. Serve as is.

Accompaniment: Boiled potatoes

NOTE: This recipe should be served with finger bowls and bibs since enjoying the taste of the crab means digging deep inside the shells.

Preparation time: 40 minutes	**Cooking time:** 25 to 35 minutes
Servings: 4	**Cost:** $$$$

SNOW CRAB AND QUEEN CRAB

Chionoecetes opilio

Incorrect name: spider crab

Characteristics: Hard, smooth shell. Small tail folded in under the shell. Five pairs of flat legs, all longer than the width of the shell. The first pair have strong claws.

Habitat: North Atlantic

Where & When to Find It: From June to October, in abundance; rarely available whole and fresh where fish is sold

Processed & Sold: Deep-frozen in packages of 1 lb (454 g). Also possible to buy with legs in their shell

Cooking Method: Steamed, poached in a *court-bouillon*, grilled or in the oven

Value: A fine taste

$$$$

Snow Crab Claws with Almond Milk on a Bed of Glasswort and Saltwater Cordgrass

3 1/2 cups (350 g)	Glasswort (brown seaweed)
1/3 cup (60 g)	Saltwater cordgrass
7 oz (200 mL)	Cream (35%)
1/3 cup (70 mL)	Almond milk
To taste	Salt & pepper
1/3 cup (60 g)	Lobster butter (see "Basic Ingredients for Some Recipes")
1	Lime (juice)
1 1/4 lbs (600 g)	Snow crab claws, cooked and shelled
1/2 cup (80 g)	Sweet butter

- Blanch the glasswort and the saltwater cordgrass separately to desalt, if necessary.
- **Sauce**: Heat the cream, add the almond milk, season with salt and pepper. Reduce slightly and thicken with the lobster butter. Add the lime juice; gently heat the snow crab claws in the sauce. Set aside and keep warm.
- In a skillet, heat the sweet butter, and sauté the glasswort and the saltwater cordgrass together. Season with salt and pepper.
- Stack the glasswort in the center of the plate and arrange the pieces of crab and the sauce around the glasswort.

Preparation time: 30 minutes **Cooking time:** 10 minutes
Servings: 4   **Cost:** $$$$

Avocado with Snow Crab Stuffing

4	Ripe and fresh avocados
2	Lemons (juice)
approx. ³/₄ lb (320 g)	Snow crab meat
¹/₃ cup (80 g)	Mayonnaise (see "Basic Ingredients for Some Recipes")
1 tsp (20 g)	Shallots, minced
To taste	Salt & pepper
4 sprigs	Dill

- The avocados should be very ripe, but stored in the refrigerator so they stay cold.

- Open the avocados, remove the pit and, using a melon baller, make small balls (as round as possible). Sprinkle immediately with the lemon juice.
- Combine the crab meat, the mayonnaise and the shallots, then, with the avocado balls, season and garnish the avocado halves with the preparation. Garnish with the sprigs of dill.

NOTE: This recipe is very simple, but individualized creations are also possible, as shown in the photograph.

> **Preparation time:** 30 minutes
> **Servings:** 4 **Cost:** $$$$

WHITE SHRIMP AND GLASS SHRIMP

Pasiphaea multidentata

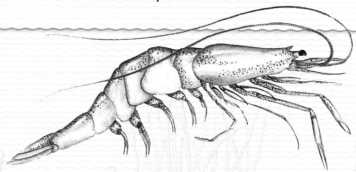

Characteristics: Flexible and transparent shell when fresh. Shell and abdomen are compressed laterally.

Habitat: North Atlantic

Where & When to Find It: Irregular availability on the market

Processed & Sold: Deep-frozen, rarely fresh

Cooking Method: Poached in a *court-bouillon*, steamed, sautéed or grilled

Value: A high-quality crustacean

Comments: As is the case with all shrimp, white shrimp should not be overcooked.

$$$$

White Shrimp Fricassee with Aniseed

3 ¹/₂ cups (300 g)	Firm, white mushrooms
approx. ³/₄ cup (150 g)	Sweet butter
To taste	Salt & pepper
approx. 1 lb (480 g)	Shrimp, shelled and deveined
¹/₃ cup (75 mL)	Ricard or Pernod
4 Tbsp (60 g)	Shallots, chopped
3 ¹/₂ oz (100 mL)	White wine
approx. ²/₃ cup (160 mL)	Shrimp bisque (see Lobster bisque, in "Basic Ingredients for Some Recipes")
approx. 1 cup (40 g)	Chives, cut with scissors

Preparation time: 30 minutes   **Cooking time:** 10 minutes
Servings: 4   **Cost:** $$$$

- Cut the mushrooms into quarters. Wash and cook without water with 4 ¹/₂ Tbsp (50 g) of butter. It is important that the mushrooms be very fresh, i.e., very firm, so that, once cooked, they remain firm and white. When cooked, season with salt and pepper and set aside.

- Heat the remaining butter, and sauté the shrimp quickly to stiffen without browning. Pour the Ricard or the Pernod into the pan, then flambé. Using a skimmer, remove the shrimp, then add the shallots and cook gently until tender. Pour in the white wine and reduce by ⁹/₁₀. Incorporate the shrimp bisque and let simmer for a few minutes.

- In another saucepan, add the mushrooms and the shrimp. Strain through cheesecloth or a fine mesh strainer and let simmer (do not boil). Season and, just before serving, sprinkle with the cut chives.

Accompaniment: Boiled white rice or rice pilaf

NOTE: If you buy unshelled shrimp, store the shells in the freezer. Once you have enough, they can be used to prepare a bisque.

Photo on next page →

Sautéed Shrimp with Coconut Milk on a Bed of Brown Seaweed

3 cups (300 g)	Glasswort (brown seaweed)
1/2 cup (120 mL)	Peanut oil
approx. 1 lb (480 g)	Shrimp (15 to 18 per pound)
approx. 2/3 cup (80 g)	Currants
1/2 cup (120 mL)	Coconut milk
approx. 3/4 cup (150 g)	Sweet butter
1	White onion, minced
approx. 1 cup (200 g)	Coconut meat, diced
To taste	Salt & pepper
2/3 cup (40 g)	Fresh parsley, chopped

- Taste the raw glasswort. If it is too salty, blanch, i.e., bring to a boil and immediately refresh in cold water. Drain and set aside.
- Heat the peanut oil and quickly sear the shrimp until they brown. Drain and set aside on a paper towel.
- Soak the currants in the coconut milk for a few minutes.

- With 1/3 cup (60 g) of butter, braise the chopped onion, add the diced coconut and let simmer until the dice are cooked. Add the coconut milk and currant mixture as well as the glasswort. Leave at low heat so that the entire mixture is hot, yet crunchy. Season with salt and pepper.
- With the remaining butter, reheat the shrimp, season with salt and pepper to taste.
- In the bottom of each plate, make a bed of brown seaweed. Arrange the shrimp in a crown around the glasswort and sprinkle with chopped parsley.

NOTE: Garlic should not mask the flavor of crustaceans. If garlic is truly desired, it is better to use "fake shrimp" (surimi), which are much less expensive.

Preparation time: 25 minutes	**Cooking time:** 10 to 15 minutes
Servings: 4	**Cost:** $$$$

RED SAND SHRIMP AND SCULPTURE SHRIMP

Sclerocrangon boreas

Incorrect name: slipper lobster

Characteristics: When fresh, it has a rough, hard shell and abdomen, covered with brown and white spots. The shell is 5 times as long as it is wide. The body is compressed, the maximum length being 5 inches (12.5 cm).

Habitat: North Atlantic

Where & When to Find It: Irregular availability wherever fish is sold

Processed & Sold: Whole, fresh and deep-frozen

Cooking Method: Poached in a *court-bouillon*, steamed, sautéed or grilled

Value: Very tasty

Comments: As with all shrimp, these must be eaten fresh or deep-frozen.

$$$$

Vanilla-Flavored Shrimp with Pattypan Squash

12	Yellow pattypan squash (small)
7 oz (200 mL)	Lobster sauce (see "Basic Ingredients for Some Recipes")
To taste	Vanilla bean or vanilla extract
As needed	Peanut oil
4	Oyster mushrooms
To taste	Salt & pepper
2/3 cup (100 g)	Butter
approx. 1 lb (480 g)	Shrimp, shelled and deveined
2	Green onions, cut with scissors
4 tsp (20 mL)	Cognac
1/2 cup (120 mL)	White wine
approx. 1/2 cup (80 g)	Fresh tomatoes, blanched, peeled, seeded and diced

- Cook the pattypan squash in boiling, salted water. When cooked, set aside and keep warm.
- **Sauce:** Heat the lobster sauce, add the inside of one vanilla bean or natural vanilla extract and let simmer. Caution: The vanilla taste must not be too strong; it should remain subtle. Set aside.
- On the grill or in a thick skillet, with a little peanut oil, cook the oyster mushrooms that have been seasoned with salt and pepper. Drain and set aside.
- Heat the butter and sauté the shrimp, seasoned with salt and pepper. Remove and

keep warm. Add the green onions, then pour in the cognac, flambé, pour in the white wine as well as the lobster sauce. Let simmer for several minutes, then add the shrimp.

- At the bottom of each plate, place one oyster mushroom, then the shrimp and, on each side, the pattypan squash and the diced tomatoes.

NOTE: Why yellow squash? It is simply a question of presentation. Otherwise, it is possible to use any that can be found on the market. Pattypan squash are used for their neutral taste because it does not hide the taste of the shrimp.

Preparation time: 40 minutes	Cooking time: 6 to 8 minutes
Servings: 4	Cost: $$$$

Photo on page 265

Shrimp Steamed in Seaweed with Lemon Butter

1 1/4 cup (300 mL)	*Court-bouillon* (see "Basic Ingredients for Some Recipes")
5 oz (150 g)	Fresh Irish moss* (seaweed)
approx. 1 lb (480 g)	Shrimp, shelled and deveined
1 cup (160 g)	Lemon herb butter (see "Basic Ingredients ...")

Preparation time: 15 minutes	Cooking time: 8 to 12 minutes
Servings: 4	Cost: $$$$

- To prepare this recipe, a three-part steamer is required. In the bottom pot, pour in the *court-bouillon*, then place the seaweed in the first insert, and the shrimp in the second insert.
- Heat the *court-bouillon*. Add the first insert, in which the seaweed has been placed. Cover and boil for 4 to 5 minutes to allow the seaweed to develop its flavor, then place over it the second insert, in which the shrimp have been added. Steam until the shrimp are soft.
- Serve immediately with the hot lemon herb butter.

* Irish moss can be found where fish is sold, during lobster season.

BROWN SHRIMP AND SAND SHRIMP

Crangon septemspinosus

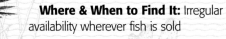

Where & When to Find It: Irregular availability wherever fish is sold

Processed & Sold: Whole in the shell or deep-frozen

Cooking Method: Poached in a *court-bouillon* or steamed

Value: Much smaller than the red sand shrimp; can be eaten whole

Comments: In Europe, the brown shrimp is the species *Crangon vulgaris*.

$$$$

Characteristics: Flexible and smooth shell. One spine in the center of the shell, another one on each side. Compressed body

Habitat: North Atlantic and Europe.

Shrimp Consommé

1 ¹/₂ cups (600 mL)	Fish fumet (see "Basic Ingredients for Some Recipes"), light and clarified
¹/₂ cup (120 mL)	White wine
approx. 1 lb (500 g)	Shrimp shells
To taste	Salt & pepper
¹/₂ lb (250 g)	Puff pastry
1	Egg
4 oz (120 g)	Shrimp, shelled, deveined and cooked
1 ¹/₃ cups (120 g)	White mushrooms, diced and cooked
1 ¹/₂ cups (90 g)	Chervil leaves

- Heat the light fish fumet, then add the white wine and the shrimp shells. Cook gently for about 20 minutes and strain through cheesecloth or a fine mesh strainer. Let cool after checking the seasoning. For this recipe, the consommé must be cold.
- Use four bowls with a slight rim.
- Roll out the puff pastry, beat the egg with a little water to make the glaze.
- In the bottom of each bowl, place equal amounts of shrimp and mushrooms, then the chervil leaves and fill the bowl ³/₄ full with cold consommé. Brush the outside edge of the bowl with the glaze. Cut any chervil leaves that are ³/₄ inches (2 cm) longer than the diameter of the bowl, and place a slice of pastry on each bowl, ensuring that the pastry sticks to the glaze. Brush the top of the pastry and let cool for about 15 minutes.
- Place in the oven at 500°F (260°C) to brown the pastry, then lower the heat. Cover with

aluminum foil. After 20 to 25 minutes, the consommé should be ready to enjoy.

NOTE: Shrimp shells can be kept and frozen. When there are enough, a shrimp consommé can be prepared.

Preparation time: 1 hour	Cooking time: 20 to 30 minutes
Servings: 4	Cost: $$$

Photo on next page →

Brown Shrimp with Three Sauces

14 oz (400 g)	Brown shrimp
As needed	White wine (Optional)
1 cup (250 mL)	Mayonnaise (see "Basic Ingredients for Some Recipes")
3 to 4 tsp (15 to 20 mL)	Orange juice, reduced
3 to 4 tsp (15 to 20 mL)	Oyster juice, reduced
1/3 cup (80 mL)	Maltese sauce
As needed	Orange zest, blanched
To taste	Salt & pepper
1/3 cup (80 mL)	Lemon mayonnaise
1/2 cup (20 g)	Chives, cut with scissors
1/3 cup (80 mL)	Mayonnaise with oyster juice
2	Lemons (juice)

- Using a steamer, cook the shrimp. A little white wine can be added to the water, if so desired. *Caution*: The shrimp should remain soft, i.e., not overcooked. Never put the shrimp in the water. Stop them from cooking further by putting them on crushed ice and, once they are sufficiently cold, wrap them in a cloth and store in the refrigerator.

- **Mayonnaise**: Prepare 1 cup (250 mL) of mayonnaise according to the basic recipe, then divide into three equal parts. The day before preparing the sauces, reduce the orange juice and the oyster juice to produce concentrates.

- **Maltese sauce**: Add the reduced orange juice as well as the blanched orange zest. Season to taste.

- **Lemon mayonnaise**: Add the lemon juice and the cut chives. Season to taste.

- **Oyster juice mayonnaise**: Add the concentrated oyster juice. Season to taste.

NOTE: These small but very tasty shrimp can be eaten whole. All the sauces that accompany the shrimp, whether hot or cold, must enhance the flavor of these magnificent crustaceans and not mask it.

Preparation time: 30 minutes	Cooking time: 2 to 4 minutes
Servings: 4	Cost: $$$$

PINK SHRIMP
Pandalus borealis

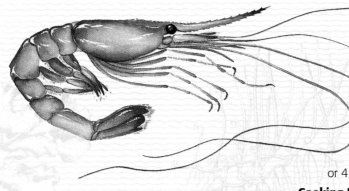

Habitat: North Atlantic

Where & When to Find It: All year round, deep-frozen, wherever fish is sold

Processed & Sold: Rarely fresh, deep-frozen in packages of 1 lb (454 g) or 4 1/2 lbs (2 kg)

Cooking Method: Poached in a *court-bouillon* or steamed

Value: High-quality shrimp

$$$$

Characteristics: A uniform bright red or finely flecked, with red diagonal bands on its shell and abdomen. Flexible shell. Abdomen and shell laterally compressed

Pink Shrimp Salad with Soya Beans

14 oz (400 g)	Pink shrimp, cooked or raw
8 oz (240 g)	Dried soya beans
1	Onion, cut in rounds
1	Carrot, cut in rounds
2	Lemons (juice)
1/2 cup (120 mL)	Sunflower oil
To taste	Salt & pepper
1 cup (40 g)	Chives, cut with scissors

- If the pink shrimp are raw, poach in a *court-bouillon* (see "Basic Ingredients for Some Recipes"). *Caution:* When the *court-bouillon* comes to a rolling boil, stop cooking the shrimp (by adding ice cubes), otherwise they will be overcooked. Set aside.
- Soak the soya beans in cold water for a few hours. Next, cook with the onion and carrot rounds. Leave in the cooking stock until completely cool.
- Pour the beans and the shrimp into a strainer, applying a light pressure to the shrimp to extract as much liquid as possible. Store the two ingredients in the refrigerator for a few hours.
- Combine the lemon juice and the sunflower oil with a little salt and pepper, then add the shrimp and the soya beans. Adjust the seasoning and serve in small dishes. Sprinkle with the cut chives.

Preparation time: 30 minutes **Cooking time:** 35 minutes
Servings: 4 **Cost:** $$$$

Pink Shrimp and Asian Vegetable Stir Fry

14 oz (400 g)	Pink shrimp, shelled and deveined
1/4 cup (60 mL)	Roasted sesame oil
2	Green onions, cut with scissors
1/2	Garlic clove, minced
approx. 3 oz (100 g)	Rehydrated shiitake mushrooms
approx. 5 oz (160 g)	Snow peas
To taste	Salt & pepper
1 1/2 cups (160 g)	Chinese cabbage
3 1/2 oz (100 g)	Bamboo shoots (canned)
3 1/2 oz (100 mL)	White chicken stock (see "Basic Ingredients for Some Recipes")
1/4 cup (60 mL)	Oyster sauce (commercial)
1/4 cup (60 mL)	Soya sauce (commercial)

- Drain the pink shrimp to remove as much liquid as possible. Set aside.
- Heat the roasted sesame oil and cook the cut shallots with the garlic until tender.
- Finely slice the shiitake mushrooms, squeezing them to remove the water used for rehydrating. Blanch the snow peas in salted water, drain and set aside. Finely chop the Chinese cabbage and set aside. Cut the bamboo shoots into sticks and set aside.
- Once the shallots and the garlic are tender, add the first of the sliced shiitake mushrooms and braise for a few minutes. Then, one after the other, add the Chinese cabbage, the snow peas and the bamboo shoots. Mix, then pour in the white chicken stock and let simmer for several minutes, keeping a watchful eye so that the vegetables remain crunchy.
- Pour in the oyster and the soya sauces. Adjust the seasoning, then, a few minutes before serving, combine the vegetables and the pink shrimp. Serve immediately.

Preparation time: 20 minutes   **Cooking time:** 15 minutes
Servings: 4   **Cost:** $$$$

Photo on page 271

ARCTIC ARGID
Argis dentata

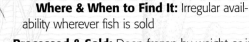

Where & When to Find It: Irregular availability wherever fish is sold

Processed & Sold: Deep-frozen by weight or in packages of 1 lb (454 g)

Cooking Method: Poached in a *court-bouillon* or steamed

Value: More delicate and fragile than the other types of shrimp, but excellent flavor

$$$$

Characteristics: Flexible shell with two spines in the middle and one on each side. Compressed body, and small close-set eyes pointing upwards

Habitat: North Atlantic

Grilled Shrimp with Saffron and Rouille Sauce

approx. 1 lb (480 g)	Shrimp (15 to 18 per pound, with the shell)
1 ¹/₂ to 2 tsp (6 to 8 g)	Saffron threads, chopped
¹/₂	Garlic clove, minced
1 ¹/₄ cups (300 mL)	Olive oil
ROUILLE SAUCE	
4	Egg yolks
3 Tbsp (40 mL)	Dijon mustard
To taste	Salt & pepper
1	Lemon (juice)

Preparation time: 20 minutes **Cooking time:** 10 minutes
Servings: 4 **Cost:** $$$$

- Thread the shrimp onto skewers, then sprinkle lightly with chopped saffron threads as well as the minced garlic. Brush with 3 Tbsp (50 mL) of olive oil and set aside.
- **Rouille Sauce**: Combine the egg yolks, Dijon mustard, salt, pepper and the lemon juice. Whisk, add saffron threads and chopped garlic. Let sit for about 15 minutes. During this step, the lemon juice helps the saffron to infuse the mixture. Emulsify with the remaining olive oil. Set aside.
- Grill the seasoned shrimp brochettes, careful not to brown them too much, which would give them a bitter taste.

Accompaniment: Mashed potatoes or boiled rice

274

NOTE: The shells can be left on or removed when preparing the shrimp. Both methods have their advantages. When the shells are left on, the shrimp stay soft. On the other hand, the meat cannot be grilled directly. When the shells are removed, the opposite is true.

Shrimp Mousse and Sugar Cane Shoots with Wild Rice, Five Spices and Star Anise Sauce

approx. 1 lb (500 g)	Shrimp for the mousse (small or mixed)
approx. 3 oz (100 g)	Flounder fillets
To taste	Salt & pepper
2	Eggs
2/3 cup (160 mL)	Cream (35%), cold
4 to 6	Sugar cane shoots
2/3 cup (160 mL)	Oyster sauce or clam juice
3/4 cup (180 mL)	Shrimp bisque (see Lobster bisque, in "Basic Ingredients for Some Recipes")
5 to 6 pieces	Star anise
approx. 1 cup (150 g)	Wild rice
4 tsp (12 g)	Five spice powder

- Chop the shrimp and the flounder fillets in a food processor, season with salt and pepper. Add the eggs, then the cream. Strain and set aside. Create a large dumpling with the shrimp mousse and surround with the sugar cane sticks. Refrigerate for 30 minutes; then, in a saucepan and using a basket steamer, poach covered for a few minutes before serving.

- **Sauce**: Boil the oyster sauce or the clam juice with the star anise for 10 minutes, then cover and let infuse. Heat the shrimp bisque and, in small quantities, add the star anise infusion until the desired taste has been obtained. Set aside and keep warm.

- **Wild rice**: Boil enough water to allow the rice to float freely. Add the five spice powder, the salt and the pepper. Cook the wild rice until it "bursts." Leave it in the cooking water and stop it from cooking further by adding ice cubes.

Presentation: Drain the rice, heat in a microwave, set the shrimp mousse on top and serve the sauce separately.

NOTE: What is five spice powder? It is a mixture of star anise, fennel, clove, cinnamon and Szechuan pepper.

Preparation time: 1 hour	**Cooking time:** 35 minutes
Servings: 4	**Cost:** $$$$

Photo on next page →

CRAYFISH
Orconectes

Where & When to Find It: Irregular availability wherever fish is sold

Processed & Sold: Whole live, and tails removed

Cooking Method: Poached in a *court-bouillon*, sautéed or in a sauce

Value: Of great culinary quality

Characteristics: Hard shell. Large, well-developed tail. Five pairs of legs, the first equipped with claws with elongated digits

Comments: This freshwater crustacean is remarkable for its fine taste; its flavor bursts in your mouth.

$$$

Habitat: Lakes of eastern North America

Crayfish Tail Gratin *

As needed	Court-bouillon (see "Basic Ingredients for Some Recipes")
2 ¼ lbs (1 kg)	River or lake crayfish, live
⅔ cup (100 g)	Butter
1 cup (100 g)	Shallots, minced
3 Tbsp (50 mL)	Cognac
½ cup (120 mL)	Good-quality dry white wine
1 ⅓ cup (320 mL)	Crayfish coulis (see "Basic Ingredients ...")
7 oz (200 mL)	Cream (35%)
To taste	Salt & pepper

- Boil the *court-bouillon*. Gut the crayfish and poach 1 to 2 minutes, drain and shell the tails. Keep the carcasses in the freezer to use at another time (for crayfish bisque or crayfish sauce).
- Cook the shallots in the butter until tender, add the crayfish tails and flambé in the cognac. Remove the crayfish and the sauce, set aside and keep warm. Add the white wine, reduce by half to remove any acidity and pour in the crayfish coulis.
- Whip the cream until stiff. Then, just before serving, carefully mix the whipped cream with the crayfish and the sauce. Adjust the seasoning. Choose four small round ceramic or copper plates (individual servings), then pour in equal parts of the crayfish *gratin* preparation.

- Bake in the oven at 325°F to 375°F (160°C) for 5 to 8 minutes to reheat the mixture, then, just before serving, broil for 2 minutes to form a *gratin*.

Presentation: Directly onto plates garnished with rice

* Dedicated to chef Carlo Dell'Ollio.

Preparation time: 1 hour	**Cooking time:** 15 to 20 minutes
Servings: 4	**Cost:** $$$$

LOBSTER
Homarus americanus

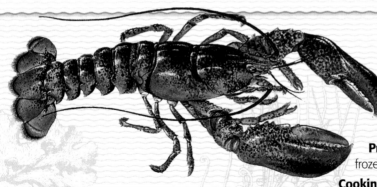

Processed & Sold: Whole live, deep-frozen tails, packaged or canned meat

Cooking Method: Grilled, roasted, poached, steamed, in the oven or in a ragout

Characteristics: Very hard shell. Large, very developed tail. Five pairs of legs, the first equipped with flat, wide claws, one much larger than the other

Habitat: Various Atlantic coastal areas

Where & When to Find It: Available all year round.

Comments: The lobster of the Magdalen Islands is considered the best.

$$$+ (depending on the season)

Braised Lobster *

9 cups (2.25 L)	Court-bouillon (see "Basic Ingredients for Some Recipes")
4 × 1 ¹/₂ lbs (675 g)	Live lobsters
¹/₂	Slice of bread
To taste	Thyme
2	Shallots *brunoise*
To taste	Salt & pepper
3 Tbsp (40 mL)	White wine
2 tsp (10 mL)	Cognac
³/₄ cup (120 g)	Whipped butter
1 cup (175 g)	Butter
1	Lemon (juice)
¹/₂ bunch	Chives, chopped

- Bring the *court-bouillon* to a boil and submerge the live lobsters one at a time so that they do not lose their meat. Cook for 2 to 3 minutes; let cool. Cut the lobsters in half and remove the meat from the body and the legs. Set the coral aside. Cut the lobster meat into large cubes.
- After removing the crust, pulverize the bread in a food processor. Add the thyme, shallots and the seasoning. Pour this bread-crumb mixture into a bowl and gradually add the white wine, coral, cognac and the whipped butter.
- Wash the lobster shells and dry. Spread the lobster meat into each half shell. Cover each half with the coral preparation. Bake in the

Preparation time: 40 minutes   **Cooking time:** 15 to 20 minutes
Servings: 4   **Cost:** $$$+

oven at 350°F (180°C) for 15 to 18 minutes. Place the two lobster halves on each plate and serve immediately.

- Accompany with clarified lemon butter, then garnish with the chives.
* Dedicated to chef Marcel Beaulieu.

Lobster Whisky Ragout with Small Vegetables

1 1/2 lbs (4 x 675 g)	Live lobsters
2	Shallots, chopped
approx. 1 cup (170 g)	Butter
To taste	Salt & pepper
3 Tbsp (45 mL)	Whisky
7 oz (200 mL)	White wine
10 oz (280 mL)	Lobster sauce (see "Basic Ingredients for Some Recipes")
7 oz (200 g)	Carrots
5 oz (150 g)	Zucchinis
7 oz (200 g)	Potatoes
As needed	Lemon juice

- Steam the lobsters for 3 to 4 minutes using a basket steamer; shell, and cut the meat into large cubes. Sweat the shallots in 4 1/2 Tbsp (50 g) of butter. Add the lobster meat and season.

- Flambé in the whisky. Add the white wine and reduce completely. Moisten with the lobster sauce and let simmer for 4 to 5 minutes. Remove the lobster meat from the sauce and set aside.
- Trim the carrot, zucchini and potato into the shape of an olive. In the liquid used to steam the lobsters, cook each vegetable separately in the order listed. Set the cooked vegetables aside.
- Thicken the cooking liquid with the remaining butter, then add the lemon juice to taste. Add the vegetables and the lobster meat, then set this ragout aside. Clean the lobster carcasses and heat them in the oven. Divide the hot ragout among the carcasses and serve immediately.

Preparation time: 40 minutes	**Cooking time:** 40 minutes
Servings: 4	**Cost:** $$$+

Photo on page 277

ROCK LOBSTER AND SPINY LOBSTER

Palinuridae
Incorrect name: lobster

Where & When to Find It: Seasonal availability, depending on the source; available all year round deep-frozen

Processed & Sold: Whole, tails deep-frozen along with the shell

Characteristics: Hard shell, very spiny. Long antennae, very strong at the base. Five pairs of legs. No claws

Cooking Method: Grilled, steamed, in a *court-bouillon* or in the oven

Value: Luxury crustacean

Habitat: South Atlantic (Caribbean)

$$$$$

Spiny Lobster Tails with Asian Aromatics

¹/₄ cup (60 mL)	Roasted sesame oil
¹/₂ cup (60 g)	Shallots, chopped
²/₃ cup (150 mL)	White wine
4 cups (1 L)	Coconut milk
2 Tbsp (40 g)	Lemongrass, finely sliced
2	Lime leaves, cut with scissors
1 ¹/₄ tsp (3 g)	Ginger powder
1 tsp (3 g)	Turmeric powder
12	Coriander seeds
14 oz (400 mL)	Lobster sauce* (see "Basic Ingredients for Some Recipes")
To taste	Salt & pepper
7 oz (4 x 200 g)	Spiny lobster tails

- Heat the sesame oil, then braise the shallots. Add the white wine, coconut milk and lemongrass, cut lime leaves, ginger powder, turmeric powder and coriander seeds. Cook until reduced by 50%. Add the lobster sauce and reduce until the desired consistency is obtained. Strain through cheesecloth or a fine mesh strainer and adjust the seasoning.
- Separate the tails from the shells and cook in the sauce at low heat, i.e., 175°F (80°C), for 5 to 8 minutes.
- Serve with a mixture of wild rice and white rice.

* Can also be made using spiny lobster shells.

Preparation time: 40 minutes **Cooking time:** 20 minutes
Servings: 4 **Cost:** $$$$

Spiny Lobster Tails in Red Wine

4	Celery stalks
2	Leeks (white part only)
7 oz (200 g)	White mushrooms
7 oz (200 g)	Carrots
approx. 1 1/4 cups (200 g)	Butter
approx. 1/2 cup (45 g)	Shallots, chopped
2 cups (500 mL)	Dry red wine
1 1/4 cups (300 mL)	Fish fumet (see "Basic Ingredients for Some Recipes")
As needed	Oil
2 3/4 lbs (1.2 kg)	Spiny lobster tails
4 tsp (20 mL)	brandy
To taste	Salt & pepper

- Cut the vegetables into a fine julienne and sweat in 2/3 cup (100 g) of butter, then set aside.

- Sweat the shallots in 1/4 cup (45 g) of butter. Add the red wine and reduce by half, then add the fish fumet and reduce by half.
- In the oil, sauté the spiny lobster tails, which have already been cut. Deglaze the saucepan with the brandy. Add everything to the red wine and fish fumet reduction. Cook for 6 to 7 minutes. Remove the spiny lobster tails from the cooking liquid. Using a spoon, scrape the meat from the carcasses, then set aside.
- Bind the sauce with the remaining butter, then season with salt and pepper. Arrange the julienned vegetables on the plates to form two semicircles that meet in the middle of the plate. Place the spiny lobster tails on the sides. Cover with the red wine sauce and serve.

Preparation time: 40 minutes **Cooking time:** 20 minutes
Servings: 4 **Cost:** $$$$$

NORWAY LOBSTER AND SCAMPI

Nephrops norvegicus

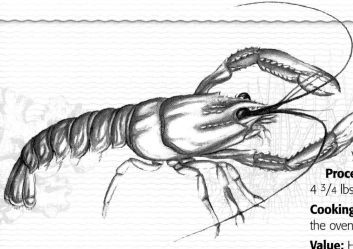

Characteristics: Reddish-yellow shell. Size varies from 6 to 10 inches (15 to 25 cm). Five pairs of legs

Habitat: North Atlantic

Where & When to Find It: Frozen, all year round wherever fish is sold

Processed & Sold: Frozen in bulk or in cans of 4 3/4 lbs (2.2 kg)

Cooking Method: Grilled, poached, steamed or in the oven

Value: High-quality crustacean

$$$$$

Scampi Fricassee with Puréed Lentils

10 oz (400 g)	Green or yellow lentils
1	Onion
1	Clove
1 sprig	Thyme
1	Bay leaf
To taste	Salt & pepper
3/4 cup (120 g)	Butter
1	Leek (white part only), julienned
2	Shallots *brunoise*
1 lb (450 g)	Scampi, shelled
1/4 cup (60 mL)	Sherry
1/2 cup (120 mL)	White wine
7 oz (200 mL)	Fish fumet (see "Basic Ingredients for Some Recipes")
7 oz (200 mL)	Lobster juice
3 1/2 oz (100 mL)	Cream (35%)

- Soak the lentils in a little water for at least 12 hours (note that some types of lentils do not need to soak). Transfer to a saucepan and cover with cold water. Heat, add the whole onion with the clove stuck in it, the thyme, bay leaf, salt and pepper. Bring to a boil and cook the lentils (the cooking time depends on the quality of the lentils). Purée the lentils in a food processor, then strain. Set this purée aside.

- In a saucepan, in 4 1/2 Tbsp (50 g) of butter, sweat the leek and the shallots. Add the scampi. Pour in the sherry and reduce completely. Add the wine and reduce completely. Remove the scampi from the saucepan and set aside.

- Add the fish fumet and lobster juice to the saucepan, then reduce by half. Incorporate the cream, and thicken the sauce with the remaining butter. Return the scampi to the sauce just before serving.

- Arrange the lentil purée in a ring around the plates, and place the scampi fricassee in the center. Serve immediately.

Preparation time: 40 minutes **Cooking time:** 20 minutes
Servings: 4   **Cost:** $$$$

Scampi Tails in Pernod

³/₄ cup (120 g)	Sweet butter
20	Scampi tails (9 to 12 per lb)
3 ¹/₂ oz (100 mL)	Pernod or Ricard
¹/₂ cup (120 mL)	Dry white wine
¹/₂ cup (60 g)	Shallots, minced
²/₃ cup (160 mL)	Cream (35%)
7 oz (200 mL)	Scampi sauce*
To taste	Salt & pepper

- Quickly heat the butter and sear the scampi tails, flambé with Pernod or Ricard, then remove the scampi tails, set aside and keep warm. Deglaze with the white wine and add the shallots. Cook for a few minutes, then add the cream and reduce by half, then pour in the scampi sauce. Let simmer for a few minutes and gently heat the scampi tails in the sauce. Adjust the seasoning and serve very hot.

Accompaniment: White rice

* Store the scampi shells in the freezer to eventually make a sauce. See Lobster Sauce ("Basic Ingredients for Some Recipes").

Preparation time: 20 minutes **Cooking time:** 15 minutes
Servings: 4   **Cost:** $$$$

Shellfish

SHELLFISH AND INVERTEBRATES

Unlike crustaceans, mollusks are animals that lack articulated appendages. They have a soft body, usually protected by a shell secreted by a skin fold in the body.

The Italians were the first to baptize shellfish "crustaceans," and other marine animals such as squid and sea urchins "fruit of the sea" for their fresh, flavorful taste.

There are three major groups of mollusks:

- *Lamellibranchia* have branchiae shaped like strips. Their soft body is protected by a bivalve shell that articulates around a hinge.
- *Gastropods* are univalve mollusks that have an unusual morphology; it is a class that includes several species.

This chapter concentrates on these two groups.

- *Cephalopods* are invertebrates. This group represents the most active and most evolved mollusks. They are characterized by 8 arms or more around their mouth. This important group is the subject of the next chapter.

In this chapter, we discuss univalve and bivalve shellfish of the Atlantic coast. We can find, however, from time to time, shellfish from the Pacific such as the abalone or the Pacific surf clam.

Common periwinkle

Common whelk

Cockle

Razor clam

American oyster

Atlantic surf clam

Blue mussel

Soft-shell clam

Abalone

Hard-shell clam

Scallop

Ocean quahog/ Iceland cyprine

COMMON PERIWINKLE

Littorina littorea
Incorrect name: whelk

Characteristics: Small round shell with a spiral shape. Opening trimmed with a small white lunule

Habitat: North Atlantic

Where & When to Find It: Irregular availability wherever fish is sold

Processed & Sold: With the shell

Cooking Method: In a *court-bouillon* with sea water (careful of the salt)

Value: A very delicate taste; either you like it or you don't.

Comments: In North America, there are approximately 20 species of periwinkles (common periwinkles). The small shellfish with the exclusive flavor that is used the most often is the common periwinkle from Europe.

$

Periwinkle Salad in Whelk Shells

1 ³/₄ lbs (800 g)	Common periwinkles in their shells
1 cup (100 g)	Carrots, julienned
¹/₂ cup (100 g)	Celeriac, julienned
approx. 1 cup (100 g)	Leek (white part only), julienned
¹/₄ cup (40 g)	Capers, chopped
²/₃ cup (85 g)	Onions *brunoise*
²/₃ cup (40 g)	Parsley, chopped
¹/₄ cup (60 mL)	Mayonnaise
1	Lemon (juice)
To taste	Salt & pepper
4	Whelk shells

Preparation time: 1 hour **Cooking time:** 10 to 30 minutes
Servings: 4   **Cost:** $$

- Wash the periwinkles several times, each time starting with fresh water to remove as much sand and dirt as possible. Cook the shellfish in a lot of unsalted water. Determine doneness by trying to remove a periwinkle from its shell using a pin; the cooking time will vary according to the size and origin of the periwinkles. Let the cooked shellfish cool in their cooking liquid. Extract the periwinkles from their shell, using a pin.
- Blanch the julienned vegetables separately, refresh, then drain. Combine the vegetables, capers, onions, parsley and the mayonnaise, then add the periwinkle meat.
- Add the lemon juice. Adjust the seasoning and put this salad into each whelk shell, arranged in such a way as to reproduce the shape of a horn of plenty.

Clam and Periwinkle Soup

approx. 1/4 lb (600 g)	Periwinkles with their shells
4 1/2 lbs (2 kg)	Clams
3 1/2 oz (100 mL)	White wine
9 cups (2.25 L)	Court-bouillon (see "Basic Ingredients for Some Recipes)
1	Shallot, chopped
1/3 cup (60 g)	Butter
1/3 cup (80 mL)	Dry white wine
2	Fresh tomatoes
14 oz (400 mL)	Cream (35%)
As needed	White roux (see "Basic Ingredients ...")
To taste	Salt & pepper

Preparation time: 1 hour **Cooking time:** 45 minutes
Servings: 8 **Cost:** $$

As needed	Parsley, chopped
As needed	Buttered croutons (Optional)

- Wash the periwinkles and boil for 2 to 3 minutes. Remove the periwinkles from their shells, using a pin. Set aside.
- In a saucepan, cook the clams with the white wine until they open; extract them from their shells. Heat the *court-bouillon* and strain through cheesecloth or a fine mesh strainer. Continue to cook the clams in the *court-bouillon*. Remove the cooked clams from the saucepan and reduce the *court-bouillon* by half. Purée the clams with the *court-bouillon* in a blender.
- Sweat the shallot in the butter. Add the white wine, and reduce completely. Moisten with the clam preparation and let simmer for 30 minutes. Blanch, peel and seed, then chop, the tomatoes.
- Reduce the cream by half and add the clam preparation. Bind this preparation with a little roux, if required, then strain through cheesecloth. Adjust the seasoning if necessary.
- Add the periwinkles to the soup when ready to serve, then add the parsley and the tomatoes. Serve this soup hot with small croutons sautéed in butter, if so desired.

Photo on next page →

COMMON WHELK, WAVED WHELK AND WHELK

Buccinidae

Incorrect name: periwinkle

Characteristics: Spiral-shaped shell. Opening rimmed in white

Habitat: North Atlantic

Where & When to Find It: If fresh, irregular availability wherever fish is sold; available all year round deep-frozen or canned

Processed & Sold: Canned; or in the shell, fresh or deep-frozen

Cooking Method: Pressure-cooked or boiled

Value: This shellfish is not well known, yet excellent.

Comments: Despite its long cooking time, the whelk remains a shellfish of choice. It should also be noted that the whelk has firm flesh which should be eaten raw or well cooked. The whelk is a member of a family that is among the most abundant and diverse of all the *Gastropods*, comprising more than 2,000 species.

$$

Whelk with Kelp and Clam Juice

8	Medium-sized whelks
1 cup (250 mL)	*Court-bouillon* (see "Basic Ingredients for Some Recipes")
1 Tbsp (12 g)	Dried kelp or 7 oz (200 g) fresh kelp (seaweed)
3 1/2 oz (100 mL)	White wine
2 1/3 cups (200 g)	Mushrooms, diced
As needed	Butter
4 Tbsp (30 g)	Dried shallots, chopped
1 cup (250 mL)	Clam juice
As needed	*Beurre manié* or white roux (see "Basic Ingredients …")
1 1/4 cups (300 mL)	Cream (35%)
1	Lemon (juice)
To taste	Salt & pepper

- Wash the whelks several times, always starting with fresh water; if necessary, parboil in salted water. Cook the whelks in a *court-bouillon* at moderate heat for 4 to 5 hours or longer, depending on the mollusks. Once they are cooked, let cool in the cooking liquid. Remove the cooked mollusks from their shells.

- Soak the kelp in the white wine for several minutes (if working with dried kelp). Blanch the mushrooms. Sweat the shallot, mushrooms and diced whelks in 1/2 cup (80 g) of butter. Add the seaweed and the white wine, then reduce to remove any acidity from the wine. Add the clam juice and the whelk cooking liquid. Let simmer for 10 minutes, then strain through cheesecloth or a fine mesh strainer. Set aside the solids and keep warm.

- Bind the sauce with the *beurre manié* or the roux. Add the previously reduced cream, then the lemon juice. Check the seasoning. Strain the sauce through the cheesecloth and pour over the solid ingredients. Thicken with the butter and serve this mixture very hot.

Preparation time: 40 minutes	**Cooking time:** 4 to 5 minutes
Servings: 4	**Cost:** $$

Whelk Salad with Hazelnuts and Pistachios

approx. ³/4 lb (320 g)	Whelks, shelled and cooked, deep-frozen or canned
¹/2 lb (240 g)	Firm white mushrooms
3	Lemons (juice)
¹/2 cup (80 g)	Pistachios, shelled
²/3 cup (80 g)	Hazelnuts, shelled
¹/2 cup (120 g)	Mayonnaise
To taste	Salt & pepper
4	Whelk shells, empty
4	Lettuce leaves
approx. ¹/3 cup (40 g)	Lovage, chopped

- Dice the firm, white mushrooms. Normally, a mushroom should not be washed, but peeled. White mushrooms do not like water.

- Cut the whelk into small cubes. Put the mushrooms into a container, sprinkle with the juice from two lemons and set aside in the refrigerator.[*] Thinly slice the pistachios and the hazelnuts. A few minutes before serving, combine the mayonnaise and the whelks, mushrooms, sliced hazelnuts and pistachios. Add the remaining lemon juice as needed. Adjust the seasoning.
- Stand an empty whelk shell upright on a plate. In the opening, place one lettuce leaf and spoon the whelk salad onto the leaf. Sprinkle with the chopped lovage.

[*] The acid from the lemon will tenderize the whelks and keep the mushrooms white.

Preparation time: 20 minutes	
Servings: 4	**Cost:** $$$

Photo on page 291

COCKLE

Clinocardium ciliatum
Incorrect name: soft-shell clam

Cooking Method: In cream, soups, served in its shell or in a sauce

Comments: Cockles are part of a group of more than 200 species. The types most often found in North American waters include the Iceland cockle (*Clinocardium ciliatum*), the northern dwarf cockle (*Cerastoderma pinnulatum*) and the Greenland cockle (*Serripes groenlandicus*). They are excellent served raw.

$$$

Characteristics: Bivalve shellfish, with several grooves in its shell

Habitat: North Atlantic and the Pacific

Where & When to Find It: All year round since, like mussels, cockles are farmed shellfish

Processed & Sold: Whole, deep-frozen or canned

Cockle with Pastry Squares and Lemongrass

3 ¹/₄ lbs (1.5 kg)	Live cockles with their shells
7 oz (200 mL)	Cockle, soft-shell clam or mussel juice (commercial)
As needed	White roux (see "Basic Ingredients for Some Recipes")
¹/₂ lb (240 g)	Firm white mushrooms
As needed	Butter
1 ¹/₂ cups (160 g)	Fresh glasswort
²/₃ cup (160 mL)	Cream (35%)
2	Limes (juice)
To taste	Salt & pepper
approx. 1 cup (120 g)	Lemongrass, chopped
4	Baked puff pastry squares, purchased at a pastry shop

- Place the cockles in a fairly large saucepan and add 7 oz (200 mL) of water. Cover and cook for a few minutes so that the cockles open. Extract the meat and strain the juice, taking care to ensure that there is no sand. Set the meat aside.
- Add 7 oz (200 mL) of cockle, clam or mussel juice to the cooking juice. Bind with white roux. Cook for about 10 minutes. Strain through cheesecloth or a fine mesh strainer. Set aside.
- Cut the mushrooms into small cubes and sauté in the butter until all the liquid has evaporated. Set aside.
- Blanch the glasswort and refresh. Drain and set aside.

294

- Reheat the sauce, add the cream, and reduce until the desired consistency is obtained; incorporate the lime juice and adjust the seasoning. Add the mushrooms, glasswort, lemongrass and, lastly, the cockles. Let simmer gently (without boiling).
- Heat the puff pastry squares. Garnish and serve hot.

Preparation time: 40 minutes	**Cooking time:** 15 to 20 minutes
Servings: 4	**Cost:** $$$

Photo on next page →

Cockles in the Shell and Garden Herb Sauce

1/2 cup (120 mL)	Dry white wine
4 Tbsp (30 g)	Shallots, chopped
48	Small cockles
approx. 2/3 cup (160 mL)	Crustacean coulis or sauce (see Lobster coulis in "Basic Ingredients for Some Recipes")
approx. 3/4 cup (150 g)	Butter
As needed	Coarse salt
approx. 3 oz (100 g)	Spinach
2 oz (60 g)	Sorrel
6	Lettuce leaves
1/2 cup (30 g)	Curly parsley
1/2 cup (30 g)	Chervil
To taste	Salt & pepper
As needed	White bread crumbs

- In a fairly large saucepan, combine the cockles, white wine and shallots with 3 1/2 oz (100 mL) of water. Cover the saucepan and let the cockles open. Let cool and remove the meat from the shells and set the meat aside.

- Reduce the cooking juice by 9/10, then add the crustacean coulis or sauce. Let simmer for about 10 minutes. Strain through cheesecloth or a fine mesh strainer. Place 2/3 cup (100 g) of butter knobs on top, set aside and keep warm.
- Wash the cockles and place in an ovenproof dish in which coarse salt has been sprinkled. This will help to keep the cockle shells upright.
- Wash the spinach, sorrel, lettuce, curly parsley and chervil, then roughly chop in a food processor. With the remaining butter, cook in a saucepan until all the liquid has evaporated. Season.
- In the bottom of each shell, place a spoonful of herbs, then the shellfish. Cover with sauce. Sprinkle with the bread crumbs and bake in the oven. Serve in the shell.

Preparation time: 30 minutes	**Cooking time:** 10 to 12 minutes
Servings: 4	**Cost:** $$$

RAZOR CLAM

Ensis directus

Characteristics: Bivalve mollusk. Pale green shell, curved and thin, longer than it is wide, and shiny

Habitat: North Atlantic

Where & When to Find It: Fresh or deep-frozen wherever fish is sold

Processed & Sold: Whole with the shell, fresh, deep-frozen raw or canned

Cooking Method: Steamed, in a cream soup or in a sauce.

Value: Surprising taste, delicate and subtle (between that of a scallop and an oyster)

Comments: Razor clams (*Solenidae*) have elongated shells in a grayish-green shade.

$$

Razor Clams with Crushed Tomatoes and Onions *

approx. 1 cup (120 g)	Spanish onions or shallots, chopped
2	Garlic cloves, chopped
3 Tbsp (50 mL)	Virgin olive oil
3 cups (320 g)	Tomatoes, crushed
1 cup (250 mL)	White wine
To taste	Salt & pepper
approx. 3/4 lb (320 g)	Razor clam meat, top grade (i.e., better part of the meat)
4	Lettuce leaves
1/2 cup (20 g)	Chives, cut with scissors

- Gently drop the onions and the garlic into the olive oil. Add the crushed tomatoes.
- Add the wine, then season with salt and pepper. Let simmer for 15 minutes.
- Add the razor clams once the preceding mixture has come to a boil and turn off the heat immediately. Let cool.
- Arrange the lettuce in the bottom of the plate, then place the clam-tomato-onion mixture on top. Sprinkle with the cut chives.

* Dedicated to chef Claude Cyr.

Preparation time: 10 minutes **Cooking time:** 8 to 10 minutes
Servings: 4   **Cost:** $$$

Razor Clam with Garlic Cream

7 oz (200 mL)	Cream (35%)
1/2 lb (120 g)	Garlic butter (see Garlic cream in "Basic Ingredients for Some Recipes")
To taste	Salt & pepper
1	Lemon (juice)
approx. 3/4 lb (320 g)	Razor clam meat, top grade*

- Heat the cream, then reduce by 25%. Incorporate the garlic butter; do not heat above 200°F (100°C). This step binds the cream.

- Season to taste. Add the lemon juice.
- Just before serving, incorporate the clams into the sauce and set aside.
- This razor clam and garlic cream mixture goes very well with pasta (spaghetti, small shells or macaroni).

* The meat of the razor clam can easily be divided inside the shell: "top grade" refers to the better part of the meat, while "second grade" refers to the digestive tract.

Preparation time: 10 minutes   **Cooking time:** 5 to 8 minutes
Servings: 4   **Cost:** $$$

AMERICAN OYSTER

Crassostrea virginica

Incorrect names: Malpeque oyster, Caraquet oyster

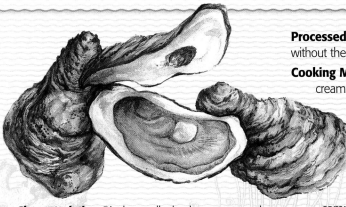

Processed & Sold: Whole with the shell or fresh without the shell

Cooking Method: Cooked with the shell, in a cream soup or steamed

Value: Raw, hot or cold, either you like it or you don't.

Comments: Some of the better-known types are the popularly named Malpeque and the Caraquet oysters. Other types can now be found commercially: flat oysters (*Ostrea edulis*)— European flat oyster; giant oysters (*Crassostrea gigas*)—Portuguese oysters.

$$$$

Characteristics: Bivalve mollusk whose upper valve is larger and flatter than its lower valve. Irregular and rough shell

Habitat: North Atlantic

Where & When to Find It: Now available all year round, but oysters are best when fresh, in the fall— during all the months that end in "r": September, October, etc.

Hot Oysters in White Wine with Mushrooms *

24	Giant oysters
1 ¼ cup (200 g)	Sweet butter
1 cup (220 mL)	Dry white wine
To taste	Salt & pepper
2 cups (250 g)	Firm white mush-rooms, chopped
2	Shallots, minced
As needed	White roux (see "Basic Ingredients for Some Recipes")
3	Egg yolks
As needed	Chervil leaves

- Shuck the raw oysters and filter their water by straining through cheesecloth or a fine mesh strainer. Set aside.
- Wash the inside of the empty valves of the shells. Set aside.
- In a saucepan, combine 2 ½ Tbsp (30 g) of butter, the filtered oyster juice and the white wine. Season with pepper, but do not add salt. Heat to 175°F (80°C); at that point, poach the oysters for a few seconds just to stiffen. Drain on a paper towel.
- With 2 ½ Tbsp (30 g) of butter, cook the chopped mushrooms until all the liquid has evaporated. Season lightly with salt and pepper. Set aside.

- In a sauté pan, cook the chopped shallots in ¹/₃ cup (60 g) of butter until tender, then add the poaching liquid from the oysters. Bind lightly with a little white roux (the mixture must remain syrupy). Strain through cheesecloth or a fine mesh strainer.
- Beat the egg yolks vigorously, then incorporate the remaining butter and the preceding sauce. Keep at 175°F (80°C). Adjust the seasoning.

Presentation: In the bottom of each shell, spoon ¹/₂ tsp (3 mL) of mushrooms, then the oyster and cover with sauce. Heat in the oven. When ready to serve, sprinkle with chervil.
* Dedicated to chef Raymond Ferry.
NOTE: To stand the oyster shells upright, cover a plate with a layer of coarse salt.

Preparation time: 30 minutes **Cooking time:** 10 minutes
Servings: 4   **Cost:** $$$$

Oyster Cream

1 ¹/₄ cups (300 mL)	Cream (35%)
7 oz (200 mL)	White chicken stock (see "Basic Ingredients for Some Recipes")
7 oz (200 mL)	Clam (hard shell or soft shell) or oyster juice
¹/₃ cup (70 g)	White rice
¹/₂ cup (70 g)	Firm white mushrooms, chopped
36	Oysters in the shell (Malpeque or Caraquet)
To taste	Salt & pepper
1	Egg
1	Lemon (juice)
6 Tbsp (70 g)	Butter
¹/₃ cup (20 g)	Chervil, cut with scissors

- Reduce the cream by half. Set aside.
- In a saucepan, at moderate heat, gently cook the chicken stock and the clam or oyster juice with the rice for 15 to 20 minutes, then add the chopped mushrooms and cook for another 5 to 8 minutes. While cooking, shuck the oysters, place them in a saucepan and, at very low heat, "reheat" them, i.e., stiffen them so that they contract.
- Drain on a paper towel and pour the juice in the saucepan containing the chicken stock.
- In a blender, emulsify the mixture, season with salt and pepper, then strain through cheesecloth or a fine mesh strainer. Reheat, but do not boil. Retain at approximately 175°F (80°C). Combine the egg yolk, the cream and the lemon juice, then incorporate this mixture into the oyster juice. At the last moment, add the butter.

Presentation: In a bowl or soup dish, spread the stiffened oysters, pour in the oyster cream and sprinkle with chervil.

Preparation time: 30 to 40 minutes
Cooking time: 25 to 35 minutes
Servings: 4   **Cost:** $$$$

Photo on page 297

ATLANTIC SURF CLAM AND SURF CLAM

Spisula solidissima
Incorrect names: cockle and soft-shell clam

Where & When to Find It: Currently, available only deep-frozen

Processed & Sold: Fresh with the shell, without the shell, frozen and canned

Cooking Method: Steamed or pressure-cooked

Value: Excellent raw in a salad, cooked or in a sauce

Comments: The Atlantic surf clam is part of a family of 24 Atlantic species. More than 80% of clams harvested in North America are surf clams. The Stimpson's surf clam is a delicacy.

Characteristics: Bivalve mollusk that has a large shell with several fine grooves

$$

Habitat: North Atlantic

Shellfish and Crustacean Timbales *

7 oz (200 mL)	Dry sparkling wine
1 cup (250 mL)	Crustacean fumet (see "Basic Ingredients for Some Recipes")
To taste	Salt & pepper
approx. 3 oz (100 g)	Small scallops with coral, raw
approx. 3 oz (100 g)	Stimpson's surf clam tongues, raw
approx. 3 oz (100 g)	Snow crab claws, cooked
approx. 3 oz (100 g)	Whelk meat, cooked
1/3 cup (100 g)	Green peas
1 1/4 cups (100 g)	Chanterelle mushrooms
approx. 1/2 cup (75 g)	Butter
3/4 cup (160 g)	Rice
As needed	White roux (see "Basic Ingredients …")
7 oz (200 mL)	Cream (35%)

- In a sufficiently wide saucepan, pour in the sparkling wine and the crustacean fumet, then place a basket steamer in the pot. Bring to a boil. Season the small scallops and coral and the Stimpson's surf clam tongues with salt and pepper. Spread the clam tongues on the bottom of the basket steamer and, after one minute of boiling, cover on, remove the clams immediately and spread out on a paper towel. Repeat this step with the small scallops, but cook for no more than 30 seconds.

- *Caution*: This step is very important. If the meat of such a delicacy is overcooked, it will become too tough.
- Drain the crab claws and the diced whelk and spread out on a paper towel to absorb as much moisture as possible.
- In the crustacean fumet and the sparkling wine, poach the crunchy green peas. Drain and set aside. Sauté the chanterelle mushrooms in butter, season with salt and pepper. Drain and set aside. Cook the white rice in salted water. There should be enough water to allow the grains of rice to move about.

- Bind the cooking stock with the white roux. Finish with the cream. Adjust the seasoning and strain through cheesecloth or a fine mesh strainer. Combine all the ingredients in the sauce, let simmer gently (175°F or 80°C) and serve with the hot white rice.

* This recipe is dedicated to Mr. and Mrs. Rail, who are always preparing seafood and researching answers to requests received from chefs.

Preparation time: 30 minutes	Cooking time: 10 to 12 minutes
Servings: 4	Cost: $$$$

Stimpson's Surf Clam Tongues with Roasted Hazelnuts

16	Orange muscles from the Stimpson's surf clam, raw
3	Lemons (juice)
3 1/2 oz (100 mL)	Clam juice (hard-shell, soft-shell or surf clam)*
1/2 cup (120 mL)	Hazelnut oil
1/3 cup (20 g)	Chervil
1/3 cup (20 g)	Flat-leafed or curly parsley
1 1/4 cups (20 g)	Sorrel
2/3 cup (60 g)	Hazelnuts
To taste	Salt & pepper

- Using a knife, finely slice the Stimpson's surf clam tongue one hour before serving. Add the juice of 2 lemons, the hard-shell, soft-shell or surf clam juice, and the hazelnut oil, and store in the refrigerator.
- Mince the aromatic herbs (chervil, parsley and sorrel) and the hazelnuts, using a knife. Just before serving, add these to the clams. Taste, season, then add, as needed, the juice of the third lemon, season with salt and pepper and serve on a bed of chopped green papaya or on a lettuce leaf.

* Small bottles of hard-shell, soft-shell and surf clam juice can be found where fish is sold.

Preparation time: 15 to 20 minutes	
Servings: 4	Cost: $$

Photo on next page →

BLUE MUSSEL AND EDIBLE MUSSEL

Mytilus edulis

Processed & Sold: Live with the shell, canned in its own juice without the shell

Cooking Method: Lightly moistened, steamed or in a sauce

Value: High-quality shellfish

Comments: In North America, there are approximately 40 members in the mussel family. In the past, cleaning rock mussels was difficult, but mussels farmed in the sea are much easier to clean.

$$$

Characteristics: Bivalve mollusk in a black shell with blue highlights

Habitat: North Atlantic

Where & When to Find It: All year round, depending on the source, wherever fish is sold

Moules Marinière

7 oz (200 mL)	Dry white wine (e.g., Muscadet)
³/₄ cup (80 g)	Shallots, minced
To taste	Ground pepper
6 Tbsp (70 g)	Sweet butter
2 ¹/₄ to 2 ³/₄ lbs (1 to 1.2 kg)	Small cultured mussels
²/₃ cup (40 g)	Parsley, minced

- Firstly, the presentation: A burner in the center of the table or a side table will be necessary to keep the mussels warm in their shells. They cool quickly once they are on the plate. A small bowl is also required beside each plate for the cooking stock.
- Use a fairly large saucepan as the mussels must be completely covered with water. Pour in the wine, add the shallots, pepper and butter. Wash the mussels, drain in a strainer, then place in the saucepan. Cover and cook at high heat. From time to time, stir the mussels so that they can open uniformly. The mussels must not be overcooked. Wait to seat your guests at the table before beginning to cook, and add the parsley at the last minute.
- Place the mussels a few at a time in a hot soup dish for each guest, then pour the cooking juice into small hot bowls. Every time a mussel is eaten in its shell, a spoonful of the juice can be taken from the bowl.

Preparation time: 10 to 15 minutes
Cooking time: 7 to 8 minutes
Servings: 4   **Cost:** $$$

Blue Mussel Pithiviers *with*
Saffron Sauce and Saltwater Cordgrass

10 oz (300 g)	Firm white mushrooms
¾ cup (120 g)	Sweet butter
To taste	Salt & pepper
7 oz (200 mL)	Dry white wine
½ cup (60 g)	Shallots, chopped
2 ¼ to 2 ¾ lbs (1 to 1.2 kg)	Blue mussels
As needed	Saffron threads
As needed	White roux (see "Basic Ingredients for Some Recipes")
1 cup (240 mL)	Cream (35%)
1 cup (160 g)	Saltwater cordgrass
¾ lb (350 g)	Puff pastry
1	Egg yolk

- Finely slice the mushrooms. Wash, and sauté in ⅓ cup (60 g) of sweet butter until all the liquid has evaporated. Season with salt and pepper. Set aside.
- In a fairly wide, large saucepan, pour the white wine and the shallots. Add the mussels, cover and cook at high heat so that the mussels open. As soon as they do, remove from the heat. Let cool, shell and set aside in the refrigerator.
- **Sauce**: Strain the mussel juice through cheesecloth or a fine mesh strainer, add a few saffron threads, and boil. Bind with the white roux, add the cream and cook until the desired consistency is obtained.
- Strain again and set aside.

NOTE: These 3 steps can be done the night before as these ingredients should be cold to prepare the *pithiviers*.

- On the day the mussels are to be cooked, bring the saltwater cordgrass to a boil and drain. Combine with the mussels, mushrooms and 2 Tbsp (30 mL) of cold sauce. Adjust the seasoning.
- Roll out the puff pastry, cut out 8 circles 4 inches (10 cm) in diameter. On 4 of the circles, place 2 large spoonfuls of the preceding preparation. Brush the surrounding pastry with the beaten egg yolk and a little water, and place another slightly larger pastry circle on top of the first and crimp the edges. Place in an ovenproof dish and refrigerate for at least 1 hour.
- Heat the sauce and combine with the remaining mushroom-mussel-saltwater cordgrass preparation. Keep warm.
- Heat the oven to 500°F (260°C). Using a small brush, brush the *pithiviers* with the egg glaze. Put in the hot oven to brown the pastry.
- As soon as the pastry is slightly hard and golden, lower the oven temperature to 300°F (150°C) and cover the dish with aluminum foil.

Presentation: In the bottom of each plate, pour a little sauce with the garnish, then place a hot *pithiviers* on top.

Preparation time: 1 hour, 30 minutes
Cooking time: 30 minutes
Servings: 4   Cost: $$$

Photo on page 305

CLAM, SOFT-SHELL CLAM AND STEAMER CLAM

Mya arenaria

Incorrect names: cockle, hard-shell clam and quahog

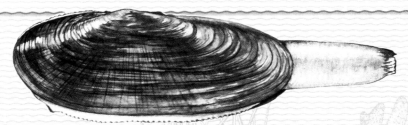

Characteristics: Bivalve mollusk in a whitish oval shell, with a few circular folds

Habitat: North Atlantic

Where & When to Find It: Rarely fresh, often canned

Processed & Sold: Fresh with the shell; frozen or canned without the shell

Cooking Method: Steamed or in a sauce

Value: Excellent raw, in soup or in a salad

Comments: The *Myacidae* family includes the edible clam (*Mya arenaria*) from Eastern Canada, (*Mya brenaria*) from the United States, and the plump clam from the Pacific coast (*Platyodon cancellatus*).

$$

Spaghetti with Clams and Cream Sauce

3 × 14 oz (398 mL)	Clams, canned
	or
2 ¹/₂ to 2 ³/₄ lbs (1 to 1.2 kg)	Fresh clams
1 cup (250 mL)	Cream (35%)
approx. ²/₃ cup (160 mL)	Clam juice (commercially available)
As needed	White roux (see "Basic Ingredients for Some Recipes")
¹/₂ lb (250 g)	Spaghetti of choice*
To taste	Salt & pepper
1 cup (60 g)	Parsley, chopped

Preparation time: 30 minutes **Cooking time:** 15 to 30 minutes
Servings: 4 **Cost:** $$$

- If the clams are fresh, cook them like *moules marinière* in a wide saucepan with a little water. *Caution:* The shell is very fragile. When removing the meat, check that there are no bits of shell. Set the clams aside on a paper towel.
- Strain the juice through a small strainer.
- Reduce the cream by half, then add the two clam juices. Bind like a sauce with the white roux and strain through cheesecloth or a fine mesh strainer. Incorporate the clams and keep warm (175°F or 80°C).
- Cook the spaghetti, then mix with the clam sauce. Adjust the seasoning and serve in soup dishes. Sprinkle with chopped parsley.

* Different types of spaghetti can be used: squid ink, spinach or herb.

Clam Soup with Angel Hair Pasta and Pink Shrimp

4	Dried tree-ear mushrooms
³/₄ lb (350 g)	Soya vermicelli (angel hair pasta)
1 can	Soft-shell clams in their own juice
approx. 5 oz (160 g)	Pink shrimp, cooked
As needed	Peanut oil
1	Onion, minced
1	Green onion, cut with scissors
¹/₂	Garlic clove, minced
To taste	Salt & pepper
1 tsp (5 mL)	Nuoc mam (Vietnamese fish sauce)
2 ¹/₂ cups (600 mL)	Shrimp or soft-shell clam bouillon (commercially available)
1 tsp (5 g)	Sugar
12	Fresh coriander leaves

- Rehydrate the tree-ear mushrooms in a bowl of warm water.
- Soak the vermicelli in cold water for 12 minutes, then boil for 4 to 6 minutes (be careful not to overcook).
- Drain the clams and the pink shrimp.
- In a little oil, cook the onions, shallot and chopped garlic until tender. Season with salt and pepper. Add the nuoc mam and the shrimp or clam bouillon and let gently simmer.
- Slice the tree-ear mushrooms into fine strips, then mix with the soya vermicelli. Form 4 nests with this preparation and reheat in a microwave oven just before serving.
- Also, just before serving, add the sugar to the bouillon, and add the clams and the shrimp. Adjust the seasoning. Do not let this reach boiling point as the clams and the shrimp will become too tough.

Presentation: In the middle of a soup dish, place the vermicelli. Surround with the shrimp or clam bouillon and sprinkle with the coriander leaves.

Preparation time: 25 minutes **Cooking time:** 15 minutes
Servings: 4   **Cost:** $$$$

Photo on next page →

ABALONE

Haliotis sp.

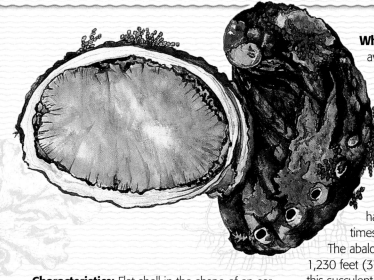

Where & When to Find It: Rarely available

Processed & Sold: Whole and shelled

Cooking Method: Sautéed, braised or in a sauce

Value: High-quality shellfish, excellent raw

Comments: There are no abalone on the Atlantic coast. This shellfish, harvested by man since prehistoric times, is one of the "gastronomic pearls." The abalone clings to rocks and can live up to 1,230 feet (375 m) below the surface. Fishing of this succulent shellfish is heavily regulated.

$$$$$

Characteristics: Flat shell in the shape of an ear, with several holes near the edge

Habitat: Pacific

Abalone Escalopes with Persillade

8 to 16	Abalone (depending on the size)
As needed	White vinegar
2/3 cup (100 g)	Sweet butter
As needed	Flour
2	Garlic cloves, minced
1/3 cup (20 g)	Parsley, chopped
2 1/2 Tbsp (10 g)	Chervil, chopped
To taste	Salt & pepper
As needed	Lemons

- Remove the abalone from the shells. Wash in the water and vinegar solution to extract the mucus. If the abalone are large, wrap in a cloth or paper towel and tap with a small wooden mallet to tenderize them. Next, cut the abalone into escalopes.

- Heat the butter, flour the escalopes and cook until each side is nicely golden. Remove from the cooking butter and from the heat. Add the garlic, parsley and chervil (*persillade*), season with salt and pepper, then cover the abalone escalopes with the *persillade*.

- Serve very hot, with lemon wedges served separately.

Accompaniment: Glasswort sautéed in butter

Preparation time: 30 minutes	**Cooking time:** 15 minutes
Servings: 4	**Cost:** $$$$

Pan-Roasted Abalone with Artichokes

8	Large abalone
4	Medium-sized artichokes, diced or cut into strips
14 oz (400 g)	Mini potatoes
1/2 cup (60 mL)	Peanut oil
approx. 2/3 cup (120 g)	Butter
To taste	Coarse sea salt
As needed	Flour
2/3 cup (160 mL)	Brown veal stock (see "Basic Ingredients for Some Recipes")
As needed	Chervil leaves

- Remove the abalone from their shells, wash and tenderize (see preceding recipe).
- Cook the artichokes in a lot of salted water, refresh, remove the leaves and keep in the cooking liquid.
- Blanch the mini potatoes, then sauté with the peanut oil and 1/3 cup (60 g) of butter, sprinkle with the coarse sea salt and bake at 300°F (150°C).
- Cut the abalone into escalopes, flour and cook *à la meunière* in 1/3 cup (60 g) of butter. Remove the abalone and keep warm. In the same butter, heat the artichokes.

Presentation: Place the artichoke cubes or strips in the bottom of the plate, then arrange the abalone escalopes on top. Surround with the mini potatoes. Pour the bound brown veal stock over the abalone and finish with the chervil leaves.

Preparation time: 45 minutes **Cooking time:** 15 to 30 minutes
Servings: 4   **Cost:** $$$$

313

HARD-SHELL CLAM AND QUAHOG

Venus mercenaria

Incorrect names: cockle, soft-shell clam

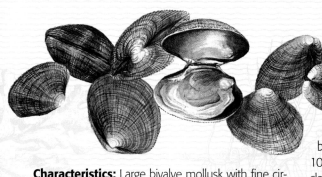

Processed & Sold: Whole with or without the shell

Cooking Method: Steamed or in a sauce

Value: Excellent raw

Comments: The hard-shell clam is a member of the *Veneridae* family that includes about 100 species. The true name of this clam is northern clam-quahog (*Mercenaria mercenaria*) (Canada and Florida). There is also the southern clam-quahog (*Mercenaria campechiensis*) (Virginia and Florida).

$$

Characteristics: Large bivalve mollusk with fine circular grooves on its shell

Habitat: North Atlantic

Where & When to Find It: Irregular availability wherever fish is sold

Clam Soup with Kombu Seaweed and Tree-Ear Mushrooms

3 Tbsp (15 g)	Dried kombu seaweed (kelp)
1 1/4 cups (300 mL)	Hard-shell clam juice
1 1/2 cups (160 g)	Raw potato, diced small
24	Average-sized hard-shell clams
14 oz (398 mL)	Tree-ear mushrooms (canned)
1	Lime (juice)
2 tsp (10 mL)	Soya sauce
To taste	Salt & pepper

- Rehydrate the seaweed in the clam juice, then gently cook the diced potato in the same juice.
- In a saucepan, with a little water, open the clams, recover the meat and add the juice to the preceding preparation.
- When the potatoes are cooked, using a whisk, emulsify until the excess starch is released and will easily bind the soup. Add the drained tree-ear mushrooms, the clams, lime juice and soya sauce to the soup.
- Adjust the seasoning and serve very hot.

Preparation time: 30 minutes **Cooking time:** 20 minutes
Servings: 4 **Cost:** $$$

Bacon and Clams with Hollandaise Sauce

4	Bacon slices
24	Average-sized hard-shell clams
4	Bread slices
1	Garlic clove
To taste	Coarse salt
1/2 cup (120 mL)	Hollandaise sauce (see "Basic Ingredients …")

- In a microwave oven, between several sheets of paper towel, cook the bacon, then cut into fine strips.
- Open the clams in a saucepan, while letting them cook sufficiently. Remove the meat from the shells and save.

- Find the best-looking shells (24); wash and dry them. Save.
- In a toaster, toast the 4 slices of bread, cut in half diagonally, then rub with the garlic. Keep warm.

Presentation: In a soup dish, pour the coarse salt, then place a paper doily on top. Push the six shells per plate into the paper doily and salt so that they remain upright. In each shell, lay a few strips of bacon, then arrange the clams and cover each clam with 1 tsp (5 mL) of hot hollandaise sauce.

Preparation time: 30 minutes	**Cooking time:** 15 minutes
Servings: 4	**Cost:** $$$

SCALLOP
Pectinidae

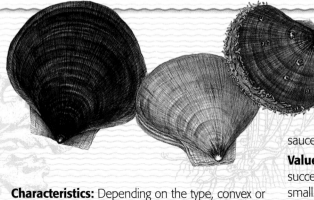

Where & When to Find It: All year round, depending on fishing cycles

Processed & Sold: Whole and live with the shell, without the shell but with the coral or the muscle only

Cooking Method: Grilled, steamed, in a sauce or poached

Value: In Europe, Coquille St. Jacques is a culinary success. On the European coast, the scallop is very small. In North America, the scallop is king and larger than the Coquille St. Jacques. It can also be eaten raw.

Characteristics: Depending on the type, convex or flat valves, numerous threadlike or irregular grooves and not very scaly

Habitat: North Atlantic

$$$$

Scallop Mousseline *with Coral Cream*

approx. 1 lb (500 g)	**Scallop meat with the coral**
To taste	**Salt & pepper**
1	**Egg white**
7 oz (200 mL)	**Cream (35%)**
2/3 cup (100 g)	**Butter**
7 oz (200 mL)	**Fish *velouté* (see "Basic Ingredients for Some Recipes"), lightly bound**

- Separate the coral from the scallop muscle.
- Dry the scallop muscle. Chop in a food processor. Season with salt and white pepper, incorporate the egg white, then the very cold cream.

- With the whipped butter, brush 4 ovenproof ramekins. Fill each one with the preceding preparation and gently cook in a *bain-marie*, in the oven at 350°F (180°C) for 15 to 25 minutes.
- Transfer the scallop coral to a blender. Heat the lightly bound fish *velouté* and gradually incorporate the coral, tasting regularly as the coral has a strong flavor. Strain through cheesecloth or a fine mesh strainer. Keep warm.

Presentation: Turn the scallop *mousseline* out of the mold and place in the bottom of the dish. Cover with sauce.

Accompaniment: Rice pilaf, boiled rice or boiled potatoes

Preparation time: 30 minutes	**Cooking time:** 15 to 25 minutes
Servings: 4	**Cost:** $$$$

Fishmonger's Scallop Crown

8	Fresh tomatoes
1/2 cup (90 g)	Butter
1	Onion, chopped
2 1/3 cups (280 g)	White mushrooms, finely sliced
To taste	Salt & pepper
1 lb (450 g)	Scallop meat
As needed	Parsley, chopped
2	Sweet basil leaves, chopped
1 cup (250 mL)	*Mousseline* sauce* (see "Basic Ingredients for Some Recipes")
As needed	Steamed potatoes (Optional)

- Blanch, peel and seed the tomatoes, then chop. Brown the onion in 1/3 cup (60 g) of butter. Add the tomatoes and the mushrooms. Season with salt and pepper, and cook to remove as much moisture as possible, then set aside.

- With the remaining butter, grease the bottom of an ovenproof dish and place the shelled scallops, cut in half, in the dish. Broil at high heat for 1 to 2 minutes, depending on the thickness.

- Reheat the tomato and mushroom preparation. Add the parsley and the basil, then arrange this preparation in a ring around on the plates. Place the scallops on the vegetables.

- Cover the scallops with a little *mousseline* sauce. Glaze under the broiler and serve immediately with the steamed potatoes.

* If the sauce is not used immediately, set aside in a warm place as it does not tolerate wide swings in temperature.

Preparation time: 20 minutes	**Cooking time:** 20 to 30 minutes
Servings: 4	**Cost:** $$$$

OCEAN QUAHOG
Arctica islandica

Characteristics: Bivalve mollusk with an almost perfectly round shell, decorated with grooves radiating out from the center

Habitat: North Atlantic

Where & When to Find It: Very rarely on the market

Processed & Sold: Whole, with the shell or deep-frozen meat

Cooking Method: Steamed, pressure-cooked or canned

Value: Delicate taste

Comments: This shellfish with the orange meat is a member of the *Articidae*. Its true name is "Iceland cyprine."

$$

Iceland Cyprines with Sea Urchin Sabayon

24	Iceland cyprines or northern quahogs
2/3 cup (150 mL)	White wine
1/4 cup (40 g)	Shallots, chopped
24	Sea urchin roe
2/3 cup (140 mL)	Melted butter, warm
To taste	Salt & pepper

- In a large saucepan with a little water, open the cyprines, extract the muscles and keep on a paper towel.
- Recover the cyprine juice, add the white wine and the shallots. Reduce by half. Let cool until still warm. Whisk the sea urchin roe vigorously, and strongly emulsify. Gradually incorporate the melted butter. Strain through cheesecloth or a fine mesh strainer. Adjust the seasoning.

Presentation: In a small gratin dish, place the cyprines and cover with the sea urchin sabayon.

Accompaniment: Boiled white rice

Preparation time: 20 minutes	**Cooking time:** 15 to 20 minutes
Servings: 4	**Cost:** $$$

Ocean Quahog Salad with Almond Milk and Celeriac Slivers

approx. 1 lb (500 g)	Celeriac
2	Lemons (juice)
1/2 cup (120 mL)	Cold Maltese sauce (see "Basic Ingredients for Some Recipes")
1/4 cup (60 mL)	Almond milk
To taste	Salt & pepper
4	Lettuce leaves
32	Ocean quahogs or Iceland cyprines
1/3 cup (20 g)	Parsley, chopped

• Slice the celeriac in slivers the size of grated carrot. In a container, combine the celeriac and the lemon juice, then add the Maltese sauce and the almond milk. Season. Save.

Presentation: Place lettuce leaves on a plate. Create a nest with the celeriac slivers. In the center, place the ocean quahogs or Iceland cyprines. Sprinkle with chopped parsley.

Preparation time: 25 minutes
Servings: 4   **Cost:** $$$

Invertebrates

CEPHALOPODS

Squid, octopus and cuttlefish form a particular class: *Cephalopods*. These are not fish, but rather mollusks like *Gastropods* (periwinkle, abalone and limpet) and *Lamellibranchia* (oysters, mussels, scallops, clams, and razor clams).

The head of these mollusks is equipped with huge eyes surrounded by numerous tentacles that have suckers. In the middle of these tentacles is the mouth, with corneous jaws that are shaped like the beak of a parrot. The body consists of an external envelope or mantle that holds the animal's organs. Generally, it is this mantle which is consumed. The head of the animal can also be eaten.

Squid
Boreal squid
Green sea urchin
Octopus
Cuttlefish

SQUID
Loligo paelei

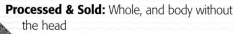

Processed & Sold: Whole, and body without the head

Cooking Method: Pan roasted, fried, sautéed or in a sauce

Value: Enthusiasts find it succulent.

Comments: Among the numerous squid families in the Americas, two include the common species that are consumed in North America. These are the long-finned Atlantic squid (*Loligo paelei*), measuring 2 to 3 1/4 ft in length (60 cm to 1 m), and the short-finned squid (*Lolliguncula brevis*), measuring 7 to 8 1/2 inches (18 to 22 cm) in length.

$

Characteristics: Elongated body. The head has 10 tentacles, 2 of which are much longer than the others. The fins are triangular in shape and make up half the length of the body.

Habitat: Atlantic and Pacific

Where & When to Find It: All year round, deep-frozen, wherever fish is sold

Fried Squid

2 1/4 lbs (1 kg)	Small squid
To taste	Salt & pepper
As needed	Peanut oil for frying
As needed	Flour
1 1/3 cups (80 g)	Parsley
4	Lemon wedges

- Clean the squid (see the recipe for Squid Stuffed with Ham, in this chapter).
- Cut the body or mantle into pieces or rounds, then set aside the heads and the tentacles.

- In a saucepan, without any fat, cook the squid quickly to release their water. Drain, then season with salt and pepper on a paper towel.
- Heat the peanut oil in the deep fryer.
- Flour the squid pieces and cook rapidly in the hot oil 3 to 4 minutes, stirring frequently. Once the pieces and the tentacles are golden, drain. Drop the parsley in the oil and drain.
- Place the fried squid on the plates, sprinkle with the fried parsley and serve with the lemon wedges.
- This recipe can be served with lemon mayonnaise.

Preparation time: 20 minutes	**Cooking time:** 7 to 10 minutes
Servings: 4	**Cost:** $$

Stuffed Squid with Mollusk Ink Sauce

36	Squid
1/2 lb (225 g)	Lobster meat
2	Small egg whites
To taste	Salt & pepper
2/3 cup (160 mL)	Cream (35%)
1 1/4 cups (300 mL)	Fish fumet (see "Basic Ingredients for Some Recipes")
As needed	Fiddleheads (Optional)

- In a food processor, combine the squid tentacles and the lobster meat. Add the egg whites, all the while mixing, then season with salt and pepper. Gradually incorporate the cream and set the forcemeat aside in the refrigerator.

- Clean the squid, and garnish 24 of them with the forcemeat; seal each squid and keep closed with a needle or a toothpick. Purée the other squid in the food processor and set the mixture aside in a saucepan.
- Bake the stuffed squid in the fish fumet, in the oven at 250°F (120°C) to ensure that they do not burst open; drain. Heat the squid purée to obtain a sauce made from the ink of the squid.* Place the stuffed squid on hot plates or on a serving dish. Cover with the ink sauce. Serve the squid very hot.

Accompaniment: Fiddleheads, if so desired
* Can also be prepared using squid ink.

Preparation time: 1 hour	**Cooking time:** 10 to 25 minutes
Servings: 6	**Cost:** $$

BOREAL SQUID, SHORT-FINNED SQUID AND SQUID

Illex illecebrosus

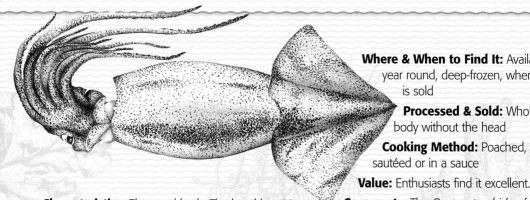

Where & When to Find It: Available all year round, deep-frozen, wherever fish is sold

Processed & Sold: Whole, and body without the head

Cooking Method: Poached, fried, sautéed or in a sauce

Value: Enthusiasts find it excellent.

Characteristics: Elongated body. The head has 10 tentacles, of which 2 are much longer than the others. The fins form a triangle and are one-third the length of the body.

Habitat: Pacific

Comments: The *Ommastrephidae* family with the small eyes includes the boreal squid or the short-finned squid (*Illex illecebrosus*), which can measure 1 to 16 1/2 ft (30 cm to 5 m).

$$

Squid Stuffed with Ham

8	Average-sized squid
10 oz (300 g)	Pressed ham
1	Egg white
To taste	Salt & pepper
7 oz (200 mL)	Cream (35%)
2 1/2 Tbsp (30 g)	Butter
1/2 cup (60 g)	Shallots, chopped
2/3 cup (150 mL)	White wine
3 1/2 oz (100 mL)	Fish fumet (see "Basic Ingredients for Some Recipes")
7 oz (200 mL)	Crustacean bisque or sauce (see Lobster bisque, in "Basic Ingredients …")
1 1/2 cups (240 g)	Cooked white rice

- Separate the heads from the squid, extract the bone called the "pen." Cut the tentacles into sections right up to the eyes, and remove the beak by pressing down with two fingers around the mouth situated in the middle of the tentacles. Carefully recover the ink sac and set aside. Wash the body and the tentacles. Dry completely with paper towel.
- Slice half the ham into fine strips and set aside.
- In a food processor, chop the remaining ham and the squid tentacles, add the egg white, season with salt and pepper, then slowly add the cream. Strain the forcemeat through a sieve and set aside in the refrigerator for 30 minutes.
- Using a pastry bag, stuff the squid bodies (not too full) and close the openings, using a few intersecting wooden toothpicks.

- Grease an ovenproof dish with butter and sprinkle the chopped shallots in the dish. Place the squid head to tail, pour in the white wine and the fish fumet. Cover with aluminum foil and bake at 300°F (150°C), about 25 to 30 minutes. If the oven is too hot, the squid will burst.
- When cooked, pour the cooking juice into a saucepan and reduce by 9/10. Add the crustacean bisque or sauce. Let simmer for a few minutes and strain through cheesecloth or a fine mesh strainer. Keep warm.
- Place the cooked rice around the rim of the soup dish. Harmoniously arrange the hot squid. Sprinkle with the strips of ham and cover with sauce. Garnish to taste.

Preparation time: 40 minutes	**Cooking time:** 30 to 35 minutes
Servings: 4	**Cost:** $$$

Photo on next page →

Squid Curry

2 1/4 lbs (1 kg)	Squid
2 cups (500 mL)	White chicken stock (see "Basic Ingredients for Some Recipes")
To taste	Salt & pepper
As needed	Sunflower oil
2	Onions, minced
2	Garlic cloves, chopped
6	Large tomatoes, blanched, peeled, seeded and diced
1 Tbsp (60 g)	Curry powder
1 Tbsp (10 g)	Soft sugar
As needed	Corn starch
14 oz (398 mL)	Straw mushrooms, canned
1 1/3 cups (200 g)	Cooked white rice
1/2 cup (100 g)	Grated coconut

- Clean the squid (see "Squid Stuffed with Ham," in this chapter).
- Cut the body or mantle into pieces. Poach the pieces in the chicken stock and season. Drain and set aside.
- In the sunflower oil, brown the chopped onions and the chopped garlic until nicely golden, then add the diced tomatoes and let simmer for a few minutes. Next, incorporate the curry powder and the sugar. Moisten with the chicken stock. Bind with corn starch until the desired consistency is obtained, and set aside.
- Using a wok or a large skillet, brown the squid pieces for 3 or 4 minutes, then season with salt and pepper. Remove the cooking fat, then add the sauce. Carefully mix, then add the straw mushrooms. Let simmer for a few minutes, and serve very hot with the rice mixed with the grated coconut.

Preparation time: 20 to 30 minutes	
Cooking time: 4 to 8 minutes	
Servings: 4	**Cost:** $$$

GREEN SEA URCHIN, SEA EGG AND SEA URCHIN

Strongylocentrotus droebachiensis

Where & When to Find It: Irregular availability wherever fish is sold

Processed & Sold: Whole and live, frozen roe

Cooking Method: Creamed, in a soufflé or with scrambled eggs

Value: A delicacy, but either you like it or you don't. Can be eaten raw.

Comments: The Greek name for sea urchin means "hedgehog." There are several types: the large, round ones with tightly packed spines, common to the Atlantic; the flat ones, with long and pointy spines, brownish-green or purple in color. A full sea urchin should contain 12% of its weight in roe, the best part.

Characteristics: Brownish-green or purple invertebrate, with a flat shell and long, pointy spines. Its size ranges from 2 1/4 to 3 inches (6 to 8 cm). The spines can reach 3/4 inches (2 cm) in length.

Habitat: Atlantic

$$

Green Sea Urchin Cream

4 Tbsp (30 g)	Shallots, chopped
1/2 cup (80 g)	Sweet butter
12	Green sea urchins
1 1/2 cups (350 mL)	White wine
1 cup (250 mL)	Water
1 sprig	Thyme
2	Eggs
14 oz (400 mL)	Cream (35%)
To taste	Salt & pepper
2 slices	Bread, diced
4 sprigs	Chervil
2 sprigs	Parsley

Preparation time: 30 minutes **Cooking time:** 15 minutes
Servings: 4 **Cost:** $$$

- Braise the shallots in 2 1/2 Tbsp (30 g) of butter for 5 minutes. Open the sea urchins and recover the liquid, strain through cheesecloth. Set aside the roe. Add the white wine, sea urchin liquid, water and thyme to the shallots. Cook for 5 minutes and remove the thyme from the saucepan.

- Dilute the egg yolks in the cream. Pour this mixture into the saucepan in a thin stream, stirring constantly. Adjust the seasoning. Add half the sea urchin roe and cook at a simmering boil for 3 minutes. Sauté the bread cubes in 4 1/2 Tbsp (50 g) of butter; distribute among the bowls or soup dishes.

- Divide the remaining sea urchin roe among the bowls and pour the sea urchin cream on top. Garnish with the chervil and parsley sprigs.

Scrambled Eggs with Green Sea Urchin

12	Green sea urchins, live
12	Eggs
To taste	Salt & pepper
To taste	Nutmeg
¼ cup (60 mL)	Cream (35%)
¾ cup (120 g)	Sweet butter

Preparation time: 10 minutes   **Cooking time:** 3 minutes
Servings: 4   **Cost:** $$

- Open the sea urchins and remove the roe.
- Beat the eggs, season with salt and pepper, grate in a little nutmeg and add the cream.
- Heat the butter in a round metal mixing bowl placed in a *bain-marie*. Pour in the beaten eggs as well as the sea urchin roe; mix with a wooden spoon until the desired consistency is obtained.
- Serve immediately in ramekins or in the shells.

OCTOPUS

Octopus sp.

Where & When to Find It: Available all year round, deep-frozen, wherever fish is sold

Processed & Sold: Generally whole

Cooking Method: Steamed, fried, in a sauce or grilled

Value: Enthusiasts like it a lot.

Comments: There are about a dozen species of octopus in Canadian and American waters. The common Atlantic octopus can reach a weight of 44 lbs (20 kg). *Octopus vulgaris* can easily exceed 3 1/4 ft. (1 m) in length, unlike *Eledone commune* or *Eledone cirrosa*, which reach a length of 16 inches (40 cm), and *Eledone moschata*, which can measure 14 inches (35 cm) in length.

$$

Characteristics: The body resembles a bag. The head has 8 tentacles equal in size, each one with 2 rows of suckers.

Habitat: Atlantic

Octopus with Fennel and Rosé Wine

3 1/4 lbs (1.5 kg)	Octopus
1	Onion, minced
1/3 cup (80 mL)	Olive oil
3 Tbsp (40 mL)	Ricard or Pernod
1 cup (250 mL)	Rosé wine
2 cups (200 g)	Fennel, chopped
6	Tomatoes, blanched, peeled, seeded and diced
To taste	Salt & pepper

- After having emptied and washed the octopus, cut the sac as well as the tentacles into small rounds 3/4 to 1 1/4 inches (2 to 3 cm) wide.
- In a saucepan, cook the onion in the olive oil until tender, add the octopus, flambé with Ricard or Pernod, moisten with the wine, then let simmer covered for 20 minutes. Next, add the fennel and the diced tomatoes. Season with salt and pepper and mix.
- Cook for at least 1 hour (depending on the size of the octopus). Check for doneness using the tip of a knife. If, during cooking, more liquid is needed, add fish fumet or water.

Accompaniment: Mashed potatoes

NOTE: If the octopus has 2 rows of suckers, it is an *Octopus vulgaris* or an *Octopus macropus*. It must be "beaten" with a mallet to tenderize the meat.

Preparation time: 20 minutes	
Cooking time: 1 hour–1 hour 20 minutes	
Servings: 4	**Cost:** $$$

Octopus Savarins *with a Shrimp Garnish*

1 ³/₄ lbs (800 g)	Octopus
approx. 3 oz (100 g)	Flounder
4	Egg whites
14 oz (400 mL)	Cream (35%)
To taste	Salt, pepper and cayenne pepper
As needed	Butter
16	Average-sized shrimp
2 cups (500 mL)	*Court-bouillon* (see "Basic Ingredients for Some Recipes")
1 ¹/₄ cups (300 mL)	White wine
7 oz (200 mL)	Lobster coulis (see "Basic Ingredients …")
1	Lemon (juice)
¹/₃ cup (20 g)	Parsley, chopped
As needed	Steamed potatoes (Optional)

- Parboil the octopus in fresh water; clean to remove as much ink as possible. Purée the octopus with the flounder in a food processor. Add the egg whites, gently whisking, then add the cream. Season with salt and pepper, add the cayenne pepper and strain through a strainer.
- Butter the *savarin* molds and fill with this preparation. Cook in a *bain-marie*, in the oven, at 160°F (70°C) for 10 to 15 minutes.
- Cook the shrimp in the *court-bouillon* and white wine. Heat the lobster coulis; thicken with 1 cup (175 g) of butter, and add the lemon juice and the chopped parsley. Pour this sauce in the bottom of each dish. Turn the octopus *savarins* out of the molds and arrange one *savarin* in the middle of each dish. Hang the shrimp from each side of the *savarin*. Serve very hot.
- Place the steamed potatoes in the center of each *savarin*, if so desired.

Preparation time: 1 hour	**Cooking time:** 20 minutes
Servings: 8	**Cost:** $$$

Photo on page 327

CUTTLEFISH
Sepia officinalis

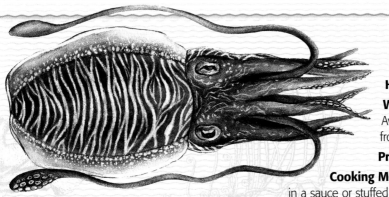

Habitat: Atlantic

Where & When to Find It: Available all year round, deep-frozen, wherever fish is sold

Processed & Sold: Whole

Cooking Method: Poached, fried, sautéed, in a sauce or stuffed

Value: For enthusiasts

Comments: The cuttlefish and squid have an ink sac that can be used in cooking to prepare ink sauces and to color pasta.

$$

Characteristics: Cephelapod mollusk with an oval body. One fin runs almost the entire length of the body. The head has 10 tentacles, 2 of which are much longer, all equipped with suckers. The internal shell is called a "cuttlebone" or "pen."

Cuttlefish with Tomatoes and Papaya Juice

7 oz (200 mL)	Papaya juice
32	Small cuttlefish (only the body)
2	Red onions, chopped
1/4 cup (60 mL)	Olive oil
4	Tomatoes, blanched, peeled, seeded and diced
1/2	Garlic clove, chopped
24	Black olives, pitted
To taste	Salt & pepper
1/3 cup (20 g)	Parsley
8	Sweet basil leaves

- Soak the cuttlefish body in half the papaya juice for 3 or 4 minutes, as the papaya juice will tenderize the meat.
- Cook the chopped red onion in the olive oil until tender, then add the tomatoes, chopped garlic and the black olives. Moisten with the remaining papaya juice, season with salt and pepper, and cook for about 10 minutes. Next, add the papaya juice and cuttlefish.
- Cook gently, checking to see if done by using the tip of a knife.
- Finish by sprinkling with the parsley and chopped sweet basil.

Accompaniment: Small boiled and diced potatoes

Preparation time: 20 minutes	**Cooking time:** 8 to 15 minutes
Servings: 4	**Cost:** $$$

Butterfly Cuttlefish with Lobster Sauce

14 oz (400 g)	Small cuttlefish (the body only)
1/2 cup (120 mL)	Dry white wine
1/2 cup (80 g)	Shallots, chopped
1/2 cup (40 g)	Fresh coriander, chopped
1/4 cup (60 mL)	Ricard
1/4 cup (60 mL)	Olive oil
To taste	Salt & pepper
6	Tomatoes, blanched, peeled, seeded and diced
3/4 cup (180 mL)	Lobster sauce (see "Basic Ingredients for Some Recipes")
approx. 1 cup (160 g)	Cooked Puy lentils

- Place the cuttlefish in a bowl; add the white wine, shallots, coriander and the Ricard. Macerate for 1 hour. Next, drain the cuttlefish. Heat the olive oil, quickly sauté the cuttlefish, season with salt and pepper, and keep warm. Reduce the macerating juice by 9/10. Add the diced tomatoes, lobster sauce and let simmer for 7 to 8 minutes. Adjust the seasoning just before serving. Add the lentils and the cuttlefish. Let simmer for 2 minutes and serve in a soup dish.

Preparation time: 25 minutes **Cooking time:** 8 to 10 minutes
Servings: 4   **Cost:** $$$

SEA LETTUCE, ARAMÉ, NORI AND OTHERS

Seaweed

In Japan, edible seaweed has been found in funerary ruins and in peat dating back 10,000 years.

If seaweed is one of the most valued dishes in Asia, its use is much more limited in the West. Whether in South America, North America or Europe, seaweed has its own history.

At the beginning of this century, in Ireland, children sold dried seaweed in paper cones. The seaweed was eaten like french fries. The Indians who crossed the Andes Mountains carried a small leather pouch around their necks containing seaweed to give them energy.

In France, there is a cake made with a seaweed gelling agent. In Canada, seaweed is unknowingly consumed every day in the form of agar-agar. We are only beginning to use seaweed, of which we have a rich abundance, as an accompaniment to our meals.

Sea lettuce
Porphyra
Dulse
Hijiki
Blade kelp
Horse tail
Aramé
Irish moss
Nori

SEA LETTUCE
Ulva lactuca

Characteristics: The fronds can measure 4 to 24 inches (10 to 60 cm). Pointed, oval or rounded edges, with tears and holes

Habitat: All year round on rocks and mudbanks

Where & When to Find It: Available all year round in specialty stores

Processed & Sold: Dried, in packages of 2 to 3 oz (50 to 100 g)

$$

HOW TO COOK FRESH SEAWEED

Blanch: Gently boil the seaweed that is to be used, to increase the flavor or to make it greener (wakame, fucus and all the types of brown seaweed).

Steam: This technique works well with thin seaweed as it keeps its beautiful color and, with thicker seaweed, as it precooks it.

Fry: Quickly deep-fried, porphyra is delicious. It can also be prepared ahead of time to garnish the plates. In general, seaweed has very beautiful shapes and colors when it is fried.

Grilled: Japanese seaweed produced in sheets is sometimes grilled over an open flame or on an electric griddle. It can be served as a condiment.

Sautéed Red Snapper with a Sea Lettuce Garnish

1/3 cup (30 g)	Dried sea lettuce
1/2 cup (120 mL)	White wine
6 Tbsp (60 g)	Shallots, chopped
1 cup (170 g)	Butter
3/4 cup (160 g)	White rice, uncooked
1 cup (250 mL)	Mussel or soft-shell clam juice
To taste	Salt & pepper
4 tsp (15 g)	Fresh ginger, chopped
4 × 7–9 oz (200–250 g)	Red snapper
approx. 1/3 cup (70 mL)	Peanut oil

Preparation time: 30 minutes **Cooking time:** 30 minutes
Servings: 4   **Cost:** $$$

- Rehydrate the sea lettuce in the white wine. Cook the chopped shallots in 4 1/2 Tbsp (50 g) of butter until tender. Add the rice, letting it swell slightly, i.e., heat it, then add the mussel or clam juice, half the seaweed (rehydrated sea lettuce) and season with salt and pepper; cover and bake at 400°F (200°C) (do not add salt immediately) for 20 to 25 minutes.
- Gently cook the remaining sea lettuce with the white wine and the chopped ginger. At the last moment, bind together with 6 Tbsp (70 g) of butter.
- Season the fish with the peanut oil and the remaining butter. Fry the red snapper in a skillet. Using a spoon, baste often with the fat from the skillet during cooking.

Presentation: Mold the rice in a dariole mold. Pour the sea lettuce stock onto the edge of the plate, lay the red snappers in the plate, and turn the rice and seaweed out of the mold upright in the middle of the plate.

PORPHYRA
Porphura laciniata

Characteristics: The frond resembles a flat leaf. In the winter, the thallus is cut into straight strips, with curved edges. In the summer, these strips become larger with irregular projections in the shape of leaves. Color: reddish-brown. Size: 2 to 8 inches (5 to 20 cm)

Habitat: Coastal shelf, at the same level as *Fucus spiralis*

Where & When to Find It: Available all year round, dried, in specialty stores

Processed & Sold: Dried, in packages of 2 to 3 oz (50 to 100 g)

Comments: This is a variation of *Porphyra tenera*, a Japanese seaweed that is used in the production of nori seaweed.

$$

GLASSWORT OR SALTWATER CORDGRASS

Glasswort grows in salty soil. This is not a seaweed, but it is used extensively in cooking. Some botanists recognize two species in North America: Atlantic (*Salicornia europaea*) and that of the center and west (*Salicornia rubra*), which has moved inland onto very salty soil (salt mines). Harvested from May to September, these "sea beans" explode in the mouth; they have a fresh, salty taste. Neither contains vitamin C.

Other Edible Plants from the Edge of the Sea

SEASIDE PLANTAIN (*Plantago maritima*—Linnaeus). The plantain family; the young leaves are eaten in salads.

SEABEACH SEAWORT (*Arenaria peploides*). The carnation family. The young shoots are eaten raw or blanched.

SEA MILKWORT (*Glaux maritima*). The primrose family. A little bitter, sea milkwort is usually eaten marinated.

HALBERDLEAF ORACH: Lamb's-quarters family. The young leaves are eaten in a salad; the less tender leaves are cooked like spinach.

Oyster Aspic with Seaweed Jelly and Avocado Cream

24	Oysters in the shell
7 oz (200 g)	Spinach leaves
1 ½ Tbsp (15 g)	Agar-agar, dried (gelatin)
2 cups (500 mL)	Fish fumet (See "Basic Ingredients for Some Recipes")
4 Tbsp (20 g)	Shallots, finely sliced
2/3 cup (85 g)	Carrot rounds
1/2 bunch	Chives
3	Egg whites
6 servings	Avocado cream (see recipe on next page)
As needed	Chervil leaves
3/4 cup (150 g)	Tomatoes, diced

- Shuck the oysters, and keep the juice. Poach the oysters in their juice for 10 seconds; set aside. Blanch the spinach, and wrap each oyster in one spinach leaf.
- Place 3 oysters in each small mold (ramekin) and set aside in the refrigerator. Cook the agar-agar at low heat in the fish fumet until tender.
- In a blender, purée the shallots with the carrots, chives, the remaining oysters, oyster juice and egg whites. Mix this preparation

with the fish-and-seaweed aspic. Bring to a rolling boil and cook for 20 minutes. Clarify. Strain through cheesecloth or a fine mesh strainer. Fill the ramekins with this preparation and let set in the refrigerator.

- Pour one serving of the avocado cream (1 oz or 30 mL) into the bottom of each dish. Turn out the aspic onto each plate.
- Garnish with the chervil leaves and a little of the diced fresh tomato.

Preparation time: 50 minutes **Cooking time:** 10 minutes	
Servings: 6	**Cost:** $$$

Avocado Cream

2	Ripe avocados
4 Tbsp (20 mL)	Cognac
3 ½ oz (100 mL)	Cream (35%)
1	Grapefruit (juice)
To taste	Salt & pepper

- In a blender, purée the avocado with the cognac, cream, grapefruit juice, salt and pepper. Strain through cheesecloth or a fine mesh strainer.

Preparation time: 5 minutes	
Servings: 4	**Cost:** $$$

DULSE
Palmaria palmata

Characteristics: Flat blade about 16 inches (40 cm) in length. Color: red. Average size (20 inches or 0.5 cm), notched, often at two intervals, with lobes 2 to 4 inches (5 to 10 cm) long. Elongated and rounded shape towards the top.

Habitat: Rocks in the lower level of the coastal shelf and below

Where & When to Find It: Available all year round in specialty stores

Processed & Sold: Dried, rarely fresh

Comments: This hardy seaweed can be found in Europe, Iceland and Canada. A traditional dish in Iceland, it is used to flavor seafood tortes. Common name: dulse.

$$

Shrimp Ragout with Dulse

approx. 1 lb (500 g)	Fresh tomatoes
2 oz (60 g)	Red peppers
3/4 cup (100 g)	Small new carrots, cut into an olive shape
To taste	Salt & pepper
1/2	Coconut or coconut juice
2 1/2 Tbsp (12 g)	Dried dulse
3 Tbsp (30 g)	Roasted peanuts
4 tsp (15 g)	Ginger root, in pieces
1 3/4 lbs (800 g)	Red sand shrimp, shelled
3 Tbsp (30 g)	Onions, chopped
2 Tbsp (30 mL)	Oil
2 sprigs	Coriander
1	Lemon (juice)
3/4 cup (80 g)	Celery stalks, cut into an olive shape

- Blanch and peel the tomatoes and the red pepper, then seed and dice. Cook the olive-shaped carrots and celery in boiling, salted water; keep crunchy. Season these vegetables.
- Recover the coconut juice and add the seaweed. Peel the peanuts and the ginger and mince. Sauté the shrimp and onion in the oil for 1 to 2 minutes. Season with salt and pepper. Add the peanuts, ginger and the coriander leaves.
- Remove the shrimp from the skillet and set aside. Add the diced tomato and pepper to the skillet and cook for 1 to 2 minutes. Add the coconut juice and the seaweed to bind the sauce. Add the lemon juice, then season with salt and pepper.
- Reheat the shrimp and the vegetables in the sauce just before serving. Serve this ragout in soup dishes.

Preparation time: 45 minutes	**Cooking time:** 4 to 8 minutes
Servings: 4	**Cost:** $$$$

Photo on page 342

Crayfish Tails with Seaweed and Cider

3 to 4 lbs (1.4 to 1.8 kg)	Live crayfish
8 cups (2 L)	*Court-bouillon* (see "Basic Ingredients for Some Recipes")
1/4 cup (20 g)	Dulse (or seaweed of choice)
2 3/4 cups (700 mL)	Cider
approx. 1 cup (160 g)	Butter
1/2 cup (85 g)	Carrot, julienned
1/3 cup (40 g)	Celery, julienned
1 cup (100 g)	Leek (white part only), julienned
To taste	Salt & pepper
2 Tbsp (20 g)	Shallots *brunoise*
3 Tbsp (40 mL)	Calvados
2/3 cup (160 mL)	Cream (35%)
7 oz (200 mL)	Crayfish coulis (see "Basic Ingredients …")
1	Lemon (juice)

- Gut the crayfish, cook in the *court-bouillon* for 1 to 1 1/2 minutes, depending on their size, then let cool. Remove the tails and shell, then set aside. Stack the remaining carcasses and set aside to prepare the coulis. Rehydrate the seaweed in the cider.

- Sweat the carrots, celery and leek in 4 1/2 Tbsp (50 g) of butter. Season the julienned vegetables with salt and pepper, then set aside.
- Brown the crayfish tails and the shallot in 4 1/2 Tbsp (50 g) of butter. Flambé with the calvados. Add the cider and the seaweed, cook for 1 minute, then remove the crayfish so that they do not become tough.
- Reduce the cooking liquid to eliminate any acidity. Add the cream and reduce by half. Incorporate the crayfish coulis and thicken with the remaining butter. Set this Nantua sauce[*] aside and keep warm.
- When ready to serve, reheat the julienned vegetables. Reheat the crayfish tails in the Nantua sauce, at low heat, without boiling. Adjust the seasoning. Add the lemon juice.
- Arrange the vegetables to form a ring on the plates. Place the crayfish preparation in the center of the plates.

[*] Dishes and sauces which bear the name "Nantua" always include crayfish tails, whole crayfish, a crayfish purée, mousse or coulis.

Preparation time: 14 minutes **Cooking time:** 20 minutes
Servings: 4 **Cost:** $$$$

HIJIKI
Hizikia fusiforme—cystophyllum fusiformyo

Characteristics: Grows in warm seas like small trees. Hijiki resembles sprigs of hard, dried herbs. This seaweed is very popular in Japan, where it is eaten daily.

Where & When to Find It: Available all year round in specialty stores

Processed & Sold: Dried, in packages of 2 to 7 oz (50 to 200 g)

Comments: Hijiki reduces cholesterol levels.

$$

SEAWEED, HIGHLY SOUGHT-AFTER DIETARY COMPLEMENT CAPABLE OF STABILIZING THE IMBALANCES IN OUR FOOD INTAKE

Low in lipids (fats), seaweed contains more vitamins, folic and pantothenic acids and niacin than vegetables and fresh fruit. Its unsaturated fatty acids are closer to those of fish. The carbohydrates it contains are very healthy, and the carbohydrates that cannot be digested facilitate gut motility and prevent the retention of dietary cholesterol. Seaweed is rich in iodine, calcium, iron, magnesium, cobalt and vitamin B12.

Shellfish Cooked in a Court-bouillon *with Hijiki and Hollandaise Sauce*

7 oz (200 g)	Cockles, without the shell
7 oz (200 g)	Stimpson's surf clams, without the shell
7 oz (200 g)	Scallops, without the shell
7 oz (200 g)	Blue mussels, without the shell
6 cups (1.5 L)	*Court-bouillon* (see "Basic Ingredients for Some Recipes")
7 oz (200 mL)	Dry white wine
3 Tbsp (15 g)	Hijiki seaweed, dried
To taste	Salt & pepper
²/₃ cup (160 mL)	Hollandaise sauce (see "Basic Ingredients ...")

- It is crucial that the shells be removed while the shellfish is still raw. If some are too difficult to open, place them in a saucepan with a little water, then heat just enough to cause them to open. Recover the meat from the shells and store in the refrigerator.
- Heat the *court-bouillon* with the white wine and the hijiki. Season. Cook for 5 to 6 minutes.
- Prepare the hollandaise sauce so that it is still hot, and ladle into a small bowl for each guest.
- Poach the shellfish, one type at a time, as some take longer to cook than others. When they are poached, combine and, when ready to serve, place in a soup dish with the juice and the seaweed.

Accompaniment: Boiled potatoes

Preparation time: 1 hour	**Cooking time:** 8 to 10 minutes
Servings: 4	**Cost:** $$$

Photo on facing page →

BLADE KELP (BROWN SEAWEED)

Laminaria longicruris

Characteristics: Hollow stemmed, about the same length as kelp, and with a wavy blade thicker in the middle, this seaweed can reach more than 33 ft (10 m) in length.

Habitat: Attaches to rocks and wood structures, just below the low tide level. It is always submerged.

Where & When to Find It: Available all year round (kombu), dried, imported from Japan

Processed & Sold: Dried, in packages of 2 to 7 oz (50 to 200 g) in specialty stores

Comments: Blade kelp grows only in northeastern North America, where it moves up into the St. Lawrence estuary. This seaweed is used to produce kombu. In Japan, kombu is made with *Laminaria japonica*.

$$

SEAWEED AS A GELLING AGENT

Red seaweed produces carrageen and agar-agar.

Carrageen (*Chondrus crispus*)

Carrageen is made up of two similar types of seaweed. They contain both gelling and thickening substances. Currently, carrageen is used for industrial and pharmaceutical purposes: it clarifies beer and wine. It is also used in the production of industrial ice cream, sherbet, fruit in syrup, cheese and instant soup.

Agar-agar (*Gracilaria verrucosa*)

Agar-agar consists of about 15 types of red seaweed. It absorbs water, softens and expands at 170°F (85°C). It then becomes liquid and viscous. It gels between 77° and 86°F (25° and 30°C). Agar-agar is used to stabilize jams and jellies that coat canned meat. Jell-O is essentially made of agar-agar.

Mussels with Kombu Cream

2 1/4 lbs (1 kg)	Mussels, with the shell
1/2 cup (120 mL)	White wine
6 Tbsp (60 g)	Shallots, chopped
1/3 cup (30 g)	Kombu seaweed, dried
7 oz (200 mL)	Cream (35%)
To taste	Salt & pepper
1 cup (160 g)	Cooked white rice

- Wash the mussels, then place in a large saucepan with the white wine and the chopped shallots. Cover and cook until they open.
- Stop the cooking by sitting the saucepan in cold water.
- Recover the cooking juice, add the dried kombu and let it infuse for a few minutes. Reduce the cooking juice by 2/3 and add the cream. Season, set aside and keep warm.
- Remove 1/2 of each mussel shell and arrange in an ovenproof dish.
- Heat the rice.

Presentation: Place the rice in the middle of the plate, with the mussels or shells around it. Cover these with the kombu cream sauce.

Preparation time: 30 minutes **Cooking time:** 10 to 15 minutes
Servings: 4   **Cost:** $$$

Photo on facing page →

HORSE TAIL AND KELP (BROWN SEAWEED)

Laminaria digitata

Characteristics: Split blade, with a straight edge and dark brown coloring. Adheres to rocks using filaments that penetrate in and around a central conical cavity. Can reach 6 1/2 ft (2 m) in length.

Habitat: All of the Atlantic, both sides

Where & When to Find It: Available all year round in specialty stores

Processed & Sold: Dried, in packages of 2 to 7 oz (50 to 200 g)

$$

THE USE OF SEAWEED IN INDUSTRY

It was in the combustion of plants (glasswort and sodium hydroxide) that it was discovered that seaweed produced alkali. Up until 1791, this sodium hydroxide was referred to as "kelp ash." It was used in the production of glass, soap and paint. Then, doctors and photographers claimed the iodine in the kelp ash for their work. Where can we still find seaweed derivatives today? In linoleum, printer's ink, paint, wood sealant, cosmetics, etc.

Sautéed Spiny Dogfish with Kombu and Soya Sauce

2 1/2 oz (70 g)	Rehydrated kombu seaweed
1	Red onion, chopped
1/2	Garlic clove, chopped
3/4 cup (160 g)	Zucchini, diced
4	Tomatoes, blanched, peeled, seeded and diced
To taste	Salt & pepper
1/3 cup (60 g)	Sweet butter
1/4 cup (60 g)	Peanut oil
As needed	Flour
12 × 2 oz (50 g)	Spiny dogfish sections
1 1/3 cups (160 g)	Cooked wild rice
3 1/2 oz (100 mL)	Soya sauce

- Cut the kombu into fine strips. Cook the chopped onion and chopped garlic until tender, then add the zucchini and the diced tomatoes. Season with salt and pepper and cook gently. When half done, add the kombu seaweed and let simmer. Set aside.
- Heat the sweet butter and the peanut oil. Flour the spiny dogfish sections, season with salt and pepper and cook *à la meunière*.
- Combine the rice with the tomato-zucchini mixture and place in the middle of the plate. Surround with the spiny dogfish sections and cover with soya sauce.

Preparation time: 20 minutes **Cooking time:** 10 minutes
Servings: 4 **Cost:** $$

Photo on facing page →

ARAMÉ
Eisenia bicyclis

Characteristics: This plant has fronds reaching 12 inches (30 cm) in length and 1 1/2 inches (4 cm) in width. Thicker than the other types of seaweed, aramé needs to be cooked for several hours before drying.

Habitat: Along the Pacific coast of Japan

Where & When to Find It: Available all year round in specialty stores

Processed & Sold: Dried, in packages of 2 to 7 oz (50 to 200 g)

Comments: A thousand years ago, this seaweed was offered up in the famous sanctuary of Isis. Today, it is still harvested each spring at low tide.

$$

SEAWEED WE EAT WITHOUT KNOWING IT

Seaweed certainly constitutes the biggest culinary "secret." We have all eaten seaweed and, moreover, we eat it daily.

Here are a few of the dietary preparations that include seaweed in one form or another: cream, custard, ice cream, milk drinks (fermented or not), industrial meats, cooked meals, fruit paste, mayonnaise and vinaigrette.

• Products that are described as "light" often contain authorized additives made from seaweed extracts.

Monkfish Medallions in an Orange Saffron Sauce with Aramé and Etake Mushrooms

1 tsp (4 g)	Saffron threads
1/3 cup (80 mL)	Noilly Prat, white
3	Oranges (juice)
3 1/2 oz (100 mL)	Fish *velouté* (see "Basic Ingredients for Some Recipes")
To taste	Salt & pepper
approx. 3/4 cup (150 g)	Butter
2 3/4 oz (80 g)	Rehydrated aramé
2 3/4 oz (80 g)	Etake mushrooms
As needed	Flour
12 × 2 oz (60 g)	Monkfish medallions
3/4 cup (60 mL)	Olive oil

• Rehydrate the saffron threads in the Noilly Prat and the orange juice.

• Heat the fish *velouté* and add the saffron threads and the Noilly Prat. Adjust the seasoning and cook until half done, for 5 to 6 minutes. Strain through cheesecloth or a fine mesh strainer, thicken with 6 Tbsp (70 g) of butter, set aside and keep warm.

• Sauté the seaweed and the mushrooms that will serve as the vegetables in 4 1/2 Tbsp (50 g) of butter. Season with salt and pepper and set aside.

• Flour the monkfish medallions and, with the remaining butter and oil, cook *à la meunière*. Season with salt and pepper and let sit.

Presentation: Arrange the monkfish medallions to form a circle. Place the mushrooms and seaweed to one side, then cover with the sauce. Cooked rice can be added to the seaweed.

Preparation time: 15 minutes **Cooking time:** 15 minutes
Servings: 4 **Cost:** $$$

Photo on facing page →

IRISH MOSS (RED SEAWEED)

Chondrus crispus
Incorrect names: white kelp or curly kelp

Characteristics: This seaweed resembles a tuft of about 4 to 6 inches (10 to 15 cm). It has straight, flat blades and coloring that varies from dark red to yellowish-green.

Habitat: North Atlantic

Where & When to Find It: Available all year round in specialty stores

Processed & Sold: Dried, rarely fresh, in packages of 2 to 7 oz (50 to 200 g)

Comments: Eaten as a jelly, boiled in milk or in lemon oil, or coated in sugar

$$

Steamed Lobster with Seaweed and Melted Lemon Butter

4 cups (1 L)	Court-bouillon (see "Basic Ingredients for Some Recipes")
7 oz (200 mL)	White wine
4	Lemons (juice)
1/2	Bay leaf
1/2 sprig	Thyme
To taste	Salt & pepper
1/3 cup (25 g)	Dried kombu
10 oz (300 g)	Fresh Irish moss
1/3 cup (25 g)	Dried hijiki
4 × 1 1/4 lbs (560 g)	Lobsters
1 1/4 cups (200 g)	Sweet butter

- To prepare this recipe, a three-part steamer (with a lid), with two perforated inserts, is essential: (1) the lower part for the *court-bouillon*; (2) the first insert for the seaweed; (3) the second insert for the lobster.

- Heat the *court-bouillon*, add the white wine, the juice of the first lemon, bay leaf, thyme, then season with salt and pepper. Place the seaweed in the first insert, cover and cook for 10 minutes.
- The next step is very important. Since not all the lobsters can be cooked at once, they risk emptying. Place them one at a time in the second insert and boil 1 to 2 minutes each, again one at a time, to kill them.
- Once this step is completed, group the 4 lobsters together and steam for 12 to 20 minutes.
- Cut in half and serve immediately with the melted butter to which the juice of 3 lemons has been added.

Accompaniment: Chayotes cooked in butter

Preparation time: 30 minutes   **Cooking time:** 20 minutes
Servings: 4   **Cost:** $$$$

Endives and Smoked Salmon with Seaweed Sauce

¹/₂ cup (40 g)	**Dried Irish moss**
2 ¹/₂ cups (600 mL)	**Milk**
1 ¹/₂ lbs (750 g)	**Endives**
²/₃ cup (100 g)	**Butter**
2	**Lemons (juice)**
To taste	**Salt & pepper**
As needed	***Beurre manié* or white roux (see "Basic Ingredients for Some Recipes")**
approx. ³/₄ lb (325 g)	**Smoked salmon**

- Rehydrate the seaweed in the milk. Remove the base of the endives by cutting away with a knife a small cone approximately 1 inch (2.5 cm) in length. This will eliminate any bitterness. Arrange the endives in a buttered sauté pan. Add enough lemon juice so that the endives are half-covered. Season with salt and pepper, then cover and cook at low heat. Set the cooked endives aside.
- Strain through cheesecloth or a fine mesh strainer. Mince the seaweed. Bind the milk with the *beurre manié* or the white roux. Season with salt and pepper. Squeeze the endives to remove as much cooking liquid as possible. Wrap each endive in a thin slice of smoked salmon.
- Place each endive in a buttered gratin dish. Add the chopped seaweed to the sauce, then the juice of the second lemon when ready to use. Cover the endives with this sauce and bake in the oven at 350°F (180°C).

Preparation time: 45 minutes	**Cooking time:** 30 minutes
Servings: 4	**Cost:** $$$$

NORI (GREEN SEAWEED)

Porphyra lineari or *tenera*

Characteristics: This seaweed looks somewhat like a floating herb. It is grown in deep water on wooden frames along the shore of quiet bays. Once harvested, it is dried on bamboo flakes and then squeezed into thin leaves.

Where & When to Find It: Available all year round in specialty stores

Processed & Sold: Dried, in packages of 2 to 7 oz (50 to 200 g)

Comments: This seaweed has the highest level of protein.

$$

Scallops with Nori Seaweed and Fettucine

1/2 lb (240 g)	Fettucine pasta
1/4 cup (60 mL)	Olive oil
8	Tomatoes, blanched, peeled, seeded and diced
approx. 1/2 cup (80 g)	Carrots, cooked
3 Tbsp (50 mL)	Cognac
2/3 cup (160 mL)	Pineau des Charentes
2	Ripe avocados, diced
2 3/4 oz (80 g)	Rehydrated nori seaweed
To taste	Salt & pepper
As needed	Flour
1 1/2 lbs (650 g)	Fairly large scallops (without the shell)
3/4 cup (120 g)	Butter
2/3 cup (160 mL)	Brown veal stock (see "Basic Ingredients for Some Recipes")

- In salted water, cook the fettucine and refresh.
- In the olive oil, cook the diced tomatoes and the cooked carrots until tender. Flambé with the cognac, add the Pineau des Charentes, then the diced avocados and the rehydrated nori seaweed. Gently mix in the fettucine and keep warm, after having adjusted the seasoning.
- Flour the scallops and gently cook *à la meunière* in the butter; season with salt and pepper and set aside.

Presentation: Arrange the fettucine in a circle, surround with the scallops or place them on top, and cover with the hot brown veal stock.

Preparation time: 20 minutes **Cooking time:** 15 minutes
Servings: 4 **Cost:** $$$$

Photo on next page →

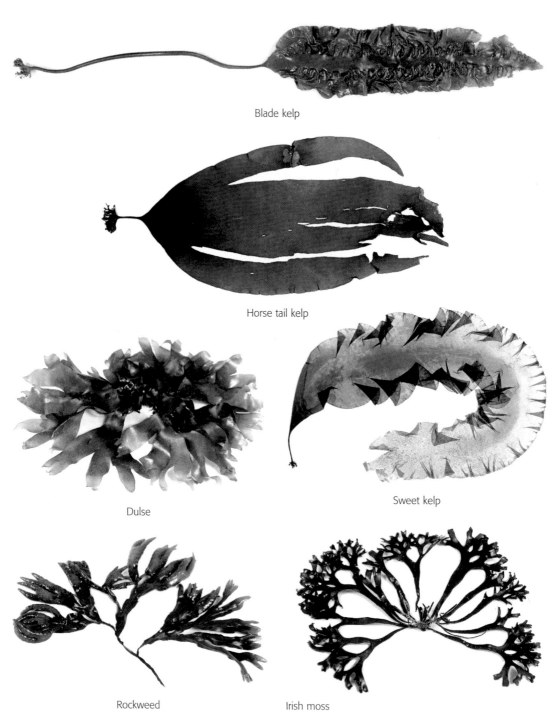

Blade kelp

Horse tail kelp

Dulse

Sweet kelp

Rockweed

Irish moss

NOTE: These are the types of seaweed most often found on the Atlantic coast of North America.

The Marriage of Wine and Fish

I n a classic marriage of wine and food, the character of the food and of the wine must be as compatible as possible.

The marriage of wine and fish follows the same principle. And, according to the well-known rule, to ensure that the marriage is a happy one, the fish must not overpower the wine and the wine must not overpower the fish.

In each of the tables that follow, the fish are classified according to the type of flesh (more or less fatty or more or less dry), the cooking method and the type of sauce. These tables provide a few guidelines. In bringing together a wine and a dish, you should consider taste, context and intuition in selecting the right wine. The sole objective is to achieve the greatest pleasure.

BASIC RULES

Just as we have our preferences when it comes to food, so too do we have them when it comes to wine. So much the better, or we would all have the same taste, which would eventually become boring.

However, certain basic rules need to be followed when combining a wine and a fish, mollusk or crustacean.

First of all, the fat level of the seafood, the cooking method and, if there is an accompanying sauce, the type—sweet, spicy, fruity, acidic vegetable or strong-tasting seaweed—need to be determined. The cost of the wine is another factor.

Obviously, the same wine would not be chosen for a festive occasion and for everyday use. The same rules apply when selecting a fish, mollusk or crustacean.

The choice of wine as outlined in the tables that follow was prepared by Jean-Marc Barraud, professor of wine stewardship at the Institut de tourisme et d'hôtellerie du Québec.

Wines for Lean, Lighter-Tasting Fish

Windowpane, sole, flounder family, halibut, skate, cod, pollock, haddock, cusk, hake, whiting, tilefish, ocean pout, capelin, American smelt, monkfish, swordfish, walleye, yellow perch, burbot, goldeye, panfish, smallmouth bass, grouper, Atlantic tomcod and many others

Grilled	Fried or à la meunière	Poached	In a sweet sauce	In a spicy sauce	In a red wine sauce
Fumé blanc (California)	Coteaux de Franconie	Rully	Auxey-Duresses	Clairette du Languedoc	Bardolino
Crozes-Hermitage	Gaillac (dry)	Pouilly-Fuissé	Chablis 1er cru	Côtes de Provence White	Valpolicella
Tokay Pinot gris	Reuilly	Graves	Coulée-de-Serrant	Vergelesses	Bandol
Riesling	Roussette de Savoie	Riesling	Côteaux du Layon	Riesling	Volnay
Beaujolais*	Neuchâtel		Lacryma Christi	Bouzy rouge	Côtes du Jura
Chiroubles*	Sancerre		Pomino	Dôle	

* Red wine

Note: Except for those dishes that have a red wine sauce, the suggested wines are white wines.

Wines for Semi-fatty Fish with a Distinctive Flavor

Sturgeon, northern pike, red snapper, Atlantic wolffish, northern searobin, sea bream, John Dory, goatfish, redfish, conger eel, spiny dogfish, cunner, white perch, bass, all the *Salmonidae* and many others

Grilled	Fried or *à la meunière*	Braised	In a sweet sauce	In a spicy sauce	In a red wine sauce
Côtes de Provence	Côte du Luberon	Tavel	Pinot blanc	Côtes du Rhône-Villages	Graves
Pouilly-Fumé	Patrimonio	Tokay Pinot gris	Tokai del friuli	Hermitage	Pinot noir (Alsace)
Buzet	dry white Bordeaux	Riesling	Pomino	Cassis	Volnay
Graves	Lugana		Barsac	Graves	Margaux
Montravel	Lacryma Christi		Sauternes	Clairette du Languedoc	Buzet
			Gewurztraminer	Côtes de Provence	

NOTE: Except for those dishes with a red wine sauce, all the suggested wines are white wines.

Wines for Fatty Fish with a Strong Flavor

Tuna, yellowfin tuna, bonito, albacore, mackerel, sardine, anchovy, eel, American shad, bluefish, weakfish, herring, alewife, sheepshead, blue runner, brown bullhead, catfish, carp and many others

Grilled	Fried or à la meunière	Braised	In a sweet sauce	In a spicy sauce	In a red wine sauce
Sancerre	Fendant du Valais	Savennières	Lirac rosé	Condrieu	Côtes du Bourg
dry Anjou	Montlouis	Côtes du Jura	white Côtes-du-Rhône	Tokay Pinot gris	Bandol
Riesling	Reuilly	Arbois	Saint-Véran	Gewurztraminer	Faugères
Pouilly-Fuissé	Seyssel	Saint-Aubin	dry Vouvray	Puligny-Montrachet	Saint-Julien
Orpailleur (Quebec)	Gaillac (dry)		Auxey-Duresses		Pinot noir (Alsace)
Chardonnay	Niersteiner (dry)				
	Wines from Rheinhessen (dry)				

Note: Except for those dishes with a red wine sauce, the suggested wines are white wines.

Wines for Saltwater and River Crustaceans

Rock crab, dungeness crab, snow crab, white shrimp, red sand shrimp, brown shrimp, pink shrimp, Arctic argid, lobster, spiny lobster, scampi, crayfish, scallops and many others

Grilled	Poached w/butter	Baked in the oven	Fried	With a crustacean sauce	In a spicy sauce
Côtes du Rhône	Vouvray	Tavel	Albana di Romagna	Puligny-Montrachet	Riesling, late harvest
Mâcon-Villages	Riesling	Bandol	Lugana	Chassagne-Montrachet	Vouvray
Monthélie	Pouilly fumé	Côtes de Provence	Soave	Corton	Château-Chalon
Pomino	Pouilly-sur-Loire	Châteauneuf-du-Pape	Chardonnay Napa or Sonoma	Tokay Pinot gris	Fendant
Orvieto	Lugana	Condrieu		Corvo blanco	Tokay Pinot gris
Sylvaner	Meursault			Falerno bianco	
				Cassis	
				Chardonnay Napa or Sonoma	

NOTE: Except for those dishes with a red wine sauce, the suggested wines are white wines.

361

Wines for Shellfish and Invertebrates

Periwinkle, whelk, cockle, razor clam, oyster, Atlantic surf clam, mussel, soft-shell clam, abalone, hard-shell clam, scallop, ocean quahog, squid, boreal squid, sea urchin, octopus, cuttlefish and many others

Raw	Cooked natural	Cooked w/the juice	Fried	In a sweet sauce	In a spicy sauce
Muscadet	Graves	Muscadet	Sancerre	Gewurztraminer	Mercurey
Sauvignon	Entre-deux-mers	Rully	Côtes de Provence	Pomino	Chablis
Sancerre	Bandol			Orvieto	Rioja
Riesling					
Moselle					

NOTE: Except for those dishes with a red wine sauce, the suggested wines are white wines.

Conclusion

Having read this book, you should now be familiar with such names as goldeye, cunner and northern searobin. You have made new culinary discoveries, some exotic, but many that are readily available on the market. Prepared in a delicate sauce, cooked with care, served with imagination, these fish will soon be part of your preferred menus and compete with Atlantic salmon, lobster or flounder for a place on your table. The culinary miracle has occurred once again: a little warmth when cooking, a quick whisk of a sauce, a few touches of color for the eye, and the end result is ready to be savored.

We hope that the information and recipes contained in this book have expanded your knowledge and awakened in you the desire to try them. That was our primary goal, to which we devoted our imagination, faith and knowledge. That is our modest contribution to the art of cooking.

Glossary

American cowslip	This plant is eaten often. Its leaves are added to salads or cooked like green vegetables. Its blossoms, preserved in vinegar, can replace capers.
Anadromous	Term for a seawater fish that travels upriver to spawn; it lives in salt water and reproduces in fresh water.
Aspic	Cooked and chilled preparations, set in molded jelly.
Avocado	The avocado belongs to the *Lauracae* family, which primarily includes aromatic plants (bay leaf, cinnamon and the camphor tree). Its Aztec name, *ahuacatl*, means "butter from the forest." Avocado goes well with several crustaceans.
***Bain-marie* (double boiler)**	A procedure for keeping a sauce, soup or preparation warm, for cooking ingredients until tender without burning or for gently preparing some dishes. A container holding a preparation is placed in another container of boiling water. The term also refers to the piece of equipment used to cook in this manner.
Bard, to	This procedure involves wrapping a fish in bards, i.e., in thin slices of bacon, to protect and drench with fat.
Burdock	The burdock roots resemble those of parsnip or salsify.
Beard, to	Using scissors or a knife, remove the beards or lateral fins of a fish, as well as the muscles and beards (cartilage that is used as a fin) of oysters and mussels.
Beurre manié	A mixture of butter and flour used to bind some preparations, including sauces, coulis and ragouts.
Bind, to	This procedure aims to make a liquid or sauce more consistent by adding different ingredients such as eggs, flour, starch or butter.
Black mustard	Unripe berry or grape must combined with crushed mustard seeds produces this mustard. Black mustard seeds can also be used to season fish.
Blanch, to	This procedure involves boiling an ingredient in a certain amount of liquid, and during a given period, to remove some impurities or to tenderize.

Blanch and peel, to	Remove the skin from fruit, vegetables or nuts—for example, tomatoes or almonds—after having submerged them in boiling water.
Boil, to	To plunge a food in a liquid once the liquid has reached its boiling point.
Borage	Raw borage leaves go well with several types of crustaceans and mollusks.
Bouillabaisse	A dish of boiled and flavored fish containing, among other things, saffron and garlic, and including fish from the Mediterranean (scorpionfish, spiny lobsters, conger eels, rainbow wrasse, John Dory, monkfish and pollock).
Bouquet garni	Aromatic ingredient made up of celery, thyme sprigs, parsley stems and bay leaves, all tied together.
Braising	Method of cooking a variety of foods, covered and with moisture.
Braise or cook until tender, to	This is the opposite of sweating. A food is cooked covered at low heat, in very little liquid and fat. Certain vegetables are typically braised. They keep their sugars and take on the taste of the butter.
Bread, to	To dredge in breading before frying, sautéing or grilling.
Bread crumbs, white	Made with white bread with the crust removed. The bread is pulverized in a food processor.
Break the fibers of a fillet, to	To break the fibers to prevent shrinkage, wrap the fillet in aluminum foil, gently tap with the flat side of a knife.
Brunoise	This term designates both a way to cut vegetables into small dice approx. 1/8 inch (3 mm) along each side and the result of this procedure, i.e., the mixture of various vegetables that are diced in this way.
Buisson	A method of stacking an ingredient such as lobster and crayfish in the shape of a pyramid.
Burnet	Herbaceous plant generally with red flowers that are sometimes used as seasoning.
Butter, to	To coat an ingredient with butter or to incorporate butter into a preparation.
Carrot, wild	These carrots are white and are eaten raw and grated.

Cassolette	A dish including fish or crustaceans, bound with a fish *velouté* and served in a dish with short handles called a "cassolette."
Cattail	The Amerindians used dried and pulverized cattail rhizomes as flour. The inside of the stalk is called the cattail heart and the male cob is eaten like a corncob.
Celery, garden	*See* Lovage.
Chayote or christophene	This vegetable is a member of the *Cucurbitaceae* (squash) family originally from Mexico. It goes well with all fish, mollusks and crustaceans, in part because of its discreet aroma.
Chervil leaves	The delicate part of chervil that is used to season dishes.
Chiffonnade	Julienne of lettuce, sorrel or other leafy greens that can be cooked in butter.
Chinese green vegetables	Bok choy, baby bok choy, bok choy sum, yow choy sum and gai lon are all members of the same family, *Crucifirae*. Each of these vegetables has a particular taste. They go well with fish, mollusks and crustaceans.
Chinese mushrooms	Shiitake, tree-ear, straw, oyster and enoki are mushrooms that go with all the fish, mollusks and crustaceans.
Clarify, to	This procedure involves making some difficult substances like bouillon and some drinks clear; the term is also used in the case of sugar, butter and eggs. To obtain a fish *velouté* free of impurities, it is recommended that the fish fumet be clarified.
Cloudberry	A small fruit; red like a raspberry at first, it then turns yellow, amber and translucent.
Cocotte potatoes	Oblong sections of peeled potato are boiled, then drained. The potatoes are quickly sealed at high heat in butter and oil in a sauté pan then sautéed gently for about 15 minutes, and covered and baked in an oven at 200°C (400°F) for another 10 minutes. Once browned, the potatoes are removed from the oven, drained and seasoned with salt.
Cook *au gratin*, to	To cook or finish cooking in the oven or under a broiler, a dish that has been sprinkled with breading or grated cheese. Cheese should not be used for most fish, since the taste of the cheese will usually overwhelm that of the fish.
Cook until tender, to	*See* Braise.

Coriander	The seeds and leaves are often used in cooking fish, mollusks and crustaceans.
Cover with sauce, to	Pour a sauce or cream on to a dish or in a serving dish and cover the surface.
Daikon	*See* Oriental radish.
Deglaze, to	To dissolve, with a little liquid, the sugars that are caramelized in the bottom of a cooking dish.
Demi-glace	A brown sauce produced by boiling and skimming espagnole sauce (made from brown stock, brown roux, mirepoix and tomato purée). White stock or estouffade (a clear brown stock) is then added to the mixture. Sherry, Madeira or a similar wine may also be added.
Dill, sweet-smelling	An aromatic plant whose smell is similar to that of wild fennel. Dill seeds are used as a condiment.
Emulsify, to	To beat vigorously with a hand whisk or an electric beater.
Encrust, to	A procedure where incisions are made into an uncooked (round) fish and strips of fat, or truffles, etc., inserted into the incisions.
Escalope, to cut into a	To carve thin slices of fish and at an angle.
Fennel, wild	Fennel includes several wild varieties with fruit that are more or less sweet, peppery or bitter, and a cultivated variety whose bulb is eaten.
Fiddlehead	This vegetable, picked in the spring, is called a fiddlehead because its shape resembles that of a violin. Among the numerous varieties of this vegetable, there are only a few that are edible, including the ostrich fern.
Fillet, to	This procedure consists in lifting the fillets from the fish, i.e., removing them using a special knife.
Fricassee	A ragout made from different ingredients, including crustaceans initially seared in butter.
Glasswort	This plant contains a high level of iodine and has a very salty yet pleasant taste. Also called saltwater cordgrass.
Glaze, to	This involves exposing to high heat fish or crustaceans coated with a "glazing preparation" containing hollandaise sauce, fish *velouté* and whipped cream in order to obtain a uniformly golden surface.

Gut, to	This term applies in particular to crayfish. The intestine is removed by pulling the middle of the back part of the tail.
Hint	A very small quantity of a spice. For example, a hint of cayenne pepper.
Hot, to remove the skin	This procedure consists in peeling the skin of a cooked fish while the fish is still hot.
Julienne	This term refers to any substance (meat or vegetables) cut into fine strips.
Lavender	When used sparingly, lavender enhances the taste of some fish.
Lemongrass	The name of a variety of plants that contain a lemon-scented essential oil (mugwort, lemongrass, lemon balm and sweet-smelling lemon verbena).
Licorice	With a particular yet refined flavor, this plant works well with several fish and crustaceans when used sparingly.
Lovage and garden celery	Garden celery is the wild celery grown in gardens since the 16th century. It provides several varieties of edible vegetables, including those known as celery and celeriac.
Macerate, to	This involves soaking various items for a certain amount of time in an aromatic liquid.
Mango	The mango has been grown in Asia for almost 6,000 years. Its unusual taste makes it unfit for some fish.
Matelote	A fish stew, primarily involving freshwater fish, prepared in red or white wine, with bacon, small onions, mushrooms, etc.
Meurette	A matelote of river fish, or eggs, veal or chicken.
Milkweed	The young shoots are cooked like asparagus.
Mirepoix	Vegetables that have been roughly cut when preparing a sauce or a combination of vegetables (carrot, celery, onion and leek).
Milt	White and soft substance found inside fish.
Moisten, to	Add water, bouillon, fish fumet or a lobster base to different ingredients while cooking.
Moisten to the top, to	Add enough cooking liquid so that the liquid covers that which is to be cooked.
Mold, to	Place a mixture or a food inside a mold.

Mouclade	A preparation of mussels, similar to a dish that is "à la poulette" or with *poulette* sauce, but with an egg-and-butter liaison.
Nage, à la	Fish or crustaceans cooked "swimming" in a *court-bouillon*.
Nettle	"When the nettle is young, its leaf is an excellent vegetable" wrote Victor Hugo. Nettle leaves are covered with fuzz.
Noisette potatoes	A melon baller is used to create small potato balls roughly the size of a large hazelnut which are then lightly browned in butter. They typically serve as a garnish.
Northern Labrador tea	This small bush grows in peat bogs. The young leaves are excellent when infused to make the base of a sauce.
Oriental radish or daikon	This plant has a more subtle taste than that of rutabaga or turnip. It can, if used discerningly, go well with some fish.
Papaya	Originally from southern Mexico, this fruit, whether raw, cooked or as a juice, greatly enhances several fish and mollusks. Moreover, papaya juice tenderizes meat.
Parboil, to	To soak an item in cold water for a certain period of time to remove any impurities.
Poach, to	Cook a food in liquid approx. 200°F (between 90° and 95°C), uncovered and without letting it boil.
Pochouse	A dish similar to a *matelote*, with perch, eel, pike, trout, carp and monkfish.
Poulette, à la	This refers to different dishes involving fish, mussels, frogs or others, accompanied by a sauce based on a mussel or frog juice reduction and 35% cream, and flavored with parsley, shallots, etc.
Preparation	A combination of diverse ingredients.
Purslane	Purslane leaves are crunchy like those of Scotch kale and can be eaten raw or cooked.
Put on a sheet, to	The act of putting food on a baking sheet with or without an edge.
Rapini	A crunchy vegetable and a close relative of broccoli. It has less flavor than broccoli; therefore, it does not hide the taste of the fish.
Reduce, to	Boil a sauce or a stock to cause evaporation and thus make the preparation more robust and colorful.

Refresh, to	Place an ingredient or a dish in water or under cold running water to chill it quickly.
Risotto	Rice pilaf, garnished with a seafood preparation or another garnish of choice.
Safflower	A plant whose seeds are used to produce oil. Sometimes the petals are used to replace saffron, whence the name "false saffron."
Sauté, to	Cook at high heat in a cooking fat and rotate the saucepan or sauté pan to make the food "sauté" or jump to prevent it from sticking.
Sea urchin roe	Yellow or orange part of the inside of the sea urchin.
Section	A piece cut from a large flatfish to feed one or several people.
Seed, to	To remove the seeds of a fruit or a vegetable.
Set aside, to	Keep a fish warm, once it has been cooked, on a serving dish or on a plate where a paper towel has been placed to absorb any excess fat.
Shallot	There are two types of shallots: green and fresh, and "French," which is a dried shallot. In most recipes, the dried shallot is used, its flavor being finer than that of the onion.
Shell, to	This procedure involves separating the fruit or seed from its husk; to remove the shell from a crustacean or a mollusk.
Simmer, to	A liquid simmers just before it reaches boiling point.
Skim, to	This procedure consists in removing the impurities that float to the surface of a liquid (sauce) during a slow boil by using a spoon or a skimmer.
Skin a fish, to	A procedure for removing the skin of a fish by holding on to the head and pulling on the skin.
Sorrel	Cultivated sorrel leaves are acid, but go very well with fish.
Sprinkle (browned ingredients) with flour, to	This procedure involves sprinkling food with flour that, when moistened, creates a liaison for a sauce.
Steak	A thick slice, cut principally from a large round fish, that usually serves one person.
Stiffen, to	Cause meat to shrink at high heat without browning.
Sweat, to	In cooking fat, to cook a vegetable at fairly high heat to cause it to lose some of its water and to concentrate the juices.

Tarragon	This type of scented mugwort originates from Russia. Because of its scent, it must be used with discretion.
Thicken with butter, to	To sprinkle a sauce with knobs of cold butter and to incorporate the butter by using a whisk until a uniform mixture is obtained.
Timbale	A croustade that is served very hot, made with puff pastry and garnished with a preparation made from crustaceans, fish or other ingredients.
Trim, to	Eliminate the parts of meat, poultry, fish or a vegetable that cannot be used in order to improve its appearance.
True watercress	A member of the mustard family, watercress grows in running water and has a peppery taste. It can be eaten raw or used in soups and forcemeats. When very fresh, it can easily replace garden cress.
Until dry	Extract all moisture from a food or reduce a liquid by 99%.
Wrap and pack on ice, to	*See* "Method for Storing Fresh Fish," page 15.
Yellow rocket (winter cress)	The taste of this plant recalls that of watercress. It can replace sorrel.

Terms Used in "Cuisine Renouvelée," Relating to Fish

Blanc　　Thin fish fillets like those of Atlantic halibut.

Catigot　　A fish *matelote* (eel and carp) with tomatoes, onions and bacon.

Daube
(casserole)　　A stew with a stock and aromatics that can be used with, among others, tuna.

Miroton　　A meat, and by extension, fish preparation that is simmered.

Paupiette　　A thin slice of meat or fish, stuffed in the middle, then rolled up and cooked.

Ragout　　A preparation based on meat or fish, cooked with a little moisture in a bound liquid, generally with small vegetables.

Salmis　　A dish based on crustaceans, in particular crayfish, cooked "à la bordelaise," but with red instead of white wine.

Suprême　　A term which describes a chicken breast or game fillet and, by extension, the thickest part of a thin fish fillet.

Tourtière　　A round mold and, by extension, the dish cooked in the mold. The name "Tourtière d'huîtres" (Oyster *tourtière*) can be found in a text dating from 1651: it describes a mixture based on oysters with artichokes, asparagus and morel mushrooms.

Fish Index

Recipes Index